OUR NATIVE AMERICAN LEGACY
Northwest Towns with Indian Names

OUR NATIVE AMERICAN LEGACY
NORTHWEST TOWNS WITH INDIAN NAMES

Sandy Nestor

CAXTON PRESS
Caldwell, Idaho
2001

Library of Congress Cataloging-in-Publication Data

Our Native American legacy
    p. cm.
  ISBN 0-87004-401-x (alk. paper)
    1. Names, Indian--Northwest Pacific. 2. Names, Indian--Alaska. 3. Names, Geographical--Northwest, Pacific. 4. Names, Geographical--Alaska. 5. Northwest, Pacific--History, Local. 6. Alaska--History, Local.

E78.N77 097 2001
979.8'00497--dc21   2001028729

Lithographed and bound in the United States of America
CAXTON PRESS
Caldwell, Idaho
166980

Dedicated to my parents

Francis & Helen Nestor

Your love & support over my lifetime has been immeasurable!

And

Mitzy, our little missing aircraft

ACKNOWLEDGEMENTS

This book could not have been written without the help of the people who staff libraries, museums, and historical societies in the Northwest. I am deeply indebted to them for their enthusiasm with my work and steering me to a multitude of resources. I can't name them all, but must make mention of a few who really gave that extra: state of Alaska, Washougal, Tacoma, Vancouver, Pomeroy, and Asotin County, Washington, libraries. I encourage everyone to support their local libraries, especially those that receive so little funding, to purchase more books.

Elaine Poole of Menan, Idaho, bless your heart for all the good conversation and wonderful photos of your community and its history. Bud Purdy, of Picabo, Idaho, for your generosity and great photos. John Harder of Kahlotus for your most interesting letters. Roy Matsuno, village council president of Ugashik, Alaska, for the pictures you shared with me, and thank your mom, "Sassa" (careful with those skis and wayward trucks).

Special thanks to Sister Mary Cantwell, Sisters of St. Ann's, British Columbia, for Akulurak, Alaska; Chad McNeill for his photos of Attu, Alaska; Walt Goodman and Elizabeth Riley of Chewelah, Washington; Irene Martin of Skamokawa, Washington; Stewart O'Nan, for Attu, Alaska; Doug Rutan, superintendent, Kuna Joint School District No. 3, Idaho; Minidoka County Historical Society; Deborah Hazen; editor of the *Clatskanie Chief*, Oregon; Lillian Pethtel of Kamiah, Idaho; John Findlay, managing editor, *Pacific Northwest Quarterly* for Pocatello, Idaho; Ruth McCausland, for Tokeland, Washington; Donna McAlpine, Anvik Historical Society, Anvik, Alaska; Phyllis Griffith, Entiat, Washington; and James Hermanson for Chimacum, Washington.

Eve Edwards, of the United States Board on Geographic Names, in Reston, Virginia, your continued support is most appreciated. I am also thankful for the assistance of David Bigger, who was a VISTA volunteer at the village of Quinhagak, Alaska. Janie Tippett of Joseph, Oregon, for taking great pictures of Imnaha for me: best of luck in your ventures. There are so many more people I would like to mention, but I'm afraid it would take another book to do that!

Gratitude to my editor, Wayne Cornell, at Caxton Press for his guidance and words of wisdom. Working with you is a most pleasurable experience.

And "Mayor" Louie Scott of Rabbit Hash, Kentucky, for your friendship, wit, support, and great Christmas presents. Darlin', this one's for you!

Contents

ILLUSTRATIONS

INTRODUCTION

Facts altered by legends, compounded by misspellings and confusion. History hides the truth behind many names. (David Webb, 1984).

Many Northwest cities and towns bear names often linked to the American Indians who inhabited the region before the arrival of white explorers and settlers.

But what is an Indian name? The names given to many Northwest towns and hamlets are of unknown origin, and even more are corruptions of the original words. It amounts to an historian's nightmare.

Why all the confusion? In the early days pioneers were unable to pronounce many Indian names, so they adapted words that were easier for them to speak. We have to remember also that a good percentage of the settlers were not well educated and could not spell. Lewis and Clark, as shown by their diaries and field notes, misspelled many of their words. When Clark arrived at Cathlamet, he wrote in his notes, "Cathlamah." Was this the elementary Indian word, or simply Clark's rendition of the name?

In southwest Idaho there is a range of mountains and a river named "Owyhee." It was once the name of a railroad stop in that state and is still the name of a northern Nevada community. Many residents of the region assume "Owyhee" is a Native American word. The real story is that nearly 200 years ago, several natives of the Hawaiian Islands disappeared without a trace while trapping along the Snake River. The region was named in their honor. But Hawaii was corrupted to "Owyhee."

Another example is Okanogan, Washington. The original spelling (or was it?) was OkanogEn. Did it signify "rendezvous" as was interpreted for OkanogAn? It was also spelled Ookenaw, Okinakane and Oakinacken. In the Indian dialects, one letter could change the whole meaning of their words. Through the years, some of the names evolved further by the substitution of a letter, or the deletion thereof.

Alaska Indian names are a real enigma. Some of the "Indian" words may have originally been Russian because of that country's tremendous influence on the native population before the United States purchased that northern region. The small community of Ugashik was recorded as Oogashik by a Russian named Ivan Petroff. It was also called Ougatik. Repeated efforts to find the definition of this word came to naught. Was it initially a Russian word, or an actual Indian word that was translated by Petroff as Oogashik? We may never know.

Then there were historians such as W. W. Tooker, who called himself an "Algonkinist," and wrote a book in the early 1900s about place names of Indian origin. Although Tooker was very dedicated to his vocation, he was an amateur with no formal training in linguistics. When he didn't know something, he often resorted to guesswork, so his work may be problematic at best. Today, it is considered controversial by many scholars.

Ives Goddard with the Smithsonian Institute, an Algonquian language expert, analyzed Tooker's research approach:

> *Some words you could say he's probably close, but with most of them he is certainly wrong. Unless you have a complete vocabulary, defining place names is just guesswork. . . . And I'm sure he is right in some areas, and some of his cultural information is most valuable today. Tooker did the spade work, and that's good for us today.*

Henry Schoolcraft was an explorer, Indian agent, and scholar who visited Native American tribes for more than thirty years. He named counties and towns during his travels and often "made up" Indian names, combining words and syllables from Native American languages, mixing them with Latin and Arabian.

A number of communities were given the names of Indian chiefs. But many of the names were never truly defined, although some form of translation was given to them. Some Indian cultures dictated that their chiefs' real names never be spoken, and so they took assumed names, further complicating the issue.

So we had a perpetuation of interpretations stemming from these "experts" by writers going back more than ninety years, some who did no further research but took the experts at their word, stating definite meanings. Today, historians and ethnologists delve deep into finding the correct translations. This is an almost impossible task because many Indian words have been so corrupted, and other tribes no longer exist.

Name origins may have been corrupted when European men, such as French trappers, married Indian women and the languages were interchanged and new words adopted. The subverted tribes were forced to speak the white man's language. In 1868, a federal commission that was trying to make peace with Indians of the Plains decided that "In the difference of language to-day lies two-thirds of our trouble. Schools should be established, which children should be required to attend; their barbarous dialects should be blotted out and the English language substituted."

Dialects also differed with the sub-tribes or bands of Indians. For example, the Pacific Northwest Indians called the Kalapuyas. In Clackamas County, Oregon, there was the band of Ahantchuyuk Kalapuya who made their home by the Willamette River and the Atfalati resided near the Tualatin River. The Cathlamet tribe formed a dialect division of the Chinookian stock, and the Clackamas Indians were a division of the Chinook, giving their name to a dialect group.

Many of the Indian tribes completely disappeared because of the white man's diseases, such as smallpox and measles, and their language was lost to history forever. A few linguists were fortunate and able to record the Indian grammar from some the last Indian speakers before they died.

Even today, Indian words are disappearing. William Yardley wrote an article in 2000 entitled "Every time one of our elders dies, it's like a library burning down." The article was written for a Smithsonian-sponsored program about preserving American native languages. Director of the American Indian Program at the National Museum of American History, Rayna Green said, in part, "But isn't it odd that we don't also sit down and learn Navaho and Zuni, and other languages of our native land, along with the ancestral names of the ancient places we now inhabit?"

Conducting research for this book was like traveling through a maze or spider web. After locating information for a town that seemed to be complete and concise, I was led down another path that contradicted the original material, which took me to other twists and turns in the maze, where even more contradictions existed.

Chimacum, Washington, is a classic example. One source showed Reuben Eldridge as the first settler; another wrote that it was William Eldridge; and yet another that Reuben Robinson was there first. Chimacum was also spelled Chimakum and Chemakum. Which are facts or words of fancy?

At any rate, it was my desire to put down on paper the best information I could find with histories of so many of our wonderful places that seem to have been overlooked. Some of their histories were very sparse, but all that could be found was included. Stories of large cities such as Seattle are brief, because there is a wealth of information already out there; rather, I concentrated on our "forgotten" towns. Numerous librarians from small towns and villages sent me letters stating they were so glad someone was *finally* writing about their community. You are not forgotten.

I hope people who are traveling throughout the Northwest will find this book engaging enough to spark their interest and visit these communities, especially those off the beaten path, and enjoy the wealth of history they have to offer. I also wish armchair travelers an enjoyable, and occasionally humorous, journey through these pages.

Historians and other people deeply interested in history will disagree, debate, and perhaps even accept some of what is written here. The book is meant to do just that; generate discussion and a place for dissemination of information. Perhaps there may be a bit of history that has eluded historians, adding one more piece to their jigsaw puzzles.

The book is not as complete as I had anticipated because there was no available data for some of the small communities, and, unfortunately, a lack of interest by some in my research. There are several towns that no longer exist and are stated as such in the text. I felt it important to include them because of their Indian origin. Too often they are left out because they don't exist anymore and, as a result, over time their history could be lost, too.

Enjoy.

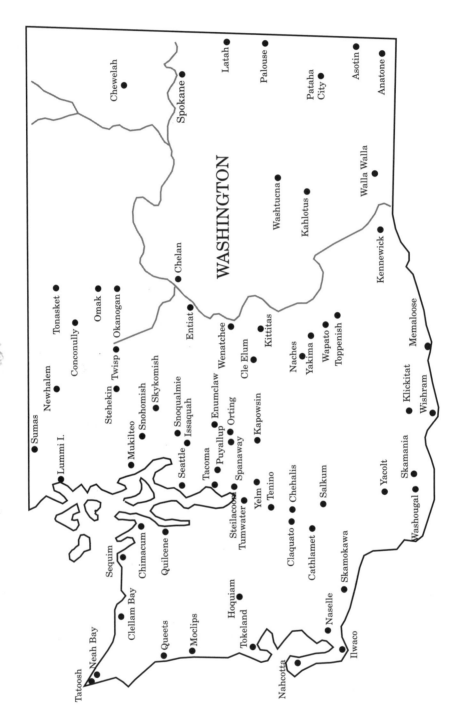

Chapter One

WASHINGTON

ANATONE

Starting out as a trading post, Anatone became part of the gold trail to the Salmon River area of Idaho in the 1860s. The post supplied the mining camps of the Imnaha and Snake River districts, and also served the surrounding area farmers. The town is located about ten miles south of Clarkston.

Few town name origins are cut and dried, and Anatone is no exception. It is believed to be named for a Nez Perce woman named Anatone. Others say the name came from a town in Greece, but there is no record of an Anatone there. Another story is that during a town meeting to select a name for the settlement, Smithville was suggested and rejected. An Irish gent allegedly popped up with "Any Town," and with his brogue it sounded like Anatone to the residents, and they adopted the name.

After the initial settlers established themselves, they found out they had to travel to Lewiston, Idaho, for supplies. In 1878, the first store in Anatone was opened by Daniel McIvor, who initially supplied only the most important necessities, such as tobacco and whiskey. As McIvor stocked more goods, it enabled the residents to travel to Lewiston less frequently.

When rumors spread of impending problems with the

Asotin County Historical Society
Anatone (1908). Main Street.

Asotin County Historical Society
Anatone (1925). Main Street. Compared to the 1908 photograph, Anatone did not grow very much.

Bannock and Paiute Indians in 1878, the settlers built a 100-foot square stockade as a precaution a few miles from the town. Soldiers on their way to the Grande Ronde River crossing stopped by the stockade to see how the people were faring, but actual hostilities never broke out, and after tensions eased the settlers returned to their homes.[1]

About the same time, William Farish arrived and built a small sawmill (eventually growing to eight mills) near Anatone. Ox teams hauled the cut lumber to the Snake River where it was loaded onto rafts and sent downstream to various destinations. In June 1878, McIvor sold his store to Charles Isecke, who freighted in supplies from the town of Dayton, about eighty miles from Anatone. During the next few years, his business was so brisk Isecke had to erect a larger structure; over time, it had to be enlarged twice. The wood from the original store was used to build a corral on W. J. Clemans' property. Isecke was also the first postmaster of Anatone, which was established in 1878. He later sold his business to Clemans.

In the 1880s, more businesses moved into town: blacksmith, feed mill, and outfitter, in addition to the general store. Clemans voiced his intentions to plat a townsite in 1893. As a result, the *Sentinel* wrote that Anatone was far enough away from Asotin, the main town in the county, that it would be assured of, ". . . good growth and prosperity which will rebound to the good of its immediate surroundings."[2] In 1901 the town was actually platted and made up a grand total of four blocks.

The year 1896 brought a devastating fire to Anatone that totally destroyed the store and warehouse. Clemans and his family lived in a house attached to the store and barely escaped with their lives. The residents feared the fire would spread to the rest of the town, but they were lucky in that only the store and warehouse burned.

Anatone never developed into a large town, as occurred with some trading points, and it remained a bedroom community. However, because of its pleasant climate, it became a summer resort that drew visitors from Lewiston and Clarkston.

ASOTIN

Asotin once was an Indian camp because of the protection it afforded. The Nez Perce called the nearby creek Has-shu-tin, which means "eel", for the species of fish. The Indians stayed here during the winters because of the light snowfall and shelter from the wind provided by high bluffs.

White settlers did not come to the region until after the Nez Perce War of 1877. Two settlements were established within a half mile of each other: Assotin and Assotin City. Assotin City was founded in April 1878 by Alexander Sumpter, but the plat was not filed until two years later. Within a ten-year period, Assotin City was absorbed by Assotin. In 1886, the Territorial Legislature changed the spelling to Asotin.

A. F. Beall, a surveyor for the district, came through the region while he was mapping a wagon road, and also surveyed the town of Asotin. The *Chronicle* wrote in 1878 that, ". . . This

Courtesy Asotin County Historical Society
Asotin and its main street (1906).

town may, in time, become an important place on the Snake River."[3]

Asotin's plat was filed in November 1881 and the townsite was laid out within the year. A man named Theodore Schank had a cabin here and was thought to have been the first settler. He and another gentleman named Reed began to promote the town. Many people purchased lots and established homes and businesses. The neighboring town of Assotin City began to dwindle in population, especially after it lost a bitter fight for the county seat, and the community died.

The first ferry at Asotin was built by J. J. Kanawyer in 1881. Other than a few rough mountain trails, the river was the only means of transportation. A sawmill was established by Frank Curtis and L. O. Stimson, followed by a flour mill, blacksmith and a warehouse, which was the sole shipping outlet for the area. The fertile land in the surrounding region became a place for raising wheat, which was shipped from Asotin by steamboat because it was the head of navigation on the Snake River. The

Oregon Railroad & Navigation Company's steamer, *John Gates,* loaded one of the first shipments of wheat. Because of the town's location on a plateau surrounded by bluffs, this was the only place through which farmers could transport their stock and grain for shipment.

By special act of the Territorial Legislature, Asotin was named county seat in 1883. That same year the *Spirit* newspaper was established and wrote some advice for Asotin, ". . . Be vigilant, for we are not out of the woods by a half section. Sharp eyes will be watching us from now until the next election and their owners will not be slow to take advantage of any mistakes we fall into. Work should be the order of the day, and never let up till we have a fixed fact for an uncertainty."[4]

The same year the *Chronicle* wrote, "Thus we have a good, solid foundation and backing for a town. . . In the next place we have some as enterprising and practical business men as can be found in any community. . . Steamboats land at the warehouse here. . . Thus you see we have all the necessary requirements to make a town, and as soon as capital notices the many natural advantages of Asotin there is not doubt but that great developments will be made here."[5]

Asotin's merchants suffered in 1883 when a diphtheria epidemic hit town. Some of the businesses closed down, along with the schools and any place of public gathering. The next year, things were back to normal; that is until 1886 when a fire broke out and burned the saloon, law offices, and the hotel. The businessmen cut their losses, moved what they could salvage and started over again.

By the early 1900s a powerhouse had been built about a mile from town and supplied electricity for the region. Asotin became a river-freighting town, and along with growing wheat, the local citizens established orchards and vineyards.

CATHLAMET

The Cathlamet Indians were a branch of the Chinook tribe who lived on the Columbia River in Oregon. They moved across the river to Washington after they became panic-stricken when a series of epidemics occurred in 1852. The race eventually disappeared. One of the last of the Cathlamet Indians named John Wallaka made a strange request just before he died. He asked to be buried in "a black diagonal suit, blue shirt with pearl buttons, a red necktie and blue socks with white toes and heels."

The town is named for the Cathlamet Indians. The tribe's name means "stone," signifying the rocky course of the Columbia River.[6]

Thomas Jefferson appropriated $25,000 from Congress to finance the Lewis and Clark Expedition, and in 1805 after many miles of exploration, the explorers arrived at Fort Clatsop, where they stayed for a few months. During the winter, Clark visited the Cathlamets, and was probably the first white man to do so. Believing the expedition would need another canoe to return home the following spring, Clark tried to make a bargain for one of their canoes, but the Indians refused. Meriwether Lewis also attempted to make the trade, which the Indians refused at first. Eventually, Lewis offered a lace-cuffed Army dress uniform and he got the canoe.[7]

It wasn't until about 1846 that the first white settler, a Scot named James Birnie, along with his Indian wife and eleven children, established his home and called it Birnie's Retreat. He was with the North West Company of Montreal when it became part of the Hudson's Bay Company. Birnie retired from the company, filed a donation claim at Cathlamet, and opened a trading post. He later became a county commissioner.

By 1850, Cathlamet had the beginnings of a prosperous little town. In the early 1900s, Alexander Birnie succeeded his father in the trading business as he wrote: "In 1846 father left the employ of the Hudson's Bay Company and moved to Cathlamet. . . Father was a good trader, a great reader and an expert at accounts, but when it came to shooting or rowing or other work of that nature he let his employees take care of it . . . He died at Cathlamet on December 21, 1864, and I took over the store and became postmaster. . ."[8]

Ulysses S. Grant often visited Cathlamet in the 1850s to escape the boredom at Vancouver where he was stationed as an Army captain. Apparently, Grant wanted to move his family here, but had to find a way to raise the money to do so. Once, he chartered a boat to ship ice to San Francisco. When that failed to deliver him extra money, he tried to grow potatoes and raise chickens at Fort Vancouver. That didn't work either, and so his family never did settle in Cathlamet. Grant went on to bigger things, including command of the Union Army during the Civil War, and the presidency.

William and George Hume started a salmon cannery in 1866, at a place called Eagle Cliff, eight miles from Cathlamet. It was the first of more than thirty-five canneries that would be established in the region. Three years later, the Warren Cannery was built at Cathlamet and produced over 30,000 cases of salmon. It was estimated that eighty-five percent of the salmon packs came from Wahkiakum County. But by 1937 there was only one cannery left in the region.

Timber was also an important industry, because the area was heavily forested with hemlock and yellow fir trees. About the same time the canneries opened, logging began at Cathlamet. The Bradley Logging Company had its operations about nine miles from town and was cutting nearly 200,000 board feet each day. The logs were rafted down the Columbia River to the Portland mills.

Cathlamet operated the only ocean rafting industry of its kind, where cigar rafts were constructed to make 1,000-mile ocean voyages. These rafts were made by chaining up to six million board feet of timber together. Ungainly craft to tow, the rafts were the most economical way to transport large amounts of timber to California markets. The first raft to make the trip broke up and the logs scattered all over the ocean when a gale came up. A man named Benson eventually perfected the raft design: the logs were assembled in a cradle while they were being bound into the famous cigar shape. The cigar rafts were used until the 1930s, and out of more than 100 rafts of Benson's design, only a few broke up.[9]

In 1851, Wahkiakum County was organized and Cathlamet was designated as the county seat. But the Legislative

Assembly of Washington Territory changed that and had the
county records moved to the town of Skamokawa. That didn't
sit very well with Alexander Birnie and C. J. Curtis, who went
to Skamokawa and somehow convinced officials there had been
a mistake, that the records should never have left Cathlamet,
and returned home with the county documents. Birnie and
Curtis then went on to establish Cathlamet as the permanent
county seat.[10]

The Cathlamet Congregational Church was built in 1895.
The old bell from the church was purchased from a New York
foundry and brought around Cape Horn, the southern tip of
South America. When the church began to age, the residents
decided they better take their precious bell down.
Unfortunately, no one had the know-how to climb way up to the
shaky bell tower. But the bell was retrieved when some experienced loggers happened to pass by, climbed up the tower and
lowered it to the thankful residents.[11]

Cathlamet was relatively isolated and the main mode of
transportation was river boats, which took residents down to
the town of Astoria to get supplies. They also went to Astoria for
medical services because, until the 1920s, there were no doctors
in town. In 1917, there were no roads in or out of Cathlamet, so
a delegation was sent to Olympia to appropriate funds for a
road. Three years later the region was surveyed for a road, but
the appropriated money was used for another part of the county. Later, the paperwork for the survey was burned when the
courthouse went up in flames, and in 1923 the road had to be
resurveyed. Cathlamet was one of the last towns in Washington
to get a road.

CHEHALIS

Said by a prominent judge to be "fit only for a frog pond," this
community was first known as Saunder's Bottom; an apt name,
because the place was quite swampy. The Chehalis, Chinook,
and Cowlitz Indians lived here before they were removed to a
reservation. Their villages were on the sandy banks of the
Chehalis River. When the Indians refused to go to the Quinault
Reservation in the 1850s, they were permitted to homestead on
what became the Chehalis Reservation at Oakville.[12]

Perhaps the first white man to lay eyes on Chehalis was a botanist named David Douglas (for whom the Douglas Fir was named), traveling and collecting specimens for the Royal Horticultural Society of London. Although Douglas was suffering from an infection from a rusty nail wound he received at Fort Vancouver, he continued on to Grays Harbor. There, he was treated for the injury by a Chehalis chief named Tha-amuxi. He continued down the Chehalis River with his Indian guides, and stopped at this site where he paid the guides for their services with tobacco, ammunition, and some flint. From here, Douglas continued on his travels to the headwaters of the Cowlitz River.

Schuyler Saunders arrived with his family in the 1850s, called it Saunder's Bottom, and for about a half dozen years only Saunders and local Indians occupied the area. During an Indian unrest in 1856, forts and blockhouses were constructed at the nearby town of Claquato. Saunders and his family, along with other area residents, took refuge while many of their homes were burned and their cattle stolen by the Indians.

Decent roads were nonexistent, and the pioneers used canoes to haul their grain to Fort Borst where it was stored, then processed into flour and shipped back up the river. Because of the difficulty in transporting the grain, the settlers decided to feed it to their livestock and drive them to market. The roads were so soggy that the settlers had an old saying: "The horns on the oxen are to show where they are in a muddy road!"[13] A judge later raised money for improving the road. Although the road was only corduroyed, at least it was a better alternative than mud. Eventually, a real road was cut between the little town of Claquato and Chehalis, and a ferry boat was put into operation at the mouth of the Newaukum River. The new road brought an influx of homesteaders.

Road conditions weren't any better for the animals, as related in an old folk tale. A man was riding his mule when it got stuck in the mud on one of the trails. Some helpful resident came by and asked what the problem was, then proceeded to put a drop of carbon disulfide (solvent) on the backside of the mule (one can only guess what part). The mule's ears began to move, then his tail twitched, and he finally pulled himself out of the mud and started running down the trail. The man asked the neighbor what he used on the mule, and to please put two drops on him because now he had to catch that mule!

A post office was established in 1858 at Saunders' home, and renamed Saundersville. After Saunders died about 1879, the post office was moved to another settler's home and the named changed to Chehalis, which was thought to mean "shifting sands,"[14] referring to the sandy banks of the Chehalis River.

William West moved here in 1864 and was considered the "Father of Chehalis." West accomplished many things in his life. He was instrumental in getting a railroad station, organized the school district, established one of the first businesses, and was mayor for three years. He was also the driving force in getting the county seat located at Chehalis.

When the Northern Pacific laid track between Kalama and Puget Sound, it bypassed the little town of Claquato, which was at that time the county seat. So residents left and moved to Chehalis, making Claquato virtually a ghost town. In anticipation of acquiring a rail station, the townspeople built a warehouse. Officials of the Northern Pacific offered Saunders' widow a ridiculous amount for her land so they could establish a station. She refused, and the railroad superintendent of the Kalama line, J. W. Sprague, purchased forty acres of land up the hill from town, built a station and called it Newaukum.

Now the train was passing right through Chehalis and not stopping. Residents were not about to slog through the swampy land and climb that big hill to take the train. They were told by someone if they waved a red flag the train would be required to stop for them. So these hardy pioneers waved their little red flag every time the Northern Pacific came through Chehalis. Rail officials finally decided it would be more economical to relocate the station, and Chehalis became a regular stop.[15]

Modern times brought the I. P. Callison Company to Chehalis. It became one of the largest producers of mint extract in the world. This area has many cascara trees, from which the extract is obtained. During an advertising campaign for the new business, the company's news releases had drops of the extract on them, and everyone who opened the envelopes got a whiff of the wonderful peppermint scent.

CHELAN

Alexander Ross and David Thompson were the first explorers to pass this way about 1811 when they were looking for a place for a trading post. Continuing up the Columbia River to a site that would become the future Fort Okanogan, they stopped here for a while and met friendly Indians who called the river Tsill-ane, from which Chelan is derived. A grandson of Chief Wapato told them his grandfather said the word meant "land of bubbling water."[16] Ross characterized the river "which descended over the rocks in white broken sheets," an apt description of the bubbling river.

A military post was built in 1879 at Chelan to protect the settlers from Indians. But the post didn't last long because of the expense, the terrible road and steep terrain, plus the rough river that made shipment of supplies too difficult. The supply wagons had to travel a road that dropped down a 2,500-foot, "widow-maker" cliff. After about four months, troops were sent to the new post at Camp Spokane.

Before 1886, this area was part of an Indian reservation. Settlers claimed their land and improved it, then later learned they couldn't get title to their claims. For unknown reasons, after the town was laid out in 1889 by surveyor Henry Carr, the plat was filed as a preemption. In 1892, a state representative asked for passage of a bill giving the town a patent. A report from Washington, D.C. in 1892 stated, . . . "The patent goes to the probate judge for use and benefit of the inhabitants of the town under the townsite laws. . . As a large number of people had taken and improved lots on the townsite this worked a great hardship. Appeal was made to representative Wilson, who promptly introduced the measure."[17] A month later the bill was approved, and the residents got title to their property.

The town was situated on a plateau overlooking the Columbia River. Industry came to Chelan when two men bought a sawmill and started a company store in 1888. The first retail business was the general store established in 1890 by C. E. Whaley. Amos Edmunds, who lived in Illinois, came out to visit his brother and ended up staying, built the first hotel and later became the town's first mayor.

The year 1889 brought two prospectors to the lake. Twenty

miles up the Stehekin River they found gold, and staked out claims they named the Black Warrior and the Blue Devil. When the word got out, the little community of Chelan was alive with miners. A man named Henry Holden discovered a mine on Railroad Creek in 1896, and called it the Holden Mine. The *Leader* wrote in 1904, "The year just closed has been one of notable prosperity for Lake Chelan. . . The Railroad Creek, twelve-mile, mining, narrow gauge railway has been made very nearly ready for the rails, and the Holden mine alone has contracted to deliver to a smelter syndicate 500,000 tons of copper and gold-bearing ore."[18] The gold was shipped by the railroad at Chelan until the mid 1950s, when the mine closed down.

Steamboat transportation started on a regular basis in 1888. Prior to that, a small steamer named *Chelan* was brought in by the army from Camp Chelan to serve their needs. When the military post was relocated, the boat went into service downriver. A retaining dam was built in the Chelan River to improve lake navigation. By the early 1900s, the Chelan Water Power Company was in operation. Tourism was booming and the hotels were filled to capacity. It wasn't long before buildings were constructed on all the sites along the lake.

Chelan made headlines in 1936 when it tested a new pension plan. One thousand one-dollar bills were circulated, with the provision that a two-cent stamp should be attached each time a bill changed hands. This was not a very popular concept and lasted only a short time.

Chelan's main industries were mining and lumber, but its most prosperous business has been apples. The town is surrounded by apple orchards and today produces some of the best apples in the world. In 1997, more than six million boxes of the fruit were produced.

An old Indian legend about Lake Chelan involves a young warrior who married an Indian girl from a Methow village. They went canoeing on Lake Chelan, and while the warrior was trying to spear a fish it turned into a dragon, which grabbed the warrior and took him to the depths of the lake. As the girl watched in horror, the dragon came up and told her that he was the spirit of the lake. "No one shall again come to my home. I will destroy anyone who dares to come." When the girl returned to the Chelan village, she told everyone the horrible thing that happened to her husband. The council decided to investigate and took their canoes onto the lake. Just before they got to the mouth of the Stehekin River, a storm came up and the dragon arose out of the water, grabbed one of the canoes and pulled it under. The other canoe paddled away in haste. For the longest time the Chelan Indians wouldn't go near the lake.[19]

CHEWELAH

The Chewelah Indians were an offshoot of the Pend Oreilles, a tribe that was part of the plateau Indians in Montana.[20] One Indian family had three sons, and one of them was slain by a neighbor after an argument. The father decided to leave the area when he thought another son would seek vengeance for his brother, and brought the family to Chewelah where there was plentiful game. As more white settlers moved in, the Indians were advised to take homesteads, which they did, and a number of them began to grow wheat on their farms. The Hudson's Bay Company later expanded its grazing areas to the Colville Valley, and when some of the employees left the company in 1845, they also came to Chewelah to live.

The first white man at this site in 1838 was probably Cushing Eells, founder of the Tshimakain Mission and First Congregational Church. Father Desmet established a mission at Chewelah in 1845, as recorded in one of his letters: "I left Kettle Falls August 4, 1845, accompanied by several of the Nation of Crees to examine the lands they had selected for the site of village. The ground is rich and well suited for all purposes, several buildings were commenced. I gave the name "Saint Francis Regis" to this new station where a great number of the mixed race and beaver hunters have resolved to settle with their families."[21] Several other families who came from Kalispel were also living in the area at this time.

Father Louis Vercruysse ran the St. Francis Regis Mission until 1851 when he was sent to St. Paul's in Kettle Falls. From time to time, the priests from St. Paul's would visit the Tshimakain Mission. When a fire destroyed part of the mission, it was discontinued in Chewelah and rebuilt between Colville and Kettle Falls.

Courtesy Chewelah Historical Society
Chewelah (1910). The town's fortune was linked to gold, silver, and copper.

Chewelah held its first Protestant church service led by Reverend Walker. He tried to teach the Indians about the life of Christ, but didn't have much success because of the language barrier, even though he used an interpreter. Reverend Eells also attempted to teach the Indians, but with the same results. They both left in 1847 after the Whitman massacre.

In the 1850s, Tom Brown and his family, on their way to the gold fields in California, had to stay in Chewelah because the winter was so severe. When spring arrived, he decided not to go to California, but instead went into farming and raised cattle in Chewelah. Brown received a contract from the government to furnish supplies to troops who were traveling back and forth to Fort Colville. Because he was one of the very few permanent white settlers at this time, his place became a rendezvous point for people traveling the old military fort to Pinkney City and other points.

Because of the rich agricultural potential in the Colville Valley, many of the Indians settled here and took up farming, and as a result the government opened an Indian agency in 1873. Agency staff taught the Indians new farming techniques, and gave them seeds and farm equipment. In the 1880s, the agency was moved to Nespelem, the present headquarters of the Colville Confederated Tribes.

When the post office was established in 1878, the town still did not have an official name. The name Chewelah comes from the Indian word s che weeleh, defined as "water" or "garter snake." The motion of the water in a spring gave the illusion of snakes moving in the water. The name may have also been spelled Chaw-wa-lah. In 1882, J. T. Lockhart established the first general store. More businesses moved in, but it wasn't until the Spokane Falls & Northern Railway was constructed that the Chewelah became a thriving town.

Chewelah was once home to the Northwest Magnesite Company, which refined the ore that was used for high-grade steel. The magnesite was normally imported from Austria, but during World War II this was not an option. Because the ore was an important commodity during the war, the plant was quite prosperous, employing more than 800 people. The company closed in 1968.

CHIMACUM

It is unclear who the first settlers were in Chimacum. Different sources show different names including Reuben Eldridge, William Eldridge, and Reuben Robinson. Some of the early events are also muddled as to who was who and who did what. It is known that the town was named for the now-extinct Chimacum Indians, and their story is full of contradictions, too. Their name was also spelled Chimakum.

The Chimacum may have been a remnant of the Quileute band of Indians who left the coast area because of extremely high tides that did not cease for many days. Supposedly an aggressive and warlike tribe, it was thought they were killed by their enemies.[22] In 1895, J. C. Costello wrote that the Chimacums disappeared because an Indian named Chetzemoka got together with a band of Skagit Indians and massacred the Chimacums while they were camping on the beach. Many human bones were found on a beach near Kuhn Spit, which was contradictory to Indian burial practices. It's also possible the Chimacums were wiped out by smallpox.

The Bishops were one of the first families here, and their

Courtesy James Hermanson, Port Townsend, Washington
Chimacum Hotel (undated). It was destroyed by fire in August 1938.

history of the community is probably the most accurate.[23] Some of Bishop's descendants still live in the area. Mrs. Stephen Bishop wrote the history of Chimacum as her father-in-law, the late Senator William Bishop, related it to her. The Chimacum Indians who lived here were annihilated by the Snohomish and Barkley Sound Indians in 1857, and the Snohomish took possession of the area.

Reuben Robinson and his wife came from the East and settled at Chimacum in 1855. Their son, Albert, was the first white child born in the town. Two men from a British merchant vessel got off the ship: William Bishop and William Eldridge. They came to Chimacum, where they met the Robinson family with whom they stayed the first winter, and in the spring acquired their own farms.

Between 1860 and 1870 there were a lot of new arrivals. Edward Strand, who was from Finland, came to Chimacum and built the first mill. Many of the new settlers were also from Finland, in addition to immigrants from Sweden and Ireland. Small businesses sprang up, and dairy farming became a thriving industry. The Chimacum Trading Company was established and also served as the post office.[24] When the Chimacum

Garage was built, it was issued business license number 4, and today may be the oldest surviving business in the state. The Chimacum Hotel was built by Dr. Kritz from Port Hadlock. Over the years it went through numerous owners, but in 1938 it was destroyed by fire.

Large stands of timber had to be cleared before farming could begin. In some boggy areas, large logs were pulled out that had floated to the top, which were then sold intact, roots and all.

A Dutch sailor named John van Trojen came to Chimacum about 1869. He married and became one of the best chicken ranchers in the valley. Speaking

Northwest and Whitman College Archives, Washington
John Palmer (late 1800s). Last of the Chimacum Indians, he was born around 1847 and died in 1881. After learning six languages, John became an interpreter for a number of Indian reservations.

of chickens, Chimacum was the locale of Betty McDonald's book, "The Egg and I," which featured the famous Ma and Pa Kettle, a comparison residents may not have appreciated.

Bishop and Eldridge, who had been in business together, went their separate ways. Bishop started raising hops on his land, and hired Indians to help him pick the product. He later sold his property and moved to Port Townsend. Eldridge ran a successful dairy farm.

During World War II, the Japanese released 9,000 balloons loaded with incendiaries. The intent was to burn our forests and cause statewide panic. One of the balloons landed at Chimacum, but it turned out to be harmless. The government kept the balloon attack secret because it didn't want the

Japanese to know that their balloons were actually landing in the United States.[25]

Chimacum has a sentinel called the Tananamus Rock, which means "fighting." It rises 400 feet above sea level and can be seen from the entire valley. The Chimacum Indians used to gather here for their worship, and whenever they were in danger, they fled to this rock. But in 1855 the Barkley Sound Indians snuck up on the Chimacums and annihilated them. (Bishop's history states the year as 1857). The Chimacums no longer pass this way, but the sentinel still stands silent guard over the valley.

CLALLAM BAY

This site was home to the Klallam Indians which is situated on the Strait of Juan De Fuca. During the 1840s, a number of the Indians went to work at a new trading post established by the Hudson's Bay Company on Vancouver Island where they grew potatoes for the company. Clallam may be derived from the Klallam's word for themselves, Nu'sklaim, which means "strong people." Their territory extended from Port Discovery Bay to the Hoko River on the north coast of the state. [26]

The town was platted in 1890 by Dave Kellogg who named it East Clallam. The people who came here to live were allowed to homestead 160 acres, but had to prove up the land according to the Homestead and Timber Act. The *Clallam Bay Record* was established by George O'Brien in 1891 because the law required publication of all patents and deeds. They were the main source of revenue for the paper. By the time all the homesteads were taken in 1908, the paper moved to the neighboring town of Sequim and was renamed the *Sequim Press*. East Clallam changed its name to Clallam Bay in 1907.

Logging became the town's main industry in 1902 when D. A. Robertson built a small railroad, in addition to building what was at the time the longest railroad bridge in the world. Crossing Charlie Creek, it was 808 feet long and 202 feet high. The logs were skidded across on grease. Robinson also built a sawmill, which he later sold to the C. A. Goodyear Lumber Company from Wisconsin. Logging slowed down for ten years until 1913, when Goodyear started a railroad that went from

Sekiu through Clallam Bay and five miles upriver where the timber was cut. Then the timber industry took off again.[27]

The California Tanning Company established an extract plant in the region. Hemlock trees were cut down, but only their bark was used, and the rest of the wood was left to rot. More than 200 people were employed at the plant, which produced at least thirty-five barrels of extract every day. It operated until 1900 when a new extraction method was discovered. Someone once attempted to mine coal not far from town. After about four years, the project was abandoned by the Star Grocery Company, the last owner of the mine.

When a fire broke out in 1907, the entire business section of Clallam Bay was lost because there was no water system, and only one store survived. The hotel was rebuilt, but it burned down again in 1947. A dock owned by Alston Fairservice was destroyed when a wicked storm came through in 1912.

Clallam was the last harbor before ships entered the Pacific Ocean, known for its dangerous storms. In 1907, the *Alice Gertrude*, a steamer coming from Neah Bay to pick up passengers and mail, ran into heavy weather in the straits. The ship had left the harbor in the face of a rising gale, but could make no headway. So Captain Charles Kallstrom turned the ship around to go back to Clallam Bay. By that time the gale had turned into a blizzard, and snowfall hindered an officer's ability to see the bay's entrance. The foghorn wasn't working that night, and the lighthouse light might have been mistaken for a dock light. Huge swells smashed the ship onto the beach at Slip Point and it was a total loss. The passengers were transferred onto tug boats and taken to Seattle.[28]

For a number of years Clallam Bay had a weather station which was in contact by telegraph with Tatoosh Island, where the lighthouse keepers kept seafarers informed of the weather conditions. This early forecast system allowed the captains to go to the station and get a weather report before sailing out to sea. It was also a great communication aid for tugboat operators, who were alerted to the ships off Cape Flattery. It was a race to see who could get to the ships first and guide them into the straits. The telegraph office was moved to Port Angeles in 1914.

CLAQUATO

The year Washington separated from Oregon Territory, Claquato became one of the earliest settlements in the region. In the Salish language, it is thought to mean "high land."[29] Claquato is located about three miles southwest of Chehalis on the Skookumchuk River.

Claquato was founded by Lewis Hawkins Davis, who came from Indiana and settled here in 1852. He had previously joined up with a wagon train that was going to the Willamette Valley. When Davis arrived at Portland, he was surprised to see how crowded the area was, which did not suit his lifestyle, so he took a donation claim on Claquato Hill. Because there were no roads yet, Davis donated part of his land to be used as a right of way that would bring a road from the Columbia River near Monticello to the Olympia area. It was built with government funding and local volunteer labor. The road brought stage-coaches through Claquato, plus military personnel traveling from Fort Vancouver to Fort Steilacoom. At a place called Adna was Claquato Landing, where the old paddlewheel steamers came up the river from Grays Harbor.[30]

Although Davis was fifty-nine years old when he first arrived in Claquato, this hardy settler built a grist mill and sawmill. Being a staunch Methodist, he gave some of his land for a Methodist church in the 1850s and supplied the lumber for it. He also offered to have a courthouse built if Claquato would become the county seat, which it did in 1862. Under Davis' leadership, the town grew and prospered. Davis died in 1864 from injuries he sustained when he fell at his mill.

Rumors flew in 1855 that the Yakima Indian War was spreading to the southwest part of Washington. Many of the set-tlers took refuge in a blockhouse that was quickly built on Davis' property. Fortunately, no problems arose in this part of the valley and the people returned to their homes.

In the 1870s, the Northern Pacific Railroad built its line between Kalama and Tacoma and completely bypassed Claquato. This little town lost its county-seat status and it was given to Chehalis. Most of the residents relocated there. Claquato became a little backwater community, and was offi-cially taken off the county records in 1902.

Claquato was home to an old Indian woman the people admired and respected. She was called "Queen Susan." The town treasurer made her coffin when she died, and the school closed down for the day so the children could go to her service. Before Susan was buried, the Indians performed an interesting ritual. They brought calico cloth to put in her coffin, then gently laid her in it. Her personal effects were put on top of her body, and finally gold pieces were placed in the coffin. Unfortunately, many years later the grave was unearthed and the gold was stolen. What's left of Claquato is a few residents and the oldest standing church in the state of Washington.

CLE ELUM

In 1880, a prospector named Thomas Gamble ran into Walter Reed who was a boyhood friend from Pennsylvania. Gamble had been traveling around the region and told Reed about the Cle Elum area, so Reed came to see for himself. He and his wife were so impressed they ended up staying and built a cabin which was completed in 1883. The town was platted by Reed on July 26, 1886. Gamble also claimed some land nearby and built his cabin on a creek.[31]

When a coal outcrop was discovered by a trapper in 1883 near Roslyn Canyon, Northern Pacific Railroad surveyors came to the territory and decided this would be a good place to extend the line. As the rails were being laid, the little town of Teanaway was being used as a depot. But Reed, with his foresight, influenced Northern Pacific officials to move the depot here and had the engineers lay out the town. The number of settlers had increased to the extent that Reed began to plat the town. The name Cle Elum was chosen, defined as "swift water."[32] The railroad tried to get the name changed, but residents refused, and Cle Elum it stayed.

Men came to find their fortunes, not only in coal, but in logging and farming. There weren't many women in the region at the time, and the *Teanaway Bugle* ran the following news item: "Partners Wanted!! Must be Females! Beauty No Object - - After roaming around this cold, cheerless and unsympathetic world for many years, with nothing to love, no-one to caress us, . . . All that is wanting to complete our happiness is partners of the

Courtesy Cle Elum Library
Cle Elum (1913). Townsmen march to honor Labor Day.

female persuasion. No capital required and but few questions asked. Women of uncertain age and questionable beauty acceptable, provided they can otherwise pass examination. Sound teeth and strong constitutions are the essential requisites."[33]

When a railroad bridge had to be built across the Columbia River near the town of Pasco, much lumber was needed. A man named Tom Johnson moved his mill from Wilson Creek and established it at Cle Elum near the railroad depot. Logs were hauled from the river to Johnson's mill, where up to fifty men were employed and produced about 40,000 feet of lumber each day. Johnson later opened a general store.

Coal mining began in earnest when the Roslyn beds were opened, and shipment of the ore started in 1886. At the suggestion of some friends, Thomas Gamble also had a coal shaft sunk on his property, which proved to be quite profitable. Later the Northwest Railroad leased the mine and Gamble got royalties to the tune of ten cents a ton. The railroad also purchased the Cle Elum Coal Company, which started quite a spat between two newspapers. People from the neighboring town of Ellensburg were concerned about this purchase, so the *Capital*

newspaper wrote: "The Ellensburg people are much concerned
... The supposition is that the N.P.C. will now boom Cle Elum
and the division of the road will be moved to Cle Elum." The
Cascade Miner retaliated with, "Ellensburg has claimed the
earth long enough. It does the people in this end of the county
good to see them scared for once!" The *Capital* responded: "The
Cascade Miner is decidedly off. The People of Ellensburg are
glad to see Cle Elum progressing!"[34] The importance of the coal
mines declined with the advent of water power.

One of the worst mining disasters occurred in Cle Elum on
July 12, 1908, when the powder house exploded, killing a number of employees. The manager and clerk were supervising the
unloading of a carload of black powder at the time, and several
other men were working in the powder magazine. Almost all the
windows in the homes for blocks around were blown out.

Timber was a big industry for the county. There was a tie and
lumber camp near Cle Elum in 1879, which sent the logs down
to the Northern Pacific mill at Ainsworth. A mill that was located at Tunnel City had exhausted its suitable timber for trestles.
It was then moved near Cle Elum, where trestle timbers were
sawed, fitted at the mill, and then moved by rail car to a switchback, ready to be swung into place and bolted.

Theron Stafford, who was a pharmacist by trade and a dentist when needed, had operated a general store and drugstore at
Teanaway, and later moved it to Cle Elum. In 1891, his son,
Charlie, and a friend were playing with matches in the store's
attic. They started a fire that destroyed the store, and before
firefighters could put the fire out, most of the business district
went up in flames. Stafford rebuilt his business and continued
operating until the Northern Pacific purchased his property.

Roads were not the best in the early 1900s and in order for
Cle Elum residents to travel to Ellensburg they had to climb
Ballard Hill. Any car that could climb the hill was considered a
pretty good vehicle, because many of their brakes failed on this
hill and they would end up on a backward ride into someone's
fence. Winter brought out the sleighs and they went into competition with the automobiles coming from the opposite
direction, and there was room for only one vehicle on the hill. It
was usually a fight for right of way with the sleighs winning

because they could not go backwards. Then they would fight over how much snow to plow off the hill. Sleds could not navigate from too little snow, and the cars could not motivate with too much. It wasn't until 1927 that a new road was built, bypassing the hill making everyone happy.

CONCONULLY

On a branch of the Salmon River (not related to Idaho's Salmon River) sits Conconully, a town that consists of about three blocks. It was first called Salmon City until it was renamed Conconully, defined as "cloudy," or in the Indians' dialect, "evil spirit," because the Indians thought there was a monster that lived in the small lake near town. Others think the name may have come from Conconulp, which meant "money hole," a place where the beaver were in great numbers and used as money by the Indians.[35]

The year 1886 brought prospectors to the Salmon River when word got out about gold and silver in the region. What began as the tents of miners turned into a settlement in a few years. A man named Boardman built a cabin, had a load of supplies freighted in, and opened a trading post. Timber was later a prosperous industry and eventually supplanted gold mining.

The first wedding in the county was held at Conconully in 1890. Jacob and Elizabeth Kornely were Germans who couldn't speak English, and the judge who married them had to struggle through the ceremony. All celebrated with cheese, crackers, and beer. The couple left and moved to another town where the husband operated a ferry crossing on the Okanogan River.

Conconully was a town of disasters: a fire in 1892; the end of the gold and silver boom in 1893; and a flash flood the following year. The fire started in an empty store, and with the wind blowing the whole town went up in flames in less than two hours. The *Spokane Review* wrote: "The entire town was suddenly illuminated by a fierce, red glare . . . a great mass of whirling sparks and cinders."[36]

In 1894 the flood hit. A huge thunderstorm with incredible lightning woke the residents. A cloudburst came down, stripping the hillsides on the Salmon River, and by morning a pent-up avalanche of water and debris was headed toward the town, where a wall of water hit the buildings and carried them away. The men had tried dynamiting all the log jams, but it didn't do any good, there was just too much water. When the flood was over, almost fifty buildings had been destroyed, the town was full of debris with boulders and household belongings strewn all over the place. A local newspaper wrote that the disaster resembled another Johnstown. By some miracle, only one person died in the flood.

By 1909, county commissioners decided the town needed a jail. It was then supplied with handcuffs, and ball and chains. Apparently, the jail wasn't built that well because inmates were always escaping and the town was ridiculed about it. At one time, two friends of a prisoner came to visit him. Finding the jailer gone, they simply unlatched the window, came in and played cards with the inmates, then left, relatching the window. So much for security.

ENTIAT

Entiat is derived from the word "Entiatqua," signifying "rushing water,"[37] an apt name for one of the major rapids of the Columbia River. At times, the river was so treacherous that shipwrecks occurred because of its strong currents. In 1902, the steamship *Camano* was destroyed near Entiat Landing. Its cargo may have shifted and its weight overturned the boat after a strong current hit the bow. That same year the steamer *North Star* sank. The current caught the boat and pushed it across the channel where it struck a rock that put a hole in the hull. In 1906, the *W. H. Pringle*'s drive shaft broke and the steamer was swept down the rapids. The channel was eventually improved.[38]

A Caribbean miner named Antoine allegedly found a gold mine at Entiat. About 1868, he was traveling from Ellensburg when he discovered the placer mine, which he called Big Antoine. Years earlier, Chinese miners had built a ditch which brought water to wash the gold that was found in the area. Antoine used the ditch for his mining operation. Sometime later, he was ordered to leave by an Army commander stationed at Camp Chelen because an Indian named Silicoe objected to his presence.

The first settler was a man named Lewis Detwiler, who came

to Entiat in 1887 and claimed land about a mile up the valley. The local Indian leader, Chief Silicoe, told Detwiler that he owned the land and, with the help of another Indian, made the white man leave. Detwiler then threatened to shoot every Indian's horse, forcing an Indian agent to intercede to make peace.

The second settler at Entiat was James C. Bonar on April 11, 1887. Two years later, Bonar helped to build a road, as shown in his journal: "August 9, rafted new lumber for new claim, . . . 23, went up river to help survey Navarre road to Entiat. 28, 29, 30, 31, I acted as ax-man, cutting trees or brush that obscured the sight on road survey, by Ole Rudd, from Entiat to Quartz Creek, W. F. Cannon, Ed Adams, and Eph. Finch assisting."[39]

As people settled in the new community, the climate and soil were foreign to them, so they began experimenting with fruit orchards. Peaches and plums did not prove to be viable crops, plus the market was poor for those products. The farmers finally turned to apples which became their principle cash product. The fruit was shipped by boat to Wenatchee, then by carload to various destinations. When the state road between Entiat and Wenatchee was completed, shipping supplies became much easier, and also brought in more settlers.

The Keystone Ranch was one of Entiat's earliest apple packers. The fruit was packed in wooden boxes and taken to the packing shed where they were graded. The apples were loaded onto boats (later by railroad) for distribution elsewhere. The farmers took quite a gamble marketing their fruit through brokers, for many of them were more interested in lining their own pockets than helping out the farmers. They did find an honest agent in a man named Conrad Rose, and established a good relationship with him.

Mail was delivered by boats that plied the Columbia River. During the winter of 1915, there was so much snow, up to five feet in Entiat, that the mail was delivered via team of horses up to a place called Potato Creek. Then it was snow shoes and skis the rest of the way. The only way one of the farmers could get his horse home that winter was to use planks alternately put in front of the horse to walk on.[40]

At the first Entiat site the post office was established in

1895, followed in a few years with a store and hotel. Gray's Mill was erected upriver. Later, a barber shop and the Blind Pig Tavern were built. Then in 1908, the mill dam was constructed, which provided electricity to Entiat and the town of Waterville. When the power plant broke down there was no one in Entiat who knew how fix it. Residents had to wait until a technician could be summoned. Installation of the town's telephone lines, which ran only fifteen miles, took two years to complete.

Water rights were filed in 1894 by the Entiat Irrigation District, and construction of an irrigation ditch was completed within eighteen months. Many of the farmers lost precious water because the ditch kept breaking. After the 1970 wildfires, there was nothing to hold back the water, and tons of debris and sand were washed into the Entiat River, causing too much wear on the irrigation pump impellers, and they went belly-up. With a loan and grant, the system was upgraded and computerized. Today, the water rights are still jealously guarded.

Because the town was populated in the early days mainly by men who came for the logging and mining industries, they needed women. In 1910, the Bachelor's Club was formed and open only to men who wanted to get married. They set up their bylaws, with the objective, "To promote interest in matrimony. To discuss the advantages and the disadvantages of the marital state. To determine what sort of woman makes the ideal wife, and to secure such a spouse for each member of the club." [41] Any correspondence between the men and prospective brides was not for public knowledge, just in case things didn't work out. Somehow word got out quickly and the club received so much mail the secretary couldn't handle it and quit.

The Great Northern Railroad laid track that paralleled the Columbia River, in 1914. As a result, the second Entiat was built along the Oroville-Wenatchee branch of the railroad. The Entiat Fruit Growers League was formed in the early 1920s, and warehouses were built to store the fruit. More than 1,000 cars of apples were shipped from Entiat in 1924.

The next year, delegations from Entiat and the nearby town of Orondo got together and proposed that a bridge be built across the Columbia River. This would have enabled everyone to have easier access to shipping and warehousing. The federal government approved the project, and Fred H. Furey & Associates got the franchise. But because they were building another bridge and there was litigation about it, the Entiat project was halted. When the depression came, the bridge project died.

In the 1950s, the public utilities department bought out Entiat because the Rocky Reach Dam was going to be built. Some of the structures were burned down, others were moved; and some were completely rebuilt at Entiat's present site.

This town moved around a lot. In 1896 it was located about one-half mile west of the Entiat River. When a mill burned down, it took most of the town with it. When the railroad tracks were built, the town relocated there in 1914. It had to move again when the Rocky Reach Dam was filled in 1960. It is now located along Highway 97A. Entiat residents hope their little town will stay where it's at; they don't want to move again!

ENUMCLAW

Named for the mountain, Enumclaw was established in 1885. The town is on a plateau between the White and Green Rivers, a gateway to Chinook and Naches Passes. Definitions of the name vary: "place of the evil spirits," "thundering mountain,"[42] or "loud, rattling noise."[43] A band of Duwamish Indians were camped at the base of the mountain when a terrific thunderstorm came through. The Indians thought the sound was coming from spirits inside the mountain, and were so frightened they called it Enumclaw. There was an old saying that when the Indians were hunting deer, the animals knew they would be safe if they headed to the mountain because the Indians would not go near it.

The first settler may have been James McClintock who came here about 1850 after the Puget Sound War. More than twenty years later, an Englishman named Frank Stevenson and his wife came to this muddy, heavily wooded area. Stevenson built a one-room cabin and began the arduous job of clearing about twenty acres of timber. Because this was just a little outpost at the time, his wife had to ride to the town of Osceola to pick up their mail.

As more people settled in Enumclaw, it was still somewhat

Courtesy Enumclaw Public Library
Enumclaw (1893). This is the oldest known photo of the town. The building on
the left is the Northern Pacific Depot. The small, square building near the
center is the General Mercantile.

isolated and transportation was limited. Residents who wanted
to cross the White River had to blow a cow's horn so a boat on
the other side of the river would come and take them across.
There was really nothing but densely forested trails. The settlers used stumps as their road, cutting down the trees and
leaving the stumps high enough for the wagon wheels to roll
over, while the tree roots held the road together.

The Northern Pacific Railroad selected Tacoma as its Pacific
Ocean terminus and came to the Enumclaw area to survey for
a rail siding. Frank Stevenson offered his land for the siding. As
the railroad began laying track in 1883, Stevenson built a hotel
in anticipation of growth, and named the site Enumclaw. He
also gave some of his lots away to encourage other businesses to
the community. Completion of the railroad linked Enumclaw to
Seattle and Tacoma.

By 1887, Arthur Griffin had opened a store with the post
office inside, and railroad workers provided the store with most
of its business. A number of saloons and a school were built, and
the first newspaper, the *Enumclaw Evergreen*, was published
by A. C. Rogers, who was the son of Governor John Rogers. At
one time, a fellow tried to open a "house of ill repute," but the
settlers ran him out of town and told him he could go across the

Courtesy Enumclaw Public Library
Enumclaw (undated). Rochdale Company Store and Vinco Flour, located on Cole Street.

river for that venture. There were no sidewalks and everyone had to walk on felled trees or planks. A man named Nelson Bennett erected the first mill, and would go on to build the Cascade Tunnel.

While the railroad tunnel was under construction through the Cascades, Enumclaw was having a problem getting funding for roads, due to politics. County commissioners were directing road money to the lower part of the valley that was flourishing with the hop industry, and Enumclaw was located in the upper valley. An upper valley resident named Johannes Mahler got a wild idea how to get enough votes for a road. Because the other towns had more people, they had more political clout. At a Republican caucus in Seattle, John Kelley attended on behalf of the "tunnel delegation." The group was composed of workers building the Cascade Tunnel and were entitled to a large number of delegates, most of whom were members of the Populist Party. Kelly cast proxy votes of the Populists. He also slipped in the names of many men who were killed while working on the tunnel. But Enumclaw got its roads.[44]

On July 7, 1887, the first transcontinental train made its way through the Cascades and Stampede Summit and into the little town of Enumclaw, where it was welcomed with a twenty-one-gun salute. The depot opened in 1888, with W. F. Giles as its first stationmaster.

In 1890, P. L. Markey took over as stationmaster. He was part of an expedition that was getting ready to climb Mount Rainier where he planned to plant a flag for Enumclaw. The day the event was to occur, Markey tried desperately to find some-one to take his place at work so he could join the expedition. Unable to do so, Markey closed the depot and went up the mountain. He lost his job for abandoning his post, but he made it to the top of the mountain.

A group of Danes who were attracted by the farmlands set-tled in Enumclaw in 1889 by taking government claims or pur-chasing lots from the railroad. They brought their principle of cooperative organization with them, which contributed greatly to the town's growth. The Enumclaw Cooperative Creamery was established, and its award-winning butter was shipped throughout the state.

HOQUIAM

Situated at the mouth of the Hoquiam River, this town saw its first white residents in 1859 when James Karr and his fam-ily made their home on the riverbank. The settlement began to take shape with the arrival of the Campbell brothers.

Although the river had some dangerous tidal flats that were full of driftwood, the waterway was a good thirty feet deep and steamboats were able to navigate the Hoquiam. The area had a wealth of timber that drew more people, and in 1867 the town got its first post office. Surveyors had originally written the name Hokium in their field notes, their interpretation of the Indian word. But when the post office was established it was spelled Hoquiam. The name may be derived from the Indian word ho-qui-umpts, which means "hungry for wood," referring to the driftwood at the mouth of the river.[45]

Land sold in Hoquiam included a requirement that the

purchasers build on their lots. In 1882, the town was progressing with two sawmills, four hotels, and an electric lighting plant. The Northwestern Lumber Company was going full steam, producing about 100,000 board feet a day, the mills were going night and day. The town reverberated with the sounds of huge saws and blowing whistles.

Some shipbuilding also occurred because of the good timber. The wooden boats were used to carry lumber. The first schooner was built in 1887 at the Northwestern Mill.

It wasn't until 1890 that a plank road was laid between Hoquiam and the neighboring town of Aberdeen. About six years later, a fire destroyed the Northwestern sawmill, but it was rebuilt within a year.[46]

The Northern Pacific Railway laid its tracks, but Hoquiam did not become the railroad's terminus because Karr would not sell his property to the company. A few years later the railroad built another line, and in 1898 Hoquiam got the railroad to extend its tracks to the sawmills. One of the first engines purchased by the Northern Pacific was named the "Minnetonka." It was eventually sold to the Polson Brothers Logging Company, which used the engine for logging until about 1928—more than fifty-five years of service. The company nicknamed the engine "Old Betsy."[47] It was later exhibited at fairs and ended up in the Lake Superior Museum of Transportation. The lumber finally played out around Hoquiam and the industry bottomed out with the depression.

Hoquiam was the first town in the state of Washington to show a talking motion picture. It is also home to the Hoquiam Castle. Built in 1897 by Robert Lytle who was a lumber magnate, the castle sits on a hillside. It is on the National Register of Historic Places. Today it is a private home, but open for tours by appointment.

ILWACO

Ilwaco is a little town on level land that faces B.
and was originally named Unity to show its residents
to the Union during the Civil War. It was later named   the
son-in-law of Chief Comcomly, Elowahka Jim (but spelled
Ilwaco). James Johnson took up a donation claim and built his
home in 1848. While paddling one day across the Columbia
River, near Astoria, with a load of goods, Johnson's canoe capsized and he drowned.

A man named Isaac Whealdon bought Johnson's property in
1859 and drove a stagecoach between Ilwaco and the town of
Oysterville, carrying mail and passengers. The stage also transported oysters, which were loaded on ships and taken to
California. In addition to the stage business, Whealdon raised
cattle. He branded them by cropping off the right ear and
underbit in the left ear.[48]

The story of Ilwaco probably starts with a sly old fox named
Elijah White, when he was looking for a place near the water
that could be built into a large city. He filed a donation claim for
640 acres at a place called Pacific City in March 1849. White
subdivided the property and advertised it for sale, claiming the
place had a hotel and other businesses. Absentee buyers didn't
know there really wasn't anything there. A year later, White
conveyed part of his claim to James Holman, who named and
platted Ilwaco, built a hotel and purchased interest in a
sawmill. Henry Feister arrived in 1851 and started an ox-team
transportation company that hauled supplies to settlers on
Shoalwater Bay. Lewis Loomis and his brother claimed land in
the 1850s and raised sheep for a while. But Loomis had bigger
ideas, so he and a group of men founded the Ilwaco Wharf
Company in 1874. Loomis later organized a stage line.

Ilwaco was a stopping point on the expanding stagecoach
and steamer ferry route between Astoria, Oregon, and the
Puget Sound country. There also was a daily schedule that ran
to Oysterville on a hard-packed beach. One of the stagecoach
drivers once stated while driving this route, ". . in addition to a
man handling the ribbons, he had to be a first-class navigator
in that business. Many a time I have had a big swell lift horses

and wagon and toss the whole shooting match up and around like a toy."[49]

In 1898, the Ilwaco Railroad and Navigation Company was founded, which later became known as the "Clamshell." The *Pacific Journal* called it the "Delay, Linger and Wait Railroad," whereupon the railroad revoked the newspaper's rail pass. Others called it the "Irregular, Rambling and Never-Get-There Railroad." The train could only run at mid flood, and schedules were constantly altered to coincide with the changing tides. The editor of an early Ilwaco newspaper got his two bits in when he printed his own train schedule: "Train Leaves Ilwaco - When It Gets Ready. Arrives at Nahcotta - When It Gets There."[50]

The old trains did not run smoothly, as described by someone who wrote to the *Willapa Harbor Pilot* in 1905, ". . .On the Ilwaco Railroad at the rate of about seven miles an hour and the whole train was shaking terribly. . . I held firmly onto my seat. Presently we settled down a bit quieter; at least I could keep my hat on and my teeth did not chatter. . . I remarked to him [another passenger] that we were going a bit smoother. 'Yes,' he said, 'we're off the track now!'"[51]

Maintenance of the railroad line and depot was less than desirable, except for the busy seasons. So the editor of the *Ilwaco Tribune*, in his tactful way, wrote a poem in 1914 about the whole situation:

> *There's a railroad they call the Peninsula Pike-*
> *. . .From Megler this railroad goes winding about,*
> *Like two streaks of rust in an alley,*
> *On low joints and high joints we're jostled about,*
> *Till the doctor can scarcely make us rally. . .*
> *Thousands of ties nearly rotten today,*
> *Bridges unsafe as the devil,*
> *The rails were aged when laid, they say,*
> *But the roadbed is not on the level.*
> *The spikes are all rusted and loose as old teeth,*
> *The fish plates have passed all redemption;*
> *The whole thing is dead; so I am weaving this wreath -*
> *As a railroad it's surely an exemption. . .* [52]

It wasn't long before a new depot was built. Loomis' company was later taken over by the Oregon Railway & Navigation (OR&N). The advent of automobiles spelled doom for the "Clamshell." The rails were eventually pulled up, except at Ilwaco and the town of Long Beach because they had been cemented in when the streets were paved.

ISSAQUAH

In a valley between the Squak and Tiger Mountains lies the historic mining town of Issaquah. This area was the fishing and hunting ground of the Snoqualmie Indians before white settlers arrived in the 1800s. The town had many names before Issaquah. The Indians called it Ishquoh, but because the white man could not pronounce the word with its guttural sound, it came out "Squak." Issaqah may have been derived from the word isquoah, which some believe means "the sound of the birds," or it could refer to a snake or a river. Whatever its real meaning, the town's name was changed to Issaquah in February 1899.[53]

The 1860s saw a lot of people coming into the area because of the fertile land. Two Norwegian brothers, Lars Ingebright and Peter Wold, pioneered the hop industry in Issaquah. They filed their homestead papers, and the following year they bought hop plants from Ezra Meeker. Many of the other settlers followed suit. After being picked by Indian and Chinese laborers, the hops were sent to Seattle where they were used to make beer. Eventually, the hops were plowed under because aphids were destroying the crops, and spraying cost too much, not to mention the spraying didn't work very well anyway.

A huge coal seam was discovered in the region in the 1870s. Issaquah's economy mushroomed when the miners came through on their way to the coal fields. With the miners came the inevitable saloons, and hardware stores that supplied the prospectors with equipment. Transporting the coal was no easy task as it had to be barged down Lake Sammamish, taken by scow to Lake Washington, then on to the Black River in Renton, and finally to the Port of Seattle. It took more than fifteen days to make the trip, and wasn't very profitable.

In 1874, George Washington Tibbetts and his family left

their home in Maine and came to Issaquah. George was one of the driving forces in developing the town. He served as postmaster, established the stage route to the town of Newcastle, and was one of the first state legislators. Tibbetts drafted a bill to build a highway over the Cascade Mountains. Today it is known as Snoqualmie Pass.

Lumbering became an important industry, and one of the first sawmills was established by the Neukirchen brothers. The mill opened the way for more settlers to come for farming and logging operations. A feed store was established, followed in 1912 by a general store. Unlike today, the merchants delivered their supplies to the family homes, and the butcher cut fresh meat for the residents right at their doorsteps.

Daniel Gilman came to Issaquah to help his brother with the coal mines. Realizing the importance of better transportation, Gilman promoted the Lake Shore and Eastern Railroad which reached Issaquah in 1888, and the first load of coal was shipped. A German count named von Alvenslaben came to Issaquah after the first World War and organized the Issaquah and Superior Coal Mining Company. The project was abandoned after more than one million dollars had been spent. With the arrival of the railroad and the creation of the Seattle Coal and Iron Company, the small miners lost out. By the 1930s, the coal mining industry dwindled and finally died. The people then turned to agriculture and dairy farming. The North Western Milk Condensing Company was established with local investment money.[54]

In 1870, William Pickering, Jr. became the first postmaster at Squak. The office was located in his cabin. The post office moved around a lot. After being resident with Pickering for about five years, it moved across the valley to another home, then in 1879 moved to the west side. It stayed there for seven years, when it was moved across the valley yet again in 1886.

When the town was incorporated, the name was changed to Gilman, because he was instrumental in bringing the railroad to this area. Postal officials said there was a town in Washington called Gilmer and there would be too much confusion with the similarity, so the name was changed to Olney, but no one knows why. In the early 1890s, the post office moved into the railroad station and was renamed Issaquah. In 1937, it was relocated in back of the bank. Finally, in the 1940s, Issaquah got a permanent post office building.

Issaquah Salmon Days Festival is held the first full weekend in October each year. Visitors can watch the sockeye salmon in the river that runs through the center of town.

KAHLOTUS

Sagebrush lines the road from Connell to Kahlotus, which is located on the west side of Lake Kahlotus. The Oregon-Washington River & Navigation Co. Railroad (OWR&N) laid a branch line from Connell to Kahlotus in 1883. Henry Villard was the president of the OWR&N, which grew from the Oregon Steam Navigation Company. His plan was to control all the steamboat and rail transport, and he tried to purchase the Great Northern Railroad. The venture failed, and then the panic of 1893 caused Villard's empire to fall around his ears.[55]

In 1886, the post office was established in the home of Thomas Winn, who was the first postmaster and also tutored some of the settlers' children. When the railroad branch was discontinued in 1890, so was the post office, but both were reinstated twelve years later. That same year, three of the citizens began promoting the town. The local improvement company believed the area would support a town if cattle were replaced by wheat fields. By 1905, there was a saloon, grain warehouses, and a hotel. Kahlotus shipped vast amounts of wheat and was considered the largest shipping point for the product. The town was platted in 1902 by the Hardersburg Townsite and Improvement Company.[56]

John Harder, great grandson of Hans Harder, wrote down some of the history he recalls about Kahlotus: "My Grandfather, Hans Harder, came from Schlevig-Holstein in Northern Germany, to settle on the Snake River at a place called Three-Spring Bar in 1883. He leased and bought land from the railroad companies, the government, and homesteaders. He rounded up wild horses, tamed and trained them for sale to the U.S. Army, settlers and prospectors. He also ran sheep, cattle and other livestock. He built his home at the spring near what would be called Kahlotus Lake."[57]

Courtesy Boyd Peterson, Pasco, Washington
Kahlotus (1907). The town became the largest wheat-shipping point in the county. OWR&N Railroad is in background.

"My father, John Harder, was Hans and Dorothea Harder's first born in 1894. He (John) began farming wheat (mainly) in 1908 which he continued to do until his death in 1952."

"The Oregon Washington Railroad and Navigation Co. (OWR&N) line was built in the 1880s and had area stops called Estes and Wacota. The railroad line which came to be called the Spokane, Portland & Seattle (SP&S) was built by Samuel Hill in 1907 and put up the first Kahlotus sign as their stop."

"Hans Harder had hired a surveyor, Otto Hanschild, to plat the town of Hardersburg in 1902, incorporated in the spring of that year. Kahlotus was incorporated in the fall of 1902. Kahlotus was the name of a Palouse Indian. The word has no other meaning [other than "hole in the ground"]. The French trappers spelled the name "Quillatose." The name Kahlotus was the only Palouse Indian name to be on the Walla Walla Treaty of 1855. This document is exhibited at the interpretive center at Toppenish, Washington. The written name is followed by an x, placed there by the person and my father told us that he (Kahlotus) put his x mark there only after Isaac Stevens promised to name a town for him."

"The town of Kahlotus boomed when the SP&S RR came through. Snake River dams were being built, open range grazing for horses, cattle and sheep. But when those factors diminished and disappeared, it floundered. Until something else rises out of the dust, Kahlotus as a town or community will exist only for those of us who have subsistence from other sources. Oil and mineral rights are still largely unexplored. Shell Oil is at present paying landowners lease money and some test wells have been drilled, the results of which have been kept secret. At best this is a longshot as the lottery for any sustenance assistance for the town."

Courtesy Centennial History of Oregon, *1912*
Railroad magnate Henry Villard tried to control Eastern Washington rail transport. He was president of the OR&N Railroad.

"The climate here can be very harsh - it's hot and dry for a good four months most summers. Farming is marginal financially even on the best land. It is not in the Columbia Basin Irrigation Project, so irrigating is difficult because wells go dry. A lake which is beautiful during the "good" years dries up completely about every 15 years."

KAPOWSIN

About twenty miles southeast of Tacoma lies the tiny community of Kapowsin, with a population of less than 200 people. This was the home of a tribe of Indians led by Chief Kapowsin (or Kapowsen). There were no white men here until 1888, when F. W. Hilgert and his family arrived from the East. They found their way to Kapowsin from the town of Orting about ten miles to the north using a compass, because there were no roads and the land was heavily timbered. Hilgert took squatter's rights on a piece of property next to the lake, and then the family had to go back to a place called Morgan Lake and literally carry their furniture on their backs to the newly acquired property. It took them more than ten years to clear their land, where they subsequently planted orchards. Hilgert and his wife also built the road to the town of Orting.

After returning from a trip to their hometown in Germany, the Hilgerts discovered that the Tacoma Eastern Railroad had built its tracks right through their orchard. So they sold their land rights to a timber company that wanted to build a mill on the lake. With the railroad in place, Kapowsin was connected to Tacoma, and when the mill began operating it brought many people to the area.

The number of residents justified the establishment of a post office in 1890 and the place was called Kapousin, with August Neubauer as postmaster. The chief's name was thought to mean "shallow," [58] referring to the lake, but the lake is more than fifty feet deep in the middle, and it was assumed the name referred to one end of the lake that was shallower. The post office operated until 1899 and then closed. In 1901, it was reopened as Hall, with Charles Fix as postmaster. When civil service exams were required, Fix's wife became postmaster because Mr. Fix had little education and would not have been able to pass the test. She distributed the mail on horseback. In 1903, the name was changed back and spelled Kapowsin.[59]

With the increase in population, sawmills began to pop up around Kapowsin Lake which was used as a log pond and could hold the booms of a number of logging companies. The logs were sent down chutes into the lake. One of the chutes was located under the road and railroad. It must have been interesting to see the look on railroad passengers' faces when they spotted a log flying down the chute which no doubt looked like it was going to land right in their laps. By 1904, the Tacoma Eastern was moving 400,000 board feet of lumber each day.

Entertainment for the men consisted of the saloons and the cat house on a small island in the middle of the lake.

Kapowsin suffered at least five fires between 1915 and 1928, and each successive one burned a little more of the business district. When the last one engulfed an entire block, it was not rebuilt. Then the timber industry slumped, and the loggers left town, along with the supporting businesses. When Tacoma bought land around the lake to use it as a municipal water supply, the mills were put out of existence and Kapowsin became a bedroom community.

KENNEWICK

In 1805, Lewis and Clark passed the site that would eventually become Kennewick. They met a group of Indians who welcomed them to their camp and offered them a meal of fish. The expedition members were a little leery because they had seen rotten salmon on the beach, and instead opted to purchase some dogs to use for food.

A so-called road crossed the river at this site in the 1850s and went between Naches Pass and Walla Walla. The road must have been in sorry shape because Captain George McClellan was ordered by Jefferson Davis to "at least endeavor to fix the line of the road." He also told McClellan to repair the worst places so the settlers could "render the route practicable by their own exertions."

The name Kennewick may have been derived from a number of sources. One states the Chemnapam Indians called this place "winter haven;" another that the word was derived from kin-i-wack, meaning "grassy place." A civil engineer named H. S. Huson wrote in 1883, . . . "They called this place 'Kone Wack,' meaning a grassy place or glade. I wrote it down mindful of the clerk of the telegraph instrument and the swing of the pen in the hands of those who would write the name millions of times, I wrote underneath 'Kennewick.'" Other sources call it "winter paradise."[60] Whatever the true meaning, Kennewick was a haven for the Indians because of its mild winters, and the land before the white man came was covered with bunchgrass. The Indians fished on the Yakima River and their horses fed on the lush grass.

Construction of the Northern Pacific brought in settlers. A millwright named C. J. Beach came to work on the railroad, homesteaded about 100 acres of land, and founded Kennewick. For some odd reason, Kennewick was once called Headlight by the settlers. In 1885, the post office opened, but the name was changed to Tehe until 1891, and there is no explanation for this unusual name. Most of the people who lived here at the beginning were railroad workers, and when the tracks were completed, they moved on.[61]

By the early 1890s, more permanent people moved to Kennewick. An example was a pioneer on his way to Portland from Iowa who stopped in the community and liked it so much he stayed. A creamery and two general stores were built, along with a mail-order establishment called The Coffin Store. The Church Grape Juice Company was founded as a bottling works, and had one of the largest Concord grape vineyards in the U.S. Before the railroad bridge was built, the settlers had a rough time crossing the Columbia River when they went for supplies, and used a sail-powered ferry, which had to be rowed by hand on windless days.

By the 1930s, Kennewick was in an economic slump, as was the rest of the nation. But it was on an upswing in the 1940s when the Richland-Hanford area was being surveyed for an atomic plant. The government took over thousands of acres and many people moved into the region; with housing projects going up, new businesses were established in Kennewick. The McNary Dam and Columbia Basin Irrigation (one of the largest in the world) was expanded to accommodate the large population.

In July 1996, a skeleton dubbed "Kennewick Man" was found at the edge of the Columbia River near town by two college students. It was carbon dated as 9,300 to 9,600 years old, but much controversy has arisen about it. Archaeologists wanted to study the bones; the Indians wanted it back. After the carbon-dating was done, the Corps of Engineers wanted the studies terminated and took the skeleton with plans to repatriate it. The remains are housed at the Burke Museum of Natural and Cultural History at Seattle awaiting a verdict.

In the fall of 2000, Secretary of the Interior Bruce Babbitt believed that Kennewick Man should be returned to the Indian tribes, stating that "After evaluating this complex situation, I believe that it is reasonable to determine that the Kennewick Man remains should be transferred to the tribes that have jointly claimed him." Scientists disagreed with Babbitt, and theorized that Kennewick Man was more closely related to the Polynesians. As of this writing, scientists planned to file a law-suit to keep the remains from being returned to the Indians.[62]

KITTITAS

The only record that seems to show the early settlement of this town is the building of a school in 1893, and nothing is known of the early residents. The Milwaukee Land Company from Seattle built the Milwaukee Railroad in 1906, and platted the town of Kittitas two years later. This brought businesses in and by 1926 Kittitas was well established.

The Psch-wan-wap-pam Indians were living in the region as early as the 1700s. They were the forerunners of the Yakima Nation, and the natives who resided here were known as the Upper Yakimas. Their staple food was the camas root, which grew in abundance in the Kittitas Valley. When the white set-tlers came to the valley, the Indians were relocated and eventu-ally ended up at the Yakima Reservation.[63]

The town's name comes from various derivations. All may be correct depending on the spoken dialects. Kittitas could mean "shale rock," "white chalk," "land of plenty," or "shoal people."[64]

One of Kittitas' main industries was potatoes, and there were many potato sheds in town, because it was a railroad dis-tribution point. Yakima Valley cattle ranchers came to the Kittitas Valley to graze their cattle on the abundant bunch-grass. They later moved their herds to the north-central region in British Columbia, and by the mid-1800s other cattle ranch-ers took claims here. Over time, the herds became so numerous that beef prices dropped, but when a bad winter killed more than half of the cattle, it brought the price of beef back up.

When overgrazing occurred, the federal government stepped in, and by 1897 grazing regulations were in effect.

The 1900s brought in a newspaper, bank, general store, and other businesses. There was also the local pool hall. There always was something interesting happening there. The fellow who owned it had a monkey that had a habit of "borrowing" things from the customers. No one ever knew where the monkey hid his treasures, until years later when an old water tank was torn down and all the missing items were found there.

The monkey story doesn't stop here. Some gent stopped at the pool hall for a quick drink on his way to Ellensburg with a sled full of grain. While he was in the pool hall the monkey came out, undid the reins, the horse saw the monkey, got scared and took off like a bat out of hell, ending up jamming the tongue of the wagon against the corner of the church.

The owner decided it was time to get rid of the monkey who had become such a hellion; it beat up the dogs, tried to pluck chickens while they were still alive, and brought sundry cats into the pool hall. Finally, one of the neighbor ladies shot the monkey when it tried to nab one of her prize roosters.[65]

Kittitas has a population of about 1,200, but today some consider it a living ghost town, as most of the businesses are gone, and the residents do most of their business and shopping in other towns.

KLICKITAT

Klickitat is situated near the base of Mount Adams on the Klickitat River. The Klickitats were a Shahaptian tribe originally from the Cowlitz River area who were great mountaineers and hunters, known to be intermediaries between the Indian tribes that lived along the coast. They helped the Chinook Indians in warfare against others, and also hired themselves out as mercenaries for which they were compensated with beads and women. The Klickitats joined with the Yakima Indians in the Treaty of 1855 when they ceded their land.

When Lewis and Clark were returning to the East in 1806, they stopped at the White Salmon River where they met Timotsk, a Klickitat Indian who would become the hereditary chief of the tribe. (He was still alive in the early 1900s, which would have made him about 117 years old.[66])

Timber initially generated interest to this area and Klickitat became a small sawmill town. Residents had the foresight to avoid clear cutting; they practiced controlled timber cutting to make sure the forest would continue to flourish. At one time, the area had the largest operation that cut only Ponderosa Pines, and a number of sawmills produced lumber for the eastern markets. Precut fruit boxes were also made for the Yakima Valley, which was an apple-producing area.[67]

The town was first named Wright for Edgar Wright who settled here in 1889. He started raising cattle and built a corral between his home and the river. When the cattle were

Courtesy Centennial History of Oregon, *1912*
Hereditary Klickitat Chief Timotsk. Lewis & Clark met Timotsk as a small boy while they were camped at the White Salmon River.

ready for market, they were driven to the Lyle Steamboat Landing and shipped to Portland. About 1902, the Columbia River and Northern Railroad came through, which made the shipment of cattle a lot easier. Eight years later, a mill and logging railroad were built by the Western Pine Lumber Company. The railroad was an incline system that went up the face of a hill. This meant that log cars had to come down one at a time on a cable operated by a hydraulic engine on top of the hill. The North Bank Railroad was built along the Columbia River a few years later, which made boat traffic almost obsolete.

In 1893, a man named Stearns built a water-powered sawmill. When the post office was first established, it was in the home of the Cox family, where mail was delivered once a week by horse carrier. Later, a federal building was built to house the post office that measured twelve by sixteen feet.

Fire plagued many of the early settlements and Klickitat had its share of them. The first fire in 1911 destroyed the sawmill and planing mill, which were rebuilt. By 1914, the town was beginning to expand with the influx of a number of businesses, but in 1916 they were destroyed by fire. The years 1918 and 1927 saw two more fires, each time destroying the sawmills, which were again rebuilt, only much larger.

In 1932, an innovative business was established. The mineral springs located in the area were developed as a dry-ice plant called the Gas-Ice Corporation, which produced pure dry ice (99.6% pure) from the natural carbon dioxide found in the springs, and was the only such ice without impurities. There were many skeptics. Initially, only about 500 pounds were sold in the Northwest. But as people became more knowledgeable about the product, the demand for the dry ice increased. Four years later, the company was putting out more than eighteen tons of ice a day.

The name of Wright was changed to Klickitat in 1910. The name has several meanings: "beyond" and "robber." "Beyond" is the accepted version as it applies to the Indians' reference to the Cascade Mountains.[68]

Klickitat celebrates Klickitat Canyon Days the last week of July.

LATAH

Latah is about forty miles southeast of Spokane, and takes its name from Latah Creek, which originates in Idaho and joins the Spokane River below the falls. The creek was once known as Hangman Creek. During an uprising, the Palouse Indians defeated Lieutenant Colonel Steptoe. In retaliation, Colonel George Wright had many Indians hanged by the creek in 1858, in addition to shooting almost 800 of their horses. After more troubles with the Indians, a small fort was built on a neighbor's property for protection.

One of the early residents was Major R. H. Wimpy who arrived in the 1870s. When the post office was established, it was housed in Wimpy's cabin. Lewis and Benjamin Coplen built the first house in Latah, each taking about 160 acres. In 1886, the town was platted on Benjamin's land. But Coplen is considered the town's founder. This was rich agricultural country with an unfailing water supply from Latah Creek.[69]

The first mail for Latah was carried via horseback by Cornelius Mooney in 1877. His route went between the communities of Palouse and Pine Grove (later named Spangle). Luck was with him because many of the mail carriers were attacked by Indians. At one time, there were rumors that Mooney had been killed by Indians, but he continued to deliver the mail. One time he crossed Hangman Creek just minutes before the ice broke, a very lucky man indeed.

One of the Coplen brothers discovered the bones of a prehistoric mammoth in 1876, which weighed almost 3,000 pounds. After touring the United States, the bones were put on exhibit in a Chicago museum. Other interesting artifacts have been found. When a settler had his well dug, the excavators unearthed a redwood log that was underneath more than twenty feet of solid rock. In the hills above Latah, oyster and clam shells were discovered.[70]

Originally called Alpha, the name Latah may have its origins from a number of definitions. The Indians passed this way during their yearly fishing expeditions on Latah Creek. Here, they dug up the plentiful camas roots that were used for food. They called the river Lahtoo, a Nez Perce word meaning "the place of pine trees and pestle"[71] (stones were used as pestles for pulverizing the camas roots). Latah could also mean "stream where little fish are caught, "camping ground" or "place well supplied with food."[72]

LUMMI ISLAND

The ancient name for this island was Skallaham, so called by the Lummi Indians. It was first charted by Spanish explorers in 1792, which they named Isla de Pacheco (Pacheco was part of the Spanish Viceroy's name). Lummi could mean "the people who repelled," or "capable of being repelled," that is, they did not mix with other people. In the mid 1800s, many of the Lummis died from diseases and Indian raiding parties. Those who were left, abandoned their village and moved to the mainland, where in 1855, they signed a treaty and were subsequently assigned to the Nooksack Reservation.

Captain Christian Tuttle, a gold miner and whaler, was the first permanent settler on the island in 1871. Tuttle selected the island because it looked like a good place to raise cattle and sheep, and he claimed 160 acres. More than forty years earlier, agents of the Hudson's Bay Company were killed there by the Indians. Consequently, people avoided the island for a long time.[73]

A few years after Tuttle moved onto the island, he married a girl he had been guardian to after she grew up and was too old to stay at a convent any longer. Frederick Lane came to the island in 1880 with his Sumas Indian wife, and moved to a section he called Lane's Spit. His years were spent tending the kerosene navigation light, then later as postmaster. He picked up the mail at Fairhaven, no easy journey because he had to cross the bay in a small sailboat and the water was hazardous at times. Lane also helped establish a school district and became the island's first school superintendent.

Tuttle and other families who moved to this island raised sheep, but that endeavor was not without problems. Rustlers would come from the mainland, steal the sheep, then sell the meat. The residents finally got a shepherd to protect their animals. Then logging took over from sheep ranching. But the biggest economic boon to the island became sport fishing.

A cannery was built on the island in 1896 by the Lummi Island Packing Company. There was a shingle mill on Lane Spit, but it was refitted later as a salmon cannery. In the early 1900s, a fertilizer company operated at Smugglers Cove. Regular mail service began in 1908 and was delivered by a boat called the *Sehome*.

At first, transportation to Lummi was by canoes and other small boats, followed by steamboats and then a ferry. The residents would put up a flag on Gooseberry Point to alert the crew they needed ferry service. In 1926, the Lummi Shore Road connected the island to Bellingham. By the 1960s, Lummi Island was primarily a retirement community.

The Lummi Reservation is located on a peninsula facing

Lummi Island. Many natives traditionally rely on fishing for their subsistence. Some of the Indians are employed by the aquaculture program funded by the government. The program raises salmon and oysters for the gourmet market. The people are also taught aquaculture at the Lummi Indian School of Aquaculture.

MEMALOOSE ISLAND

This island is unpopulated and not much is left of it. One of the largest funeral islands in the Columbia River Gorge, Memaloose means "dead," or "place of the dead," and was used by the Klickitat Indians as their burial ground.

A white man named Victor Trevitt is buried on the island. Trevitt had more Indian friends than he did whites, and allegedly said, "I have but one wish after I die, to be laid away on Memaloose Island with the Indians. In the resurrection I will take my chances with them."[74]

When the Bonneville Dam was being built, the bodies of the Indians were moved from the lower section of the island. It was known that the backwater from the dam was going to submerge it, and so they were buried at the higher part of the island. Trevitt didn't have to go anywhere because he was already on the high side. The dam was completed in 1937, and indeed submerged most of the four acres. Looking down on the island between The Dalles, Oregon, and Hood River, Trevitt's gravestone can still be seen.

MOCLIPS

Moclips sits on a bluff that overlooks the Pacific Ocean in Grays Harbor County. It did not depend on logging for its economy, but was a thriving summer town and once the center of shingle and shake manufacturing. The name designates the site where young Indian maidens underwent their puberty rites; that is, they were not allowed near the rivers full of salmon during their menstrual cycle.[75]

In 1903, the Northern Pacific Railroad built a spur track to Moclips which connected numerous shingle mills with Grays Harbor, brought in many tourists, and the town became a supply point, because it was the end of the railroad tracks. Before the railroad arrived, there was only one route in and out of town and that was the beach trail. The settlers who raised cattle in the Queets Valley drove their herds to Moclips, where they were shipped by railroad to their destinations, and fisherman from Taholah brought their clams and fish here for canning.

In the early 1900s, a hotel concern began construction of the massive 300-room Moclips Hotel, and the place became a tent city. Fronting the ocean, the hotel stood on pilings a few hundred feet from the Northern Pacific Railroad depot, and only twelve feet from the beach. The investors felt this imposing structure with its beautiful view of the great Pacific would lure thousands of people to the area.

But it was not to be. In 1913, a huge storm hit the Pacific coast and seas that were almost like tidal waves hit the hotel. The hotel that had been swaying in the wind finally went down with a crash. After it hit the beach, it was ground to matchwood and scattered along the coast. A second hotel was constructed soon after the first went into the deep, but it was located much farther back from the beach on a site believed to be an old Quinault village.

Moclips reverted to a summer community after cedar became scarce, causing the shake mills to close down. After collapse of the hotel, the railroad spur went to pot.

MUKILTEO

Located on Puget Sound, this is the site where the Indians signed the Point Everett Treaty of 1855 and ceded the land where Seattle is now situated. Once an Indian ceremony and council ground, this place was called Mukilteo, meaning "good camping (or hunting) ground."

In 1858, the town's early development began along the shoreline with the establishment of a cannery and lumber mill. It became a port of entry for sailing ships because of the deep water in Puget Sound. The town founders were Jacob Fowler and Morris Frost. Fowler established the Exchange-Saloon and traded mainly with the Indians. Frost went into politics where he was involved with government affairs during the time Washington was changing from a territory to a state.[76] This region was timber country, and Fowler did a brisk business sup-

Courtesy Opal McConnell, Mukilteo, Washington
Mukilteo's first trading post started by J.D. Fowler (early 1800s).

plying goods to the loggers. As a result, he converted one of his buildings into a hotel to accommodate the large number of timber men.

As the area population increased, Snohomish County was formed in 1861 by the Washington Territorial Legislature, and Mukilteo was made the county seat until it was given to the town of Everett. The late 1800s brought in a brewery and a salmon cannery. By 1877, the cannery was handling about 5,000 fish every day. But ten years later, the Washington State Legislature passed a law banning catching salmon on Puget Sound during the spring months of each year. This was supposedly for the conservation of the fisheries. As a result of this law, plus the financial panic that occurred in 1873, Mukilteo's economy dropped and the canneries closed.[77]

At one time the town tried to get a railroad terminus located here. Someone composed a little ditty at the time: "To the dogs Olympia with her tide flats may go, but the railroad will help little Mukilteo."[78] Actually the Great Northern Railroad did serve Mukilteo's sawmills and had a depot with an office and loading dock. It was removed in the 1940s.

Growth was spurred once again when the town turned to the timber industry. The Mukilteo Lumber Company built a plant in 1903 and the population increased. Mukilteo Lumber was one of the biggest and best equipped timber businesses at the deep harbor, which enabled the larger ships to load the timber.

On December 1, 1906, the square-rigger *Great Admiral* had been loaded with lumber at Mukilteo and was on its way to San Pedro, California. Caught in a gale, the ship broke apart, hampered by the weight of the logs. Some people managed to cling all night to part of the cabin roof, and were picked up the next morning by another ship, which took them to San Francisco.[79]

In the early 1900s, Crown Lumber took over the Mukilteo Company. At one time, Crown employed more than 100 Japanese workers in its lumber yards. They lived in unpainted structures at a place called "Japanese Gulch," and were taught to read and speak English by the women of Mukilteo. Crown remained in business until 1930, when it shut its doors. Some attempts were made to cultivate orchards, but because the terrain was too steep, it did not become much of an industry.

NACHES

Fifteen miles northwest of Yakima and situated at the foot of Mt. Cleman, Naches was visited by the Charles Wilkes Expedition when it came through the region in 1842. About ten years later, James Longmire guided a group of people through the Naches Pass to the coast. Other settlers followed and ended up staying here, where they cultivated apple orchards, raised cattle, and established dairies. By 1872, there were enough children that a school was needed.[80]

In 1898, a man named Harry Painter came to Naches, bought out a creamery, and brought in more than $10,000 worth of dairy cows from Oregon. He provided the cows to "any man who owned his own land and could sign a decent note."[81] Painter's creamery fared quite well, because he not only hauled and sold his butter at Yakima, but also traveled along the coastline with his product. Painter was so successful he had to use five teams of horses to collect cream from the farmers. When his

neighbors began asking him to pick up supplies for the
his runs, he came up with the idea of adding a store. He
up on supplies and added a general store to his cl   ..cry.
Painter sold his business in 1911.

The town was laid out in 1905 by the West and Wheel Land
Company, and the post office was established the following
year. The Northern Pacific Railroad also arrived in Naches
during the period. Naches became firmly established when
reclamation projects began with the Bumping Dam and Yakima
Tieton Reservoir, which supplied water to the valley. During
construction, Naches was the end of the rail line for the building materials. A little commuter train named "Sagebrush
Annie" would later be an important link between Natches and
the Yakima markets by making two runs daily. First called
Natchez, the name was later spelled Naches.[82]

Because of Naches' proximity to timber in the Cascades, the
backbone of the town's economy was a sawmill and two apple-
packing companies. A circular sawmill was brought in by
Orville Smith and Charles Dower, and Cascade Lumber bought
them out in later years. In more modern times, the Naches Box
Company was one of the main employers, which cut shooks for
the pine boxes that were manufactured from yellow pine.

The Indians called the site Natcheez, from where Naches
was derived. It meant "turbulent waters," referring to the swift
moving river. It was also defined as "oh water!" and "one
water."[83] Yet another interpretation is that the name originated
from the Indian word nahchess which meant "plenty of water."[84]

In 1984, a privately funded beautification committee was
formed and planted dozens of trees throughout the town. The
committee also helped to restore a circa 1919 bandstand that is
situated on its original site that spans a canal.

NAHCOTTA

Located on the Long Beach Peninsula, Nahcotta was an
important oystering center, and today great mounds of oyster
shells still line the beachfront. Named for an old Chinook chief
called Nahcati who became friends with the settlers, the town
was established in 1888 as the terminus of a narrow-gauge
railroad. Chinook villages originally dotted the north peninsu-

la, and with the millions of oysters to be had, the Indians were never in want of food.

During the 1850s, the adjoining town of Oysterville was doing a booming oyster business. Although there were a few homes in Nahcotta, most of the people had settled in Oysterville. But seamen soon discovered that Shoalwater Bay (now Willapa Bay) was deeper and they could get their schooners a lot closer to shore to load the oysters. To accommodate the ships, a wharf was built at Nahcotta in 1889. James Swan, who was a scholar and writer, traveled through the area and once wrote that "Shoal-water Bay, as a harbor, will be of great importance to Washington Territory as soon as its advantages are known and the country becomes settled."[85]

The schooner *Robert Bruce* entered Shoalwater Bay in 1851 to load oysters for shipment to San Francisco, but it never made it out of the bay. Apparently Jefferson, the ship's cook, had been reprimanded numerous times by the captain because of his lousy cooking and he decided to get even. One night Jefferson laced the food with laudanum. After all the crew members passed out, he set fire to the ship. Indians living along the shore saw the fire and went out to save the drugged seamen. Luckily, no lives were lost, but what was left of the schooner sank into the Bay. The cook disappeared and was never seen again.[86]

The first person to settle in Nahcotta was J. A. Morland, who came here in the 1890s, and was soon followed by other families. By 1899, Nachotta was the terminus of a short-line, narrow-gauge railroad that began at Ilwaco. It replaced the horse-drawn stage that ran on sand the length of the peninsula whose schedule had to coincide with the tides. A. P. Osborne, the first railroad agent, said the railroad's name had changed so many times he didn't know who in the hell he worked for anymore!

The oyster industry drew many people to the area. One of the newcomers was John Crellin, a founder of the Morgan Oyster Company based in San Francisco. He sold his property to John Paul, who platted the land south of the railroad and called the place Nahcotta. Paul then sold it to Lewis Loomis.

B. A. Seaborg, who owned a cannery in Ilwaco, decided to stake out his territory on the north side of the railroad tracks, named his plot Sealand, an thus began a dispute. Both Seaborg and Loomis wanted their piece of the pie to be the official terminus of the railroad. They each scrambled to build up their towns with hotels, saloons, general stores, and other small businesses. It ended up in a lawsuit, with Nahcotta winning the prize, and the world became the town's oyster. In fact, a postcard was created showing a huge oyster that looked like it was about ten feet long being pulled up by a hoist, and was popular with tourists for many years. In the meantime, the little town of Oysterville was losing its population when its residents began to relocate here.

In addition to oysters, there was also a growing timber trade out of Willapa Bay, which kept this little town busy. Logs were rafted to Nahcotta, then loaded on railroad flatcars and sent down to Ilwaco, where they were loaded on freighters to their destination. Freight, passengers, and mail traveled to points in Willapa Bay, and a steamer made daily trips between Nahcotta and North Bend.

The oyster business was brisk and many barges were used to harvest these delicacies. Large baskets were set over the oyster beds at high tide, then at low tide the baskets were filled with oysters, pulled up, dumped on the barge, and the baskets reset over the beds for another load. They were then taken to the local processing plants. During the California gold rush, many of these oysters were shipped to San Francisco where the miners gobbled them up.

Problems arose at Nahcotta in the early 1900s when the oyster population severely declined because of over-harvesting. Told by federal biologists to leave enough oysters for propagation, the harvesters ignored the warning, and the beds were all but destroyed. In an attempt to replenish them, Eastern oysters were brought here, but they refused to propagate.

Pacific oyster seeds were then imported when the Japanese oyster men came and set up their sheds on the water. One of them was named Jeff Murakami, whose family introduced the seeds here in 1929. The shed was his family's home, and they got their supplies and freshwater by poling a bateau back and forth to shore. They even had to put up a fence around the deck to keep their chickens from falling off into the water. Jeff and

e interred during World War II, and when they
hcotta they had lost most of their holdings.[87]

logist once made a wry comment about his fair
ythical mayor of a non-existent town, but I point
with pride to the increase of pigeons from 4 to 800 under my
administration. They keep the folks looking up and we don't
have to paint City Hall. Our chief industry used to be wind-
mills, but we made so many there wasn't enough wind to push
all of them and we had to close down. We didn't have enough
money to build a freeway, so we just built an interchange. You
go up and around it and come back to where you started. Proves
we don't spend our money foolishly . . ."[88]

NASELLE

Prior to any settlement, this was home to a branch of the
Chinook Indians who called themselves Na-sil. When a smallpox epidemic hit the Washington and Oregon coast in the early
1800s, the tribe was almost decimated, leaving about six families who left their camp and settled at what they called the Na-
sil River. As early as 1808, a Belgian Catholic priest visited and
planted a number of apple trees, but in later years the river
bank washed away and took most of the trees with it.

Phillip Pierre, a French-Canadian who once worked for the
Hudson's Bay Company, arrived in 1838 with his Indian wife
and lived with the Na-sils. This region had a wealth of fur-bearing animals. Pierre taught the Na-sils how to farm. He also
helped them get fair prices for their furs at the trading post in
Astoria.[89]

Twenty-four years later, William Whealdon, along with two
Indians, Elowahka Jim and Toke, were traveling through and
stopped to visit with Pierre and the Na-sils. Whealdon wrote of
this visit in his diary, and because he was an expert in the pure
Chinook language, it is believed his account of the name origin
is accurate. When asked what Na-sil meant, he was told it was
an old Chinook word that meant "protection" and "shelter."[90]
Over time, the name went through a number of changes: Na-sil
Na-sel, and Naselle. During a conversation between Whealdon
and the Chinooks, one of the elders told Whealdon of their
meeting with the Lewis & Clark Expedition and the black man

who was with them (probably Ben York). Pierre told Whealdon that as far as he knew, nobody had come here to live on a permanent basis. Whealdon believed it would soon happen because there were already many people settling along Shoalwater Bay. With the abundance of timber and fertile ground, it wasn't long before that occurred.

In 1869, Isaac Lane claimed land along the Naselle River, promoted the region, and helped new arrivals get settled. He planned to start a town at the headwaters of the river, but when gold was discovered in Alaska, he joined the rush and the plans for a town went with him. The late 1800s brought other members of the Whealdon family, followed by an influx of Finnish families. One of the new arrivals was Jacob Pakanen, said to have trudged through the dense woods carrying a cooking stove on his back.

Before Pacific County was established, Naselle had no roads and the settlers had to travel old footpaths and Indian trails. Farm equipment and furniture were brought by way of the river with the rising tide, and furs and agricultural products down the river with the outgoing tide to the coastal towns.

Patrick O'Connor and his family moved to Naselle in 1871. Earlier, they had met a Romanian gentleman in Portland who told them about Naselle. While Patrick came here to clear the land for their new home, his wife and children stayed at a hotel in Oysterville. Patrick's wife, Mary, was the first white woman in Naselle. They established themselves as dairy farmers, in addition to cultivating an orchard. O'Conner also picked up the mail from Knappton, about seven miles away. The mail continued to be delivered this way until 1877, when the Naselle post office was established.[91]

Beginning in the 1880s, many Finnish people moved to Naselle. The Scandinavian influence is the reason for Naselle's Finnish-American Folk Festival around the last weekend in July. The festival began in 1982 to celebrate the Finnish-American culture of the people who live in the Lower Columbia region. The event has a wealth of activities: authentic Finnish food and dancing, and a variety of exhibits and demonstrations.

NEAH BAY

Neah Bay was and still is home of the Makah Indians. The community was named for a Makah chief named Dee-ah. The first European to discover Neah Bay was a navigator named Apostolos Valerianus (Juan de Fuca) who sailed these waters in 1592. In 1790 the Spaniards arrived and began trading for sea otter pelts. Captain Henry Kellett landed in 1828 for fresh water where he met Chief Dee-ah and, unable to pronounce his name correctly, called the site Neah Bay.[92]

The first settler was a wagon maker named Samuel Hancock who established a trading post about 1849. At first the Makah Indians were not pleased and tried to make Hancock leave their land, threatening to kill him if he refused to go. Hancock told them he was going to write to the "great white father" and the Indians backed off.

In the early 1850s, a ship carrying a passenger with smallpox arrived at Neah Bay. Many of the Makahs died and those left went to Hancock for aid. But all he could do was help them bury the dead. The Indians later blamed Hancock for the epidemic, until they discovered it was a Makah on the ship that was carrying the disease. Hancock finally got fed up with the Indians' distrust and left in the 1850s.[93]

Fur-trading was a big part of the Indians' lives. But by the mid-nineteenth century, the sea otters had been hunted almost to extinction, and it ended the fur trade. When Isaac Stevens became governor, he went to talk to the Makahs about selling their land. They agreed to Stevens' terms, with the stipulation that they still be able to fish and hunt on the land. In 1875, the Makah Treaty was ratified and is still in effect today.

A man named Wilbur Washburn arrived in the 1890s, took up a homestead, and later established a trading post, which he and his wife kept open twelve hours a day. Washburn also served as postmaster for about twenty-five years. Until 1931, when Neah Bay finally had a road built that connected it to Port Angeles, all transportation was by boat.

In October 1893, the Chilean bark *Leonore* got caught in a gale on her voyage from Iquique, Chile, to Puget Sound. With the waves and wind whipping around, the captain lost his bearings and the boat struck the rocks on the shore off Cape

Flattery. The captain and some of his men died in the wreck, but a few managed to survive and made their way for help at Neah Bay. The ship was so broken up that the next day there was no sign of her.[94]

The Makahs call themselves "Kwih-dich-chuh-ahtx," or "people who live by the rocks and seagulls." The name Makah itself translates to "generous with food."[95] This tribe is the only one that has the right to hunt whales according to treaty. The Makahs believe that their first whale was brought to them by a great thunderbird. In May 1999, they hunted and caught the first whale in more than seventy years. Whale hunting by modern Makahs has stirred up a storm of controversy that will probably continue for many years.

NEWHALEM

Newhalem is a small mountain community situated on the Skagit River and headquarters for the Seattle Light operation, which also gave the town its name. Built as a company town, employees lived in the homes Seattle Light built. They maintained a series of dams which produced power for Seattle. The town name comes from an Indian word that means "goat snare."[96] There was a goat trail just upstream from the town.

Before Newhalem became a company town, the region was a center of mining activity. Prospectors came in 1878 to where the dams would eventually be built near Ross Lake. They had to take the goat trail from Newhalem up to another trail that had a sheer face above the river, and hanging bridges were required to cross some of the canyons. The mines failed to produce enough gold to make it worthwhile, with the cost of the long haul to the smelters taking most of the profits.

In 1905, Seattle built a power station at Cedar Falls. When it didn't produce enough power for growing communities, Seattle developed Gorge Dam in 1917, spearheaded by James Ross, the superintendent of Seattle Light.

A railroad from the Great Northern terminus at Rockport was built to the dam's staging area. Lumber was produced by a sawmill located on Goodell Creek and also supplied wood for employee homes. The dam was completed in 1924 at a cost of more than $14 million, and its revenues exceeded $41 million by 1937. Below the powerhouse, Ross planted tropical gardens, bringing in all types of exotic plants, animals and birds from around the world.

When Franklin Roosevelt became president in 1932, he asked James Ross to come to the White House to discuss federal power development. Ross was appointed to the Securities and Exchange Commission. He later resigned and became administrator of the Bonneville Project, a position he held, along with his job with Seattle Light, at Newhalem, until he died in 1939.[97]

OKANOGAN

Peter Skene Ogden, son of a Canadian chief justice, came through the area in 1835 on his way north to St. James, where he was to become the chief factor. He went fur trapping for beaver each year, and it was estimated his catch amounted to about $250,000 worth of furs. The pelts were taken down to the Okanogan River near the future townsite, and loaded on boats where they were taken to England and made into beaver coats and hats. General G. W. Goethals, who later was chief engineer of the Panama Canal, camped at Okanogan in 1883 while exploring the Pacific Northwest.

The town is located about twenty miles from Fort Okanogan and forty miles south of the Canadian border. A fellow named Frank "Pard" Cummings operated the first trading post here in 1886. He also started a ferry for crossing the Okanogan River, because steamboats were able navigate the stream only when the water was high, usually in May and June.[98]

The town was first called Alma and named for Alma Kahlow, daughter of a Prussian man who was an ex-Indian fighter and construction worker. In 1905, the name was changed to Pogue, in honor of Doctor J. I. Pogue who was an orchardist. When the residents felt people would have difficulty in pronouncing Pogue correctly, they voted in 1907 to change it to Okanogan, much to Doctor Pogue's displeasure. He went to see a surveyor named Ben Ross who had a homestead north of Okanogan, and convinced Ross he should start another town, which he did, and it became the community of Omak.

Okanogan means "rendezvous," derived from the Indian word okanagen, an appropriate word as the Indians used this site for their potlatches. The word was spelled many ways by various authorities: Ookenaw, Okinakane, and Oakinacken.[99] Okanogan was a quiet settlement until an irrigation system was constructed at Conconully in 1906. With the water system in place, Okanogan became a region of apple orchards, which was its main source of income.

The battles between towns for county seat status were always interesting events, and Okanogan's was a wild one. Bruce Wilson wrote, "Had the Okanogan County courthouse been built on wheels, there could not have been more repeated and inflamed efforts to drag it from one community to another."[100] Ruby was the first county seat, then Conconully took it, while the town of Chelen was trying to steal it. Then the small town of Riverside decided it wanted the honors, and prepared to build a courthouse, but the project was never completed. The climax came in 1914. Because the railroad had laid its tracks through the Wenatchee Valley, Chelan figured it should have the seat, but lost out.

Then Omak announced its desire to be county seat, but Okanogan put its money up first by providing $12,000 in gold for construction of a courthouse. Now the Conconully bank was not having any of these shenanigans, and the Okanogan banker had to sneak all the gold back to town. After all that hoopla, when Omak put its money up, no one paid any attention.

Okanogan and Omak held an elimination contest with the loser promising to support the winner against Conconully. All that said and done, the two towns really went at each other with their campaigns. But Okanogan ended winning the county seat, and it still is today.

OMAK

When Doctor Pogue got into a snit because a neighboring town changed its name from Pogue to Okanogan, he convinced surveyor Ben Ross to start another town, and thus was the beginning of Omak. Ross came from Illinois and was a civil engineer for the Great Northern Railroad in 1879. After leaving Okanogan, he settled in Omak and in 1906 laid out lots for a community. Years later, he sold more of his land which added to growth of the town. Ross was also responsible for organization of the Omak School District.

St. Mary's Mission was established near Omak in 1886 by Father Etienne DeRouge. Chief Moses and his band objected to the mission and were planning to get rid of him. But fate stepped in when the priest saved an Indian child, and DeRouge was able to keep his mission. Rumor has it that there may be a cache of gold near St. Mary's, worth at least $20,000. A Colville Indian chief named Smitkin was a successful cattleman. Because he wouldn't have anything to do with banks, he allegedly hid the money and then upped and died in 1918, without telling anyone where he hid his treasure.

J. C. Biles was another man who put Omak on the map. In the 1920s, he bought a sawmill and box manufacturing factory owned by the Omak Fruit Growers, Inc., located at a place called Cougarville. The company planned to make apple boxes from the Cougarville reservation through the Bureau of Indian Affairs, but ran into financial difficulties and the contract was transferred to Biles. He proceeded to build a five-mile-long, narrow-gauge railroad on Omak Mountain. He had logs dragged by horses to the railroad, then onto flatcars to Cougarville. In the meantime, Biles purchased a stand of timber that held more than a half-billion board feet, and built a new sawmill at Omak in 1924. Biles constructed another railroad that went to Disautel which had to have nineteen bridges constructed to connect with the Omak mill. He then purchased a forty-two-ton Heisler locomotive. In a period of twenty-three years, Biles' railroad had logged 510,000 miles and was the last surviving narrow-gauge logging railroad in the state until 1948, when a bad flood hit seventeen bridges and washed out much of the track.[101]

Omak also had a reduction plant that was used, unfortunately, to put an end to the wild horse herds in the area. The farmers complained about the horses breeding with their own stock, destroying the grasslands, and just plain making a nuisance out of themselves. Roundup of the animals began in the late 1920s after the reduction plant was built. Called knotheads, these horses were shot, skinned, quartered, and boiled in vats of water. The meat was used for dog and cat food, the tanneries got the hides, and the bones were made into fertilizer. In a few years, most of the wild horses were gone.

Omak was named for the lake east of the community. It may have been derived from Omache, which means "great medicine," as the lake was thought to have medicinal powers.[102]

The Omak Stampede is a three-day event held in August, drawing thousands of people, and features the stampede and suicide race.

ORTING

In 1854, William H. Whitesell was the first settler to file a claim at Orting, and was soon followed by others. During an Indian unrest the next year, the settlers went to Fort Steilacoom until hostilities ended. It was several years before many of the settlers returned to their homes. The population did not increase substantially due to the Indian and Civil Wars.

The 1860s brought discovery of coal near the Puyallup River. As a result, the Northern Pacific Railroad built its tracks through Orting in 1877, which enabled the railroad to get the coal it needed for the locomotives. A road was later cut between Orting and the town of Carbonado, and later more railroad branches were built through the region. The first coal seams were opened in 1879 near the Carbon River.

A man named Frederick Eldredge bought some property in Orting in the early 1800s, and began promoting the new town. He wrote, ". . . Some people have come here with families and have found work as soon as they could get their coats off. The soil is good in the valley, and lumber is not high, so that one can get a nice comfortable home with little cost. . . Property is now high in Tacoma that a man of limited means cannot get a foothold there. At Orting, property is not high, but it will grow in value fast. . ."[103]

Hops became an important industry when Ezra Meeker brought the first roots into the valley. Many of the farmers grew them, but in 1892, the crops were destroyed by the hops louse. Spraying didn't help, and a lot of people lost their land.

When the train began its regular passage over the Cascade Mountains, it brought many homesteaders to Orting. In addition to coal, the advent of the timber industry in the 1880s also brought prosperity to the town. The Orting Lumber Company constructed a mill on the Carbon River, but during the 1890s it went bankrupt. Another mill took its place and was operated by the Luney brothers. They had to move the mill further downstream when a terrible flood destroyed the dam. The mill eventually was abandoned when water damaged it again.

The post office was established in 1878 and Henry Whitesell was the first postmaster. In 1888, the *Orting Oracle* printed its first newspaper. The paper was established when the law required all homesteads and timber claims be published to show proof of ownership.

The 1890s brought in the gold seekers. There was some gold found in the hills near town, but the expense of hauling it out wasn't worth the effort. When gold was discovered in the Klondike, many of the men from Orting went there to seek their fortunes, and some came back with money in their pockets. A man named George Ames, owner of the *Orting Oracle*, developed and patented a condensed food called Pemmican for the Alaska miners.

Orting was incorporated in 1889, and the first meeting of the town council was held a few days later. Some of the early-day council minutes documented their important issues: "In December, the Marshall arrested a man for drunkeness, and kept him for a few hours in jail before releasing him. He did not consider it humane to keep him overnight in the jail because of the weather conditions." "Charges were hurled prior to the election that. . . 'the root of all our municipal rotteness lies in selfishness.' The Council appointed a committee to investigate if any rotteness exists." [104]

The 1920s brought a new industry to Orting: Daffodils. The Van Zonnoveld Bulb Farm began growing daffodils at the same time a man named Karl Koehler began his own daffodil farm. When the Van Zonnoveld Farm threw away young bulbs because they weren't up to standard, Koehler took them, which included different types of hyacinths and tulips. Koehler built up his bulb farm until he had more than 1,800 varieties of flowers. *National Geographic* wrote its lead story about the flowers in the October 1942 issue of its magazine. From that beginning, other nationally known magazines came in and ran articles about Koehler's flowers, and before long he was shipping bulbs to all parts of the world.

Orting was thought to be an Indian word that meant "a prairie in the woods." But a map dating in the 1940s shows the Chinook word defined as "valley glade," or "opening between hills."[105]

PALOUSE

It is not known for sure if Palouse is of Indian or French origin. Some believe the tribe's original name may have been Palus, Palloatpallah or Pelusha. The words might have been translated by the French-Canadians into pelouse, which described the area as a grassy expanse. Some scholars think the Indians were the Palloatpallahs who were close relatives of the Nez Perce Indians. Another suggested the name came from the Appaloosa horses, which is doubtful. The Palouse Indians were not resident in the region because it presented no shelter and the winters were severe. But they did visit and used the trails that meandered through the area.[106]

Modoc Smith was one of the early settlers. He discovered a trail in 1875 that the Palouse Indians called "Our Home," which went all the way to the mountains in Idaho, where the Indians fished and hunted. It was thought that some of Quantrell's Raiders might have been early settlers too. When gold was discovered in Idaho at its Gold Hill and Hoodoo Districts, Palouse became a trading post and outfitting town for the miners. A few of the store owners also did some mining in addition to grubstaking a number of prospectors.

When the sawmill was built, it created problems for the flour mill and the water it needed in order to operate. A compromise was made to open the dam twice a week so the logs could move, and the rest of the time it was closed so the flour mill could have the needed flow of water for its waterwheel.

As more settlers came to Palouse, it became a wheat and timber producing town. More sawmills popped up, and then with Northern Pacific's arrival, Palouse became a busy shipping point, which spurred rapid growth of the community.

In 1880, residents decided to shift the town to a better location because it was then situated on the shoulder of a steep hill.

The town was literally moved downstream where the land was flatter. Unfortunately, it also was muddier, making the streets barely passable. A fire in the late 1800s took most of the businesses, but they were shortly rebuilt. The streets were filled and raised, taking the town out of its mudhole.

During the 1893 depression period, Palouse fell into a slump, but a few years later the Potlatch Lumber Company bought the Palouse River Company's sawmill, and production increased. Potlatch Company failed to buy the mill's exclusive water rights, and the prior claim belonged to William Codd, who saw an opportunity to make some money from this "error." But he asked too much money, and a company man named Deary attempted to negotiate with Codd for a fair price. But it wasn't until 1904 that he finally sold out to the Potlatch Company.

Potlatch Company also constructed the Washington, Idaho and Montana Railroad, that made river log drives obsolete. When the company no longer needed the Palouse mills, it pulled up stakes in 1905 and moved its business to Idaho. That left Palouse high and dry and the town turned to agriculture. Ironically, a year earlier the Republic printed an item about the booming lumber business thanks to Potlatch: "Palouse must inevitably become not only a town, but a city of pretension."[107] But it never happened.

PATAHA

In 1861, James Bowers was the first settler in this brush-covered land. Angevine "Vine" J. Favor acquired the property a few years later, but it wasn't until 1882 that the town was laid out. Vine was also a stagecoach driver who drove the route to Lewiston, Idaho.

When Vine offered some of his land for a mill site, J. N. Bowman and George Snyder gladly accepted and built a flour mill. In addition, a man named Cassander Woolery sold his water rights to Snyder. Born in Pataha, Snyder was a grain dealer who shipped flour to San Francisco with wheat grown in the Pataha Valley that was very high in gluten. It was in great demand by purchasers for the manufacture of macaroni. He became a millionaire many times over. John Houser also established a mill, and the flour he produced was shipped all over the

Courtesy Garfield County Museum
Early days in Pataha (1886).

world. His son later became a marketing agent in China. The mill was closed by one of Houser's sons in 1941.

Vine's real name was Angevine June Titus and Company, and he was not happy with it, and would assault anyone who called him by his full name. In 1885, the *Columbia Chronicle* wrote an article about how Vine got his illustrious name: . . . a circus came there for the first time in the history of the place. It was owned by Angevine, June, Titus & Company. . . Mr. & Mrs. Favor attended in the afternoon and were so pleased that they named their boy, born on the following day, for the proprietors of the enterprise."[108]

Pataha had a rip-roaring election in 1886 over county prohibition. The judges of the election were charged with foul play, when they allowed ballot-stuffing to occur and quite a number of "wet" votes were put in the ballot box all at once. Because the majority of voters were into "dry," they complained about it. The people in favor of liquor insisted it was not true, but lost their arguments and the town went dry.

Once known as Waterstown and Favorsburg, the settlement was renamed Pataha. This was an Indian word meaning "brush," a descriptive term for the brush growing along a creek in the area, which was mainly cottonwood and willow. When

Garfield County was formed, Pataha became the county seat, until "unseated" by its rival town, Pomeroy.[109]

Pataha's post office was established in 1879 in the back of a general store. Within two years, the first newspaper was established and called the *Pataha Spirit*.

On April 7, 1893, a devastating fire swept through Pataha, starting in a hardware store and consequently destroying most of the business district. The same year the price of wheat dropped drastically and the majority of the crops were destroyed because of too much rain. Then in 1894, everything seemed to go to pot when the railroad workers went on strike and Pataha's Harford & Son Bank failed and closed its doors.

The county seat was temporarily given to Pataha by approval of a bill from the territorial governor in 1881 until the next year when an election would be held. Pataha should have retained its status as county seat with good location, water supply, and the mill that was quite prosperous, but it was not to be. As with most county seat races, this was a bitter battle with name-calling and fist fights. A man named Jay Lynch had many friends who lived in Pomeroy and tried to split Pataha's votes. He had lots laid out and bundles of lumber dropped on the lots to show that a building boom was on. Apparently it worked, and Pomeroy citizens celebrated by riding through the town of Pataha shouting and just generally rubbing it in.

Then came Rice vs County Commissioners of Garfield County, a suit that was brought to keep the commissioners from meeting at Pomeroy. The territorial judge said the election was void because the bill by the territorial governor had a flaw in it. Pataha residents then turned the tables and went to Pomeroy, where they strutted and shouted and thumbed their noses at the people. Then the cycle started again; the commissioners decided to abide by the will of the people, and there were more lawsuits. The result of this mixed-up fight was that Pomeroy was granted the county seat by an act of Congress, the only town in the state to have this distinction.

Pataha's decline began after it lost county seat status and the Union Pacific built its Starbuck branch with its terminus at Pomeroy. The bank had earlier closed its doors, and many of the businesses relocated to Pomeroy rather than rebuild here. The

Seventh-Day Adventists who had their organization here also moved to Pomeroy, as did the Congregationalist Church. It was not until about 1950 that Pataha began to get back on its feet.

PUYALLUP

Although Ezra Meeker came through Puyallup in 1851, the first people to actually build their homes may have been the men and their families who worked for the Hudson's Bay Company located at Fort Nisqually. Meeker's first impression of Puyallup was that there was just so much timber and thought it would be too massive an undertaking to clear it out.

Formerly a dense wooded area, Puyallup was ceded by the Indians after the treaty at Medicine Creek in 1854. The name may mean "generous people," but then again it could denote "shadows," because of the shade made by the forest. It was so dense, in fact, that a family who homesteaded in the area twenty-five years after Puyallup was established didn't even know the town existed.[110]

One of the early homesteaders in the Puyallup Valley in 1852 was Willis Boatman. Because there were no roads, his possessions were brought by boat up the Puyallup River, no mean feat, as the river was full of sandbars and log jams. Then a man named Stewart claimed some land, and more settlers followed. When there was a substantial population, Stewart established a post office and called the place Franklin.

When Ezra Meeker came back in 1877, he platted the town and renamed it Puyallup. A. S. Farquharson built the first mill that was used for cutting barrel staves from cottonwood trees. Farquharson said he was the one who actually suggested the name Puyallup when Meeker wanted to name the town Meekerville. This comment made the men bitter enemies. Later, Meeker was to write: . . . I consider it no honor to be the man who named the town of Puyallup. I accept the odium attached to inflicting that name on suffering succeeding generations . . . I have been ashamed of the act ever since. . ."[111] Meeker was obviously distressed that people couldn't pronounce the name he selected.

Meeker pioneered the raising of hops in the area and made a fortune on it. He began in 1865, cleared his land, planted the hops, and eventually established a brokerage firm for buyers to bid on the hops. But the 1890's brought ruin to many of the people in the business, which had been prosperous for about twenty-five years. The crops were infested with aphids and destroyed the local economy. Many of the men lost not only their money, but their land as well.

When the Depression of 1893 hit, a group of men who called themselves the "Commonwealth Army of Christ" was formed. Led by Jumbo Cantwell at Tacoma, about 1,500 men came to Puyallup and caused much grief to the residents for a couple of days. Their intent was to form an organization and march to the state capital and demand jobs and food. They got here by riding in a boxcar on the Northern Pacific Railroad, and Puyallup residents were terrified of these men. As they marched down the streets of Puyallup, the men began to sing a tune called "Coxey's March:"

> Come now, you sons of labor, and join the noble cause
> It's time I'm sure for something to be done
> For Bread and meat is very scarce because of their cruel laws.
> We'll pack our traps and march to Washington. . .

During this time a contingent from Butte, Montana, "secured" a train and headed east. When a reporter asked Jumbo his opinion about the train being commandeered at Butte, Jumbo told him, "We'll get back there one way or another. We ain't too proud to steal a train. Them fellers in Congress has broke the law. Why can't we?"[112] When the governor came to Puyallup and threatened them with the militia, Jumbo's group finally broke up, and the majority of them returned to their homes.

The town prospered when canneries were established in the area because there was a wealth of strawberries, blackberries and blueberries cultivated by the farmers. Supporting businesses such as box factories and preserving plants were built.

Japanese-American families were evacuated to Puyallup during World War II. The camp was just outside the city limits and was surrounded by barbed wire. Compelled to leave their homes, they lived in less-than-desirable quarters, as stated by one young man:

> *The rooms here are 17' X 20' they claim, but it does not seem so big—at least it's crowded—after 8 beds and a stove (the only furnished necessities) take up 3/4 of the floor space and the baggage for 8 of us and ourselves taking up the other 1/4. Some families of over 5 members have acquired two apartments (that's what they call these rooms) but we have as yet not been so fortunate.*[113]

Those interred were later shipped off to a relocation camp at Minidoka, Idaho.

In the 1920s, Puyallup became a daffodil and tulip bulb growing community. This occurred when the bulbs from Holland were banned because of the fear of disease and foreign insects. Today, calling itself the "Daffodil Capital of the World," the town celebrates its Annual Daffodil Festival in early April.

QUEETS

The 1850 Donation Claim Act opened this area for settlers. John Banta and S. P. Sharp formed a partnership and went searching for land, and in 1889 they came to what would eventually be Queets. They were paid to guide homesteaders and help them locate their claims when they arrived at Queets in 1890. The new arrivals were charged $50 for this service, but were told they did not have to pay until they saw the land and were satisfied with it. In March of the same year, the Portland-Port Angeles and Victoria Railroad was incorporated. As a result more homesteaders staked their claims in Queets, some of them brought here by Banta and Sharp. [114]

Because this was a new settlement and no stores were established, Banta and Sharp brought tons of supplies to the settlers. Mail even came by backpack from Quinault. The postman had quite a heavy load because the settlers subscribed to the *San Francisco Call Bulletin*, which they used to paper their walls for warmth after they read the paper. Some of the early homesteaders worked off their taxes when there was little money by helping with the building of county roads.[115]

The residents lived in relative isolation until the Olympic Highway was completed in 1931. Efforts to make the region a national park started a huge conflict between those who wanted the area designated as such and those who coveted the timber resources. In the 1940s, a man named Ickes wrote in his news column that "the tree butchers, axes on shoulders, are again on the march against some of the few remaining stands of America's glorious virgin timber." His articles prompted public opposition to cutting down the forest. In the 1950s, the Queets Corridor became part of the national park. By 1953, families within its boundaries had to give up their land.[116]

Queets is derived from the Quiatso Indian tribe. The word is thought to literally mean "out of the dirt of the skin." Legend has it that when the Great Spirit crossed a cold river, he rubbed his legs together to warm them and came up with a handful of dirt. He tossed the dirt into the river and a man and woman arose from the dirt which created the Quiatso Tribe.[117]

QUILCENE

Once the home of the Twana Indians, this area was explored by the Wilkes Expedition in 1841, where they noted on their charts the name "Kwil-sid." Quilcene is located at the mouth of the Quilcene River, and the name may signify "salt water people." The town was originally situated on the banks of the river, but was later moved to higher ground.

In 1860, a logger from Maine named Hampden Cottle claimed the land near the Little Quilcene River. He took up an unusual enterprise of digging ships knees. That is, he dug up tree trunks and roots which were cut at a certain angle and used to form the ribs of boats.

As people moved in they started some logging operations and farming, and by 1880 Quilcene had a population of fifty-eight people. In the beginning, mail came by boat from the town of Seabeck, but by 1882 it was delivered overland to Discovery Bay, and eventually the route went to the community of Port Townsend. The Green Mill Company was established and put out more than 150,000 shingles a day. In 1890, a man named Will Worthington established a general store.

When the Port Townsend Southern Railroad began

extending its line to connect with Portland, the settlers envisioned Quilcene growing by leaps and bounds. The editor of the *Quilcene Queen* wrote, "If this development is carried to a successful conclusion, our harbor will be lined with ocean going ships carrying the products of factories that will be established here, while the transcontinental railroad connections will distribute such goods to the markets of the United States."[118] This line was to become part of the Union Pacific. Construction started in 1890, but then financial problems plagued Union Pacific. A judge wrote to the *Quilcene Bugler* in 1891, stating, "The jig is up. Reliable word reached me that Portland court today appointed receiver for O.I. Co. This kills all hope that road will be extended."[119] Eventually, the tracks from Quilcene to Port Discovery were pulled up.

In 1902, hopes were up again when the Tubal Cain Mining Company began operations in the region. Some gold and manganese were found, and it was intended that Quilcene would become a large smelting and refining center for the mine. The company built bunkhouses, a sawmill and powder house. The mine continued operations until the 1920s, but there was never much ore taken out.

What brought Quilcene's economy back was logging. Will Worthington years earlier started purchasing the claims of settlers who had given up. Starting out using just axes, the industry went to logging jacks, then skid roads. Before the railroads, splash dams were used. Small streams were dammed up to give the logs the extra current needed to push them to the bay. Later, rail cars took the logs that went through town and over a trestle to the bay at a place called Linger Longer.

Oystering was a business that didn't do too well at first. A man named William Fulton tried propagating Eastern oysters in 1915, but it didn't work. In 1934, the Japanese oysters were tried, and in the warm waters of Quilcene Bay they did quite well. The bay was a perfect place for the spats (young oysters). They floated on the water for about ten days, then attached themselves to gravel or a shell. At other places, the tidal currents and winds prevented them from doing so, but here they were quite protected and the tide receded without endangering the spats.[120]

In the 1940s, a new business was born, providing florists around the U.S. with sword fern and salal (a tufted plant sold by florists as "lemon leaves"). Logging has slowed down over the years, but there is still small-scale harvesting.

SALKUM

The first settler was probably Salem Plant, who came here about 1872 and began growing hops on about fifteen acres. After other people established their homes, Plant hired some of them to pick the hops, which helped financially during the winter months. Later, Plant mortgaged his farm, and ended up losing it in 1897. When the mortgage was foreclosed, the new owner was kind enough to give Plant ten acres of the property.

William Hammill and his family moved here from Tumwater in 1881, coming originally from Virginia to get away from destruction of the Civil War. Hammill was looking for a good place to built a grist mill, and Salkum was the ideal site because of a waterfall at the junction of Salkum and Cowlitz Creeks that would give him the water power he needed. He had his gear shipped up the Cowlitz River as far as the steamboat could navigate. His mill was very up to date, with a turbine water wheel that put out eighty-five horsepower. Many of the farmers in the region grew wheat, so the grist mill was a welcome addition. They had to cut their grain by hand using what was called a cradle. Similar to a scythe with a frame, the wheat was cut and then raked into bundles and taken to the grist mill. The farmers who lived in the outlying regions were welcome to stay in Hammill's barn overnight before beginning their journey back home.[121]

Most of the roads in the region were lined with split planks, called corduroyed roads, and travel was uncomfortable at best. Much of the traffic was by river steamboats; supplies were brought in and farm produce shipped out to Portland. At first the mail had to be picked up at a place called Silver Creek until a post office was established. In those days, regular post office buildings were rare, and most were either in stores or the postmaster's home, which in this case was a home, where the mail was kept safe under a bed.[122]

The settlement grew slowly with its grist mills, general

Courtesy Van McDaniel, Salkum, Washington
Salkum (undated). This is the home of Ivy Mitchell Hills. While tearing down
the house, a woman's body was found inside. Years earlier, Ivy's daughter disappeared, and it was believed this was her body. The case was never solved.

stores, bricklayers, and even a game warden. About the only
logging done was to clear the land for homesteading. In 1903,
the Fuller family came to Salkum and purchased Salem Plant's
homestead. Fuller's daughter married a minister who was
instrumental in getting the first church built in town.

At one time, someone wrote, "Salkum is a cluster of dilapidated, nondescript houses and two mills, the latter closed down
as a result of the depletion of the timber supply in the vicinity
. . . The adjacent country is largely wasteland, where willows,
alders and vine maple almost conceal the bleaching stumps,
tombstones of forest that have passed away. . .,"[123] which was
attributed to the later over-harvesting of timber.

Salkum could mean "boiling up," referring to a section on the
Cowlitz River where the falls were located. As the water hit a
deep hole at the bottom, the Indians thought it looked like it
was boiling up. When the Mayfield Dam was constructed, rocks
were blasted to change the channel and adversely affected the
waterfall.

SEATTLE

Chief Sealth was born to the Suquamish Tribe between 1786 and 1790, from whom the city got its name. It was called Seattle because that was as close as the white men could get to pronouncing the chief's name.

Seattle had its beginning in 1851 when a group of settlers came from Illinois, led by Arthur Denny, and built their first homes at a place called Alki Point. The Indian word alki meant "by and by" or "after a while." Trees were felled to build their cabins, and after completion, the men sent for their families, who arrived after about a week on the water in stormy seas. To their astonishment, all the new arrivals could see were dilapidated cabins. Some of the women sat down and cried, because this was certainly not what they expected to see.[124]

In 1852, when the brig *Leonesa* was looking for timber to take to San Francisco, the captain saw people at Alki Point and was surprised because he didn't think there were any white men here. The settlers cut the needed timber and the ship loaded 35,000 board feet of logs. It was extremely difficult to get the logs on the ship because the beach was so shallow. The residents then moved their settlement closer to the protected waters of Elliott Bay because the timber forests, along with the natural harbor, made a perfect setting for a logging industry. H. L. Yesler selected a site and built the first steam sawmill on Puget Sound. The next year the first load of logs to be shipped to a foreign port was loaded on the *Louisiana*.

Seattle's population boomed when gold was discovered in Canada and brought miners who stopped here on their way to the gold fields. When Seattle learned the Northern Pacific Railroad was laying tracks, the town thought it would be the railway's terminus, but instead it went to Tacoma. So the town organized the Seattle & Walla Walla Railroad and Construction Company in 1873.

In 1875, the clipper ship *Windward* was leaving the harbor at Seattle loaded with lumber for delivery to San Francisco. Puget Sound was shrouded in fog, there was no wind, and the ship ran into a beach on Whidbey Island. After investigation of the damage, it was decided the ship was not salvageable, but the lumber was saved. The *Windward* was raised during a flood tide and towed into Seattle. All the usable pieces of the ship were stripped, and the rest sat there and became a landmark. What was left of the boat deteriorated over the years and it finally began to sink. In the 1880s, the Seattle Lake Shore and Eastern Railroad was constructed. The company did not remove what was left of ship, instead they simply drove pilings through the timbers, added dirt and concrete, and erected a building over her. So the *Windward* sits there to this day.[125]

By 1880, Seattle saw a lot of development with shingle mills and machine shops, and a city railway was established by Frank Osgood. The logs were dragged by teams of oxen over a muddy road to the sawmill. Because of its slick surface, it was called a skid road and soon became lined with saloons and brothels. This is where the term "skid row" was born.

When the railroad was being built, Chinese workers were imported. They were deported during the 1886 depression and replaced by Japanese who later worked in laundries and farms. By 1870, a Chinese investment group had built hotels and shops, and the Japanese developed an adjacent community.

Lou Graham came to Seattle and built a four-story brick palace, which became a famous cat house. Lou made a deal with local officials where she would contribute money to the municipal fund if they would not raid her establishment. She also told city officials that they were welcome to visit her place at no charge, for which they were most grateful and the deal was struck. When Lou died in 1903, she left the bulk of her estate, about $250,000, to the county school system.

The year 1889 brought the great Seattle fire. It started about 2:30 p.m. and by midnight more then fifty blocks in the business district had been destroyed. After the fire, the city fathers decided to purchase a fireboat, which they did in 1891. But because there were no more fires, the boat was relegated to towing garbage for a number of years.

Good fortune smiled on Seattle when the ship *Portland* came into port with more than $800,000 worth of gold from the gold fields in the Yukon in 1897. This sparked the last great gold rush, and Seattle became an outfitting center and major debarkation point to the gold fields. New businesses came in, others expanded, and of course more gambling halls and saloons made their presence known.

The steamship *Flyer* was built in Portland and brought here to conduct the Seattle to Tacoma passenger runs, which continued until about 1929. Captain E. B. Coffin liked to show off the speed of the *Flyer*. He would bring the ship close to the docks at full speed and then have the engines reversed at just the critical moment. One day it didn't stop. On September 3, 1905, Coffin was doing his thing and gave the signal to put the engines in reverse, but one of the pins in the gears fell out and the ship kept going full speed ahead. The ship hit the dock and demolished a warehouse loaded with oysters. Fortunately, nobody was hurt in the incident, just Coffin's pride.[126]

SEQUIM

Sequim is located on the north coast of the Olympic Peninsula. Before the white man entered the picture, the area was home to the S'Klallam Indians. The town was first homesteaded in 1854 by John Bell, and subsequent settlers found this place had a natural port and abundant seafood, but because of lack of water, farming was poor.

In the early 1890s, a man named James Grant and a group of men formed the Sequim Prairie Ditch Company. They tried to convince the residents that an irrigation ditch was needed, but everyone thought they were nuts because water could not be made to run uphill.[127] But the men persevered, and in 1895 the first meeting of the company with about two dozen people was held. Because there was very little money available, the company got the surveyor they hired to take potatoes in lieu of cash. The settlers dug ditches by hand and the irrigation water was to come from the Dungeness River.

When it was time to open the headgates for the first time in 1896, people from all over the area came to watch the great event. When the gate was opened, nothing happened. A wagon load of clay had to be dumped at the head of the flume into gravel, then some of the children had to jump up and down on the clay so it would work its way into the gravel, and finally the water flowed into the flume. Sequim had its irrigation ditch.

The Indians called the bay Such-e-kwai-ing or possibly

Suxtcikwi'in, from where the name Sequim was derived, which meant "quiet water." The town was first named West Clallam, then Seguin, and later changed to Sequim (pronounced Skwim) in 1883. Sequim's development was augmented when a dock was built at Port Williams in 1891 and a general store was established, as was the Corner Saloon.[128]

Sequim turned out to be one of the driest and sunniest towns in western Washington by some whim of nature. People began calling the town the "Sunshine Belt," and Sequim's population boomed. It became predominantly a retirement community.

Man may have lived here for more than 12,000 years, as evidenced by a mastodon's bones with a spear point in one of its ribs found nearby in 1977 when a farmer was creating a duck pond. Also discovered were charcoal firepits and some of them contained ash from the Mt. Mazama eruption.[129]

Commemorating the first water to Sequim, the town celebrates the Irrigation Festival in May, which is the oldest continuous festival in the state.

SKAMANIA

Located about three miles east of Vancouver, Skamania was once called Butler and Mendota. It was later named Skamania, which could mean "swift water."[130] The Indians may have been of the Shahala tribe; there was a place near Skamania that was called Sahclellah and a railroad flag station with the same name between Skamania and a landmark called Beacon Rock. Below the landmark was a Shahala village of the Wahclellah tribe, which was probably used as a winter camp. Despite their appearance of flattened heads and shells in their noses, the white men found the native residents to be friendly people. The Indians' staple diet was a root called a Wapato (eaten like potatoes), which they used as their main trading commodity.

When the settlers came to Skamania, some of them had to come down the Columbia River with their covered wagons on log rafts, because there were no roads at this time.

William Butler and his family came from England about 1892. He first worked at a dairy farm at Portland, then came by steamboat to a place called Marrs Landing where he lived for a number of years until he bought land at Skamania. What started out as just a cabin grew into a store, saloon, dock, and water tower. Butler was farsighted enough to build a dock that had two levels, which enabled boats to load or pick up supplies regardless of the water height. A fellow named Cap Ives had a flatboat and brought his supplies here to sell, but he left the area when his house washed away and his boat was lost in a flood in 1894.[131]

In the early 1900s the only road went from the schoolhouse to the dock. Eventually a railroad came through, and then the North Bank Highway was constructed, which took much of the river business with it. When the post office was established, it was called Butler. The town was renamed Skamania after the county of Skamania was formed.

The 840-foot Beacon Rock landmark was bought by residents in the early 1900s when they found out that quarry operations would destroy it. The rock would have been used to build up the jetties at the mouth of the Columbia River.

SKAMOKAWA

Those who write about ghost towns and list Skamokawa as one are doing it a great injustice. Ghost towns are just that; totally uninhabited, dead relics of yesteryear. Today, Skamokawa has approximately 200 citizens and another 200 or so in the immediate area, hardly a ghost town!

After the Hudson's Bay Company established one of its posts at Fort Vancouver, it began to expand and built more trading posts. One of them was near Skamokawa where the company was supplied with fish by the Chinook Indians. The Chinooks' practice of drying fish was to grind it up for the winter, which left a less than desirable odor. Hudson's Bay employees taught the Indians how to salt their fish to preserve them rather than grinding them into powder. The Indians got along well with the company until someone killed one of the employees. Hudson's Bay thought the Chinooks had done the deed, but they later discovered it was the Hoh Indians. The Chinooks found the guilty Indian and brought him back to the post where he was dealt with accordingly.[132]

Called "Venice of the Lower Columbia," Skamokawa was established at the junction of Skamokawa Creek, Steamboat

Courtesy Irene Martin, Skamokawa

Skamokawa waterfront (1911). During the town's early settlement, Skamokawa Creek was the only means of transportation. Some of the buildings were constructed on floats so they could rise and fall with the tide.

Slough and Brooks Slough, which became highways of commerce and communication until roads were built. John Couch moved to Skamokawa in 1844. While on his boat, the *Chenamus*, he noted in his log, "At 6 a.m. got underway and proceeded up the river and 12 noon came to anchor off . . . fame town called Schummaque and landed salt and barrels with trade to take salmon . . ."[133] Hawaiian oarsmen brought supplies from Couch's trading post in the Willamette to Skamokawa via longboats. The Chenamus also went to Hawaii and delivered more than 250 barrels of salmon, which made the salteries that were established in this area quite profitable.

When the Hudson's Bay Company got wind of what they thought was competition on Couch's part, the governor of the company wrote to John McLoughlin, who was stationed at Fort Vancouver: ". . . endeavor to defeat the object of the intruder by very fair means within your power, rendering his speculations unprofitable by lowering the tariff and selling at a small and even no profit at all for the time."[134] Couch had grubstaked many of the settlers from his trading post and was in hock to the tune of about $30,000. He offered to sell his debts to Hudson's Bay, but they refused because they didn't want his competition. Couch's trading post didn't last long, and it was later taken over by Smith Hensill It was then sold to James Birnie, who later went to Cathlamet and opened the post there.

About 1852, Thomas Dawson took up a homestead and tried his hand at raising potatoes. Some of the people to come here over the next few years made their living by cutting cordwood for the river steamers, and got out timber bolts for barrel factories in Portland. Skamokawa was laid out to conform with the sloughs and creeks which were the mode of transportation. The town had no roads until after World War I.

By the 1870s, Scandinavian immigrants had made their homes at Skamokawa and established the first cooperative creamery in the state of Washington. A teacher who was boarding with one of the families wrote that she gained more than twenty pounds while living with them. By 1899, almost 1,000 gallons of cream and seventy boxes of butter had been shipped.

Early fishermen seined with their horses, which dragged the nets onshore. When the Northern Pacific Railroad was being constructed, a sawmill supplied ties to the railroad. Skamokawa had three mills by the early 1920s and logging was a big industry. Riverboats and steamers plied the rivers and the town boomed. When river traffic dwindled, so did Skamokawa.

Skamokawa means "duck's nest river" in Japanese, but the name actually came from the name of an Indian chief named Skamokawa. His name meant "smoke over the water," because of the early morning fog that settled over the town. Skamokawa was spelled many different ways: on the Wahkuakum Treaty of 1851, the chief's name was spelled Skumahqueah. Others were Skemaqueup, Skomockaway, and Skomoqui, to name a few.

As more people moved to the region, churches were established, and Skamokawa and his wife canoed two Methodist ministers named Daniel Lee and B. Frost up the Columbia. In 1844, the Wilkes Expedition arrived, and one of the men stayed a couple of days with Skamokawa to learn some of the Wahkiakum language. During this same period, some of the Indian villages broke up and dispersed to different areas, and many natives died from fever. By 1851, very few Wahkiakums were left, and it was then that the federal government offered to buy their land.

Skamokawa was just about the last of his tribe in 1855.

During this time he lost the medal given him by Meriwether Lewis, which he greatly treasured. Skamokawa died in 1857. Folklore says the Indian chief was buried behind the old school-house. But he may actually have been buried in Pioneer Cemetery at the town of Cathlamet. The grave marker says, "Chief Wahkiakum, Grave of a Friendly Indian."

SKYKOMISH

Skykomish got its start with Great Northern Railroad (GNR). In 1889, James Hill decided to extend his railroad to the Pacific Coast from Montana, and hired John Stevens as engineer to determine the route. Stevens discovered Marias Pass in Montana, then went west to the Columbia River. During his exploration of the Cascades, he figured the coast would be the best route. Stevens met a man named John Maloney and hired him as a packer for the GNR surveys.[135]

In 1890, Maloney settled at a site he named Maloney's Siding, and three years later he built the general store which supplied the railroad and its construction crews. Skykomish's population grew to about 8,000 during construction of the railroad tunnel at Stevens Pass. This town became the division point (or switching yard) which maintained a roundhouse for the helper engines that were used for the switchback section through the Cascade Tunnel. During severe weather conditions, the switchback was the point where decisions were made to allow trains to continue over the pass. The first scheduled train came through on June 18, 1893.

Patrick McEvoy was an engineer for the GNR, but after he lost an arm in an accident, he came to Skykomish and built the first saloon about 1897, which he later turned over to his son. Called the Olympia Saloon, the son renamed it the Maple Leaf Confectioners during Prohibition, then to the Whistling Post Tavern when liquor was free to flow again. The tavern's name came from the fact that some of the railroad workers said that Skykomish would never be more than just a whistle stop.

The town was platted in 1899. When the post office was opened, Maloney was its first postmaster and the name was changed to Skykomish. The same year the Skykomish Lumber Company was formed, which made railroad ties for the GNR

Courtesy Skykomish Historical Society
Skykomish, Washington.

and timbers for snow sheds. During this period, the town was inundated with workers. For more than thirty-five years, it was supported by logging companies, shingle mills and a sawmill. One of the shingle mills was owned by Malony and putting out more than 80,000 shingles each day. Later a planing mill was built, along with another shingle mill, and warehouses. Bloedel Donovan Lumber Mills took over the planing mill in 1917. The town's economy had a burst of growth during World War I when the men who were not drafted into the service came to work at the lumber mills. There was a great government demand for building lumber, shingles and boxes. Much of the timber for shipbuilding was shipped back east on special trains.[136]

The land was quite hilly and big horses were used to haul the logs out, where they were either trucked out or floated down the Skykomish River. After ordering blankets for the horses, one of the purchasing agents from Donovan's Lumber Mill complained that the blankets were too light and small for the large logging horses. The agent got the reply back that "Having in mind the tender care given domestic animals in your neighborhood, we first thought of suggesting that this particular pair of blankets be cut bias on the gore, hem-stitched, have at least three rows of ruffles trimmed on the edges with old point lace."[137]

Courtesy Skykomish Historical Society
General store of Skykomish (undated). Owned by John Maloney.

In 1926, an electric substation was built, providing power for the electric helper engines taking trains through the tunnel at Stevens Pass. Because of their fumes, traditional steam engines could not take the trains through the almost eight-mile tunnel. By 1956, powerful fans were installed at one end of the tunnel that would push thousands of cubic feet of clean air through, allowing diesel trains to run through.

The Skykomish Indians were once considered by the government as an offshoot of the Snohomish Tribe. They spent some time hunting on the Skykomish River, and also used an Indian trail that went over Stevens Pass to the eastern portion of Washington. When the Treaty of Point Elliott was signed in 1855, the Skykomish Indians left the area and went to the Tulalip Reservation. The town's name comes from two words, skaikh and mish, meaning "inland people."[138]

The town celebrates Tunnel Days the first week in August,

commemorating the tunnel at Stevens Pass, with a number of events, including a bathtub race.

SNOHOMISH

The Snohomish Indians were a relatively peaceful tribe, living in an immense area from Puget Sound to the Cascades. They were not nomadic and were engaged in agriculture. Although peaceful, the Snohomish may have been in conflict with the Clallam Indians and the Cowiche clans. Snohomish has a number of possible meanings and is the English spelling of Sdah-hob-mish. It could mean "tidewater people," "the men", "the warriors," or "the braves."

In 1855, a military road was being planned from the community of Steilacoom to Fort Bellingham. The reason for the road was in case the British decided to move their gunboats into local waters. Three men from Steilacoom came up with an idea to build a ferry where the road would cross the Snohomish River, and in 1859 each claimed his share of the land. E. T. Cady called his site Cadyville, which would later become Snohomish City. Emory Ferguson took up residence in 1860 when he found out about the military road, knowing it would be a money-making opportunity, and took squatter's rights to one of the claims. He framed a house in Steilacoom, then had it shipped by steamer to his property. He later built the Blue Eagle Saloon and also sold supplies to settlers and Indians.[139]

The military road was never completed, but Ferguson went on to became a prominent businessman and politician. More people moved in, attracted by the timber opportunities that started about 1864, and the nearby river was used to transport the logs. In 1882, three brothers built the first mill in town and brought new technology to the lumber industry. Switching from oxen dragging logs, they had the timber carried via a wheeled truck that ran on rails. They also designed a shingle saw, and were the first to use the donkey engines that hauled logs. The donkey engine was designed by John Dolbeer about 1881. It was a small steam engine that powered a capstan-like drum which reeled in logs to a landing. Women took advantage of all the timber men in town and opened up laundries on a street that was known as "Soap Suds Row."

Ferguson and Cady came up a plan to build a trail to a gold strike at the Similkameen River, which was over the Cascade Mountains. Men were hired to break a trail, but the idea failed. When the town was surveyed in 1867, it began to experience some growth when Pope and Talbot, a firm at Port Gamble, hired people to claim homesteads and then transfer their titles back to the company. Ferguson got in on the scheme and sold his own fraudulent lots in town.

Ferguson also built a hotel which was designated as the county courthouse in 1863. He tried to get the county seat moved from Mukilteo to Snohomish. Then along came the town of Everett, and town fathers arranged to get Everett residents to vote for a park to be purchased from a land company, which in turn would build a courthouse. In 1894, Everett filed a petition to have the county seat moved from Mukilteo, and the campaigns began between the two rival towns. Rumor has it that Everett added 200 dead people to its poll books. At any rate, after a two-year battle Everett won.[140]

Settlers wanted a railroad line brought into Snohomish, so in 1888 they put up $2,700 to insure a right of way, and the railroad was built this same year. By 1910, Snohomish had grown and boasted nine mills, but a fire burned down the biggest mill, and the others were later dismantled. Because the railroad was the fastest transport for perishable food, Snohomish became an agricultural community.

SNOQUALMIE

The Snoqualmie Indians lived in the Puget Sound area, and made first contact with the white man about 1833 when Fort Nisqually was built. The Snoqualmie Tribe has been classified as part of the Coast Salish Indians. In the 1860s, white settlers drove the Indians out of their villages. When the Treaty of Point Elliott was signed, some of the Snoqualmies relocated to the Tulalip Reservation, but many of them stayed on off-reservation land. Snoqualmie may be derived from Sdoh-kwahlb, which means "moon people," or just "moon." The Indians believed this is where their ancestors originated; the place where their life source came from.[141]

Snoqualmie was born during the prosperous days of

lumbering and milling. Following paths and horse trails that were used by the Snoqualmie Indians, the first settlers came to this area in 1858. One of them was Jeremiah Borst who claimed the land and began farming and raising pigs, eventually owning about 1,500 acres. In 1881, the hop growers association bought 900 acres of Borst's land and started what would become the largest hops ranch in the world.

In 1865, a wagon road was built over Snoqualmie Pass, thus saving settlers the arduous journey along the Columbia River. The townspeople raised more than $2,000 for the project. In 1869, nasty winter storms destroyed the wagon road. The year 1884 brought a new road. But when the Northern Pacific built its line near Stampede Pass, the wagon road lost revenue.

Will Taylor came about 1880 and Borst sold Taylor some land. Taylor then platted the land and laid out streets. In 1889, the site was named Snoqualmie. Another gentleman, Allen Mitten, purchased 120 acres near the railroad tracks, sold it, and that site was named Snoqualmie Falls. Because the towns of Snoqualmie Falls and Snoqualmie were only five miles apart, the Seattle, Lake Shore and Eastern Railroad made it mandatory that the names be changed to avoid confusion. So, Snoqualmie Falls became Snoqualmie, and Snoqualmie was renamed North Bend.

Timber boosted the town's economy until the area was logged over. The settlers then turned to cattle ranching and began to ship more cattle than lumber to the Puget Sound packing houses. Some of the farmers grew hops, which became a good cash crop in the 1880s. In the 1890s, logging and agriculture benefitted from the arrival of the Seattle, Lake Shore and Eastern Railroad.

SPANAWAY

Spanaway was one of the first settlements in Pierce County. When agents of the Hudson's Bay Company came through, they wrote in their *Journal of Occurrences* in 1849, "Two plows sent to Spannuch and one to Muck."[142] It is not known what the words meant, but they were thought to be Indian. Local tradition says the word yawanaps, backwards for Spanaway, meant "beautiful water."

The Old Military Road, the first constructed in the state, was built in the 1850s near Spanaway. When Congress appropriated money for a road, it sat on the project, so residents at the town of Olympia took over the enterprise themselves, and the road was built from Fort Steilacoom through the Naches Pass. Earlier, the pass was explored for a route north for immigrant trains, and a survey party said it couldn't be done, but was proven wrong.

One of the early homesteader was Henry de la Bushalier, who settled on the shore of Lake Spanaway. The first immigrant train over the Naches Pass brought the Wright family here in 1853. Their trip was rough and hazardous as they had to come over the Cascades, where a trail was in the process of being cut to connect the east side of the mountains. But someone told the crew that nobody was coming through during the winter, so they quit for the season. The Wrights had to come over this trail, no easy task with an uncompleted road. Many other settlers got discouraged when they didn't think they could make it over the Cascades, but remembering what they had been told about the wonderful country and climate, they pushed on. On the way, one of the families met a band of Indians who wanted to buy their baby. In fear of losing their child, the family traveled around the clock.[143]

In the 1870s, German residents who lived in Chicago were urged by the territorial governor of Washington to move west. More than a hundred came with prospects of a new life. One of the immigrants was Gustav Bresemann, who was a furniture maker. He first stayed at Steilacoom doing carpentry, then later staked his claim at the north end of Lake Spanaway, where he built the first furniture factory that made household goods which were sold to people in Tacoma. After Bresemann's wife died, he sold his land to the Tacoma Light and Power Company.

The Locke family also relocated to Spanaway and took up farming. When Locke got word that a new town was being platted at Commencement Bay, he took a wagonload of vegetables to Tacoma. When he came across a group of men and their tent camp, they saw Locke had fresh vegetables, which were rare commodities, and the men made a beeline to the wagon and purchased all his produce.

Andrew Simon came from Denmark and settled at this site before the town was platted. He raised grain, hauled it to Chambers Creek where a grist mill was located, and came back with flour. Some of the homesteaders raised sheep. The wool was washed, carded, and spun into clothing, then sold. Hops was an important crop grown in the bottom lands. Pickers were paid one dollar a box, and it was a wealthy person who could fill three boxes a day. The hops were dried in a kiln, cured with sulfur, and loaded into burlap sacks, then shipped to destinations in the United States and Europe. Some logging was also conducted. The logs were brought to the sawmill by tram cars that were drawn by horses. In 1890, the Lake Park Land Railway and Improvement Company was created, which built a railroad from Tacoma to Spanaway.

SPOKANE

Acting for the North West Fur Company, Finan McDonald and Joco Finlay built a trading post called Spokane House in 1810. They took the name from the Spokane Indians, which signified "children of the sun," or "sun people." The chief called himself Illim-Spokane, "Chief of the sun people." When the Hudson's Bay Company took over in 1821, the trading post was dismantled.

Settlement near Spokane Falls started in 1871 when J. J. Downing and his family homesteaded land on the banks of the river. The *Palouse Gazette* wrote in 1877, "A surveying party is now at the falls surveying town lots for the future city. Three parties of U.S. Surveyors are in the field making rectangular surveys. The need of such work has long been sought after by persons looking for homes." Downing, along with Richard

Courtesy Spokane Public Library
Spokane Falls (1887). It was renamed Spokane in 1891.

Benjamin, built a water-powered sawmill, and the following year James N. Glover and J. N. Matheny purchased Benjamin's share in the mill and took an option on the rest. Glover then opened a store and improved the mill. He wrote: ". . . My first stock was made up of Indian supplies - cheap blankets, calicoes, beads and paints (I did a big business in paints), tobacco, sugar, tea, and coffee, cutlery and all sorts of groceries. . ."[144]

Glover filed a plat in 1871 and called the town Spokane Falls, which began to expand with the addition of a schoolhouse, newspaper, and many settlers. Also encouraging settlement was the discovery of silver and lead deposits in Idaho and British Columbia, and the town became a supply point for the miners. Arrival of the Northern Pacific Railroad also added much to Spokane's economy. One of the store owners remarked, "The N.P. is coming this way and there will be all sorts of checks to cash and I might as well be ready to take care of them." He then proceeded to open a bank. Transcontinental mail service was in place by 1883 when the railroad was completed through Montana. The local newspaper began promoting Spokane. From the *Spokane Falls Review*, May 19, 1883: "New dwellings new stores, and new manufacturing establishments are springing up like magic, and the end is not yet."[145]

But it was almost the end in 1889 when fire broke out and the flames engulfed the town fanned by wind, and destroyed the whole business district. The new water works were no good to the firefighters, because there was only one man who knew how to operate it, and he was out of town at the time. Spokane became a tent city while the people rebuilt. In 1891, Spokane Falls became just Spokane by popular vote.

STEHEKIN

Stehekin was once part of the Columbia Indian Reservation, land the Indians were trying to retain after much of it had been taken by the white men. The reservation was later disbanded. When traveling through the Cascade Mountains, the Indians camped at this site situated at the head of Lake Chelan and called it Stehekin, meaning "the way through," referring to the pass through the mountains. The Indians moved seasonally to gather berries and roots, and also spent their winters here.

Alexander Ross, who was with the Pacific Fur Company, came through the region in 1814 looking for an overland route through the mountains to the Pacific Ocean. When he reached this site, he wrote in his field notes, "Country gloomy, forest almost impervious with fallen as well as standing timber. A more difficult route to travel never fell to man's lot..."[146] He and other explorers didn't give this place much more notice and never returned for further exploration. The first white men to stay in the valley were probably the early prospectors.

A Civil War veteran named John Horton arrived in the 1880s, and decided to settle here because he liked the isolation, being a solitary man. He built his home at the mouth of the Stehekin River and hung out a sign: "Horton's Cabin, The Gateway to the Mines. Our door is wide open to all square men - all others take due warning." It was thought he also began construction on a Swiss-style hotel. In the 1890s, the area really opened to settlers. Although Stehekin was an isolated place and the trail was tough going to reach the small settlement, it still drew some homesteaders who practiced subsistence farming. [147]

What few people came were followed by a small number of "loners" who moved to Stehekin. A hunter and gambler filed a homestead claim near Rainbow falls. Another came and raised milk cows and sold cream to local store owners. Residents had to bring topsoil from the banks of the rivers nine miles down in the valley in order to cultivate gardens. The total population in 1910 was an astounding thirteen.

In 1892, Merritt Field, on his way with his family to settle in
the town of Conconully, had problems with his wagon at
Colockum Pass, and one of the valley residents stopped to help
him. He apparently told Field about the Sehekin Valley, and
Field decided to stay here instead of going on. He bought a par-
tially finished hotel (probably the one Horton started), and
eventually turned it into a resort. The post office was established in 1892 with Field as its postmaster. He also became a
Chelan   County   representative   in   the   Washington
Legislature.[148] There was not much in the way of population
because Stehekin became more of a resort, and tourists flocked
here during the summer. Field encouraged the elite to visit
Stehekin and his hotel was full during the summer months.

Field decided to move out of the Stehekin in 1916 and sold
the hotel to the Great Northern Railroad, which ran the hotel
for about another ten years. The early 1900s saw about the last
of mining activities. Today, Stehekin is a jumping-off place for
hikers and backpackers who explore the Cascades, and approximately seventy people live here year-round. They get their supplies by making out a list and sending it down to one of the
stores at Lake Chelen (with a blank check), then the merchandise is delivered by boat, as is their mail. There is only one
phone in Stehekin Valley.

STEILACOOM

This site was originally an Indian village called tchil-ac-cum,
which means "pink flower,"[149] and referred to the myriad of pink
flowers that grew in the region. It may also be derived from the
chief's name, Tail-a-koom. John Work, who was with the
Hudson's Bay Company, came to Steilacoom in 1824 and wrote
in his field notes, "Chilacoom."

The British were at the Fort Nisqually trading post originally to trade for furs, but they decided to raise cattle and sheep
instead and ship them to Alaska. Tail-a-koom and his band
resented the fact that the cattle and sheep were being grazed on
their land. When Tail-a-koom was hunting on "their" land, one
of the herders shot at the chief's dog because it was chasing his
sheep. Tailakoom shot back and ended up in jail. But when

brought up for charges in front of William Tolmie, who recognized his old friend, the judge released Tailakoon.

The first person to take a donation claim in the area was Thomas Chambers in 1849, but he was ordered to leave by an agent of the Hudson's Bay Company. He not only refused, but encouraged other settlers to move here. Under the Treaty of 1846, H.B.C. claimed all the land and grazing rights, but a court sided with the settlers.

The arrival of a sea captain named Lafayette Balch, in 1851, was the real beginning of Steilacoom. An ambitious Maine mariner, he brought with him wood for a house, and supplies on his ship, the *George Emory*. Balch claimed some land under the Donation Claim Act, and immediately opened for business. He originally planned to live in Olympia, but came here instead when he saw the high prices of lots at Olympia, and named his lot Port Steilacoom, which was located just below Fort Steilacoom. He later built a sawmill.[150]

By 1855, more sawmills and a flour mill had been constructed, and the wharf was completed. It became a port of call for ships to pick up furs, cordwood, and fish headed for the California markets. A dam was built that raised Steilacoom Lake and another sawmill was established by Andrew and Marion Byrd. Andrew cut a trail known as Byrd's Mill Road that went to the community of Puyallup. Steilacoom also had a jail built in 1858, the first in Washington Territory, but when the county seat was moved to Tacoma, the jail was closed.

In 1859, the schooner *Blue Wing* was leaving Steilacoom's wharf, but it never reached its destination. Townspeople thought the boat had sunk, but it was later learned that the boat was destroyed at Vashon Island, and the entire crew had been murdered by the Haida Indians.

Steilacoom grew considerably when gold was discovered on the Thompson and Fraser Rivers, and hundreds of gold seekers descended on the town. Businesses capitalized on this opportunity and Steilacoom became an outfitting center for the miners. The town also had a barrel factory and salmon-packing plant. In 1859, a brick factory was established which fired the first bricks in the state.[151]

When the Northern Pacific Railroad Company was chartered

by Congress to build a line across the U.S., Lafayette Balch believed Steilacoom had a pretty good chance of getting the terminal, but it went to Tacoma instead. Steilacoom's importance then declined and many of its residents moved to Tacoma. When the Point Defiance Tunnel was built, the tracks finally came to town in 1910.

Old Fort Steilacoom was home to the State Insane Asylum in 1871. One of the patients was Myrtle de Montes, daughter of a well-known family. One evening after eating salmon, she got ill, but waited until the next morning before she sought help. By this time she was so sick and delirious the neighbors took her to the sheriff, who put her in a strait jacket and had her thrown in the asylum. What she actually had was ptomaine poisoning. Four months later Myrtle was released. After her terrible experience, she became the driving force in getting the laws changed and conditions improved at the asylum.[152]

SUMAS

Sumas, meaning "land without trees," referring to a flat prairie section, sits right next to Canada, just across the border from Huntingdon, British Columbia. Indians traveled the ancient trails in this valley, and in 1827 Hudson's Bay Company men used the same route for fur-trapping. Indians made it their summer camp to fish for the plentiful salmon in the Sumas River. The south bank was home to the Matsqui tribe, and to the Sumas Indians who lived near the confluence of the Sumas and Fraser Rivers.

It was thought that Thomas Jennings was the first settler in the Sumas Valley, but he actually built his home on the Canadian side. About 1849, A. R. Johnson left his home in Kentucky and stopped in California to try his luck in the gold fields, and then went on to the Frazer River in 1858. When the gold didn't pan out for him, he worked for a while at Whatcom's coal mines, then came to Sumas in 1872.

As people moved to town, their mainstay was hunting deer and elk, and bear. Loren Van Valkenburg arrived in 1882 and claimed some land, then opened a general store. Because the settlement did not have a school, Valkenburg offered the second story of his store to be used as a school room.

Sumas began as a railroad town. The *Whatcom Reveille* in 1891 wrote, "The BB & BC road arrived at Sumas at 1:00 p.m., Sunday amid great rejoicing. Col. Barker was threatened with a spasm, while many went wild. . . . The SLS & E road is expected to arrive Wednesday, when another big time will occur." [153] A short time later the Canadian Pacific reached town, and rip-roaring celebrations went on for weeks and town lots were selling like mad. There were so many people coming that some of the settlers created room and boards out of tents, and hung signs out that said "Hotel." The saloons weren't far behind. With all those rails, Sumas had three direct lines to the towns of Whatcom, Seattle and Vancouver, British Columbia.

Because the area was so heavily timbered, residents had a difficult time cutting logs for their homes. Their saws were only about six feet long and many of the trees were much wider than that, so two saws had to be brazed together. In some cases, many of the people just burned the trees. Because of the massive timber resources, lumber became a big industry; a broom handle factory was also established, as were lumber and shingle mills. Then the bottom dropped out and the mills closed, leaving Sumas in a depression, causing land values to drop.

In 1897, gold was discovered on Mount Baker, and the town was inundated with miners. Sumas was now an outfitting town. Many of the area businesses physically moved their buildings to the boundary line; one of them was the assayer's building. When a miner brought in a gold sample, the assayer already had his building up on rollers ready to move. The sample assayed out at $10,750 per ton of ore. The assayer packed up as fast as he could and headed out to make his fortune, his building still sitting on rollers in the middle of the street. His actions precipitated a mad dash for the mountain and many of the businessmen closed up shop. More than 3,000 claims were filed.

Mail was delivered at first by horses, and then when a fellow named Joe began delivering, he thought his mules would be more economical. But Joe wasn't happy with the slowness of the mules, so he bought an old motorcycle. Now he could travel his route with speed, although the backfiring of the engine scared the hell out of the domestic animals grazing alongside the road.

In the end, Joe quite the mailrun, sold the bike, moved to Canada, and became a wheat farmer.

Because Sumas was located right on the American/Canadian border, it was the ideal route for smugglers, especially when the railroads were built. Chinese workers were used for railroad construction because they were cheap labor, and much contraband was shipped, such as foodstuffs. But the largest commodities smuggled in were opium and Chinese Nationals.

TACOMA

The town was first known by the Indians as Shubahlup, or Chelaulip ("the sheltered place"). One of the first settlers to the Tacoma area was a Swede named Nicholas De Lin, who arrived in 1852. An enterprising man, he soon started developing a lumber business, and constructed a water-driven sawmill which began cutting about 2,000 board feet of lumber per day.

Tacoma's growth came to a standstill during 1855 when the Indians became hostile. The settlers left and headed to Fort Steilacoom for protection, De Lin and his family among them. But before long, the hostilities died down, and De Lin went back to work his mill again.[154]

When General Morton McCarver heard of the area, he bought the site that would be Tacoma. He also saw the need for a railroad and thought this site would be a good place for its terminus. He was going to name the town Commencement City, but a man named Philip Ritz convinced him to name it Tacoma,[155] which is thought to come from the word Takhoma or Tayma, meaning "mountain that is God," in reference to Mt. Rainier. Other definitions have included "frozen waters," "nourishing breast," and "near to heaven.".

McCarver did a lot to promote the community. He was known to sell wilderness land sight unseen, giving names to streets that didn't exist. He also promoted nonexistent places to land-hungry people and gullible investors, but his methods did bring them in.

In 1869, the Hanson and Ackerman Mill was established, and Tacoma went into the timber industry, which in turn brought in more supporting businesses, and the first mail was delivered. The mill was one of the largest sawmills on Puget

Sound. The town grew so fast there was a shortage of currency, so Hanson and Ackerman issued metal discs to be used locally for exchange. With all these people, it didn't take long for the saloons, churches, and a jail to arrive. One of the church Deacons was quite a pistol, who would come into the saloons and tell the patrons he wanted every damn one of them in church, and each was going to put fifty cents into the collection plate. So much for piety.

Because of the time-honored custom of a bartender buying someone a drink on the house, Tacoma city fathers enacted a law which forbade this practice in order to stem the continuous drinking. However, a Washington court ruled that liquor consumption was regulated by local enforcement agencies, but "treating was an ingrained American habit, whatever the police might say about it," and the custom continued.[156]

In 1873, General McCarver's dream came true when the Northern Pacific Railway selected Tacoma as its terminus. He proceeded to purchase a lot of acreage. But his hopes were dashed when the railroad decided to locate its terminus just below town at a new Tacoma. A Steilacoom newspaper wrote, "Three new stores, one blacksmith shop, and legions of whiskey mills have sprung into existence in Tacoma since the location of the terminus, and are in full blast..."[157]

Tacoma experienced phenomenal growth when the Stampede Pass Tunnel was built and a switchback was constructed over the summit of the Cascades, which brought direct transcontinental rail service to the region in 1887.

TATOOSH ISLAND

The bean-shaped island of Tatoosh is situated off the extreme northwestern point of the state near the Makah Indian Reservation. Traditionally a summer fishing village for the Makah Indians, John Meares named the island to commemorate a Nootka Indian chief named Tatoochatticus. The word Tatooche may be a Nootkan word for "milk" or "breasts." A similar Nootkan word Tatootshe, means "thunder," "fire from thunder," or "thunder bird." The Makah Indian name for Tatoosh Island was O-per-jec-ta, denoting "island."

In search of more sea otters to add to his cargo, Meares set anchor just off this island on June 30, 1788. The Makah Indians came out to meet him, along with Chief Tatoochatticus.

Meares wrote an account of his first meeting with the Makah Indians: "About five o'clock we hove to off a small island. . . In a very short time we were surrounded by canoes filled with people of a much more savage appearance than any we had hitherto seen. They were principally clothed in sea otter skins, and had their faces grimly bedaubed with oil and black and red ochre. Their canoes were large, and held from twenty to thirty men, who were armed with bows, and arrows barbed with bone, that was ragged at the points, and with large spears pointed with muscleshell. . . The chief of this spot, whose name is Tatootche, did us the favor of a visit and so surly and forbidding a character we had not yet seen. His face had no variety of color on it, like the rest of his people, but was entirely black, and covered with a glittering sand, which added to the savage fierceness of his appearance."[158]

Not much importance was given to the island until a lighthouse was built by the federal government in 1857. The lighthouse keepers led a cold and lonely life on this desolate island. When frequent storms came, the rain would blow up under the shingles of the lighthouse and the keepers were always cold and damp; so damp, in fact, moss would grow on the walls. Chimneys were so badly built that when the wind blew down the flue, it filled the lighthouse with smoke.

In the late 1930s, Tatoosh was home to about twelve families. Their supplies and mail had to be lifted from a boat by a crane and set on the island. It had a naval station, school, and even a post office at one time. Now it is a meteorological station, where supplies are still delivered by an overhanging crane. At least a six-month reserve of supplies is kept on the island; because when the seas are rough, boats cannot get near.

Tatoosh may have been a menace to ships, but it was also a haven for a number of sailors aboard the British bark, *Matterhorn*. She was carrying barley, a light grain which could shift suddenly in heavy seas. During a violent storm near the Columbia River, the wind blew so hard the barley was displaced, causing the boat to go on her beam ends. The ship drifted north for about three days while the crew tried to right her, but to no avail. They decided to abandon ship and loaded one of the small boats with emergency supplies. As the *Matterhorn* slid down into the sea, Captain Salter guided the small boat towards the reef. They were picked up by the *Umatilla Lightship's* crew after more than twenty hours. The lightship tended to their needs until the storm was over and then transferred them to Tatoosh Island, where they were eventually picked up. How they survived the sea was a miracle, with the loss of only three men, twenty-seven of them survived.[159]

At one time, the crew at the Tatoosh Island Light Station made an announcement that they were all quitting their jobs. They did so when the Indians took over the island because they said it belonged to them because the white men never compensated them for it. It was the government's job to straighten out this mess, and until that happened a gunboat was available in case of any problems. This lighthouse has the distinction of being the only one in the United States Lighthouse Service to ever have been taken over and operated by Indian pirates.

The Makahs have a legend about how the island began. Tatoosh Island and Destruction Island lived together by the Hoh River and had many children (big and small rocks along the coast). Their parents often had spats, and after a really nasty quarrel Tatoosh made up her mind to leave her husband. She took the kids into the boat and went up the coast. The longer she paddled, the angrier she got, until she reached today's Point of Arches. She told her children they would probably grow up to be just like their father, proceeded to throw them overboard, and kept on going. When she got near Cape Flattery, she decided this was where her new home would be. And there was born Tatoosh Island, and her children became the rocks at Point of Arches.[160]

TENINO

This site was once an Indian meeting ground and trading spot. Although there was an Indian trail that meandered through, it is not known if it was a permanent settlement, which probably accounts for the very few artifacts found here. The Hudson's Bay traders used this trail, which became the main route between Fort Vancouver and Fort Nisqually.

Stephen Hodgden was the first settler to file a donation claim in 1851. He originally came from Maine and moved west to work the gold fields in California. Hodgden didn't have any luck, so settled on the banks of Scatter Creek. Thomas Linklater, who was once an employee with the Hudson's Bay Company, also took up a homestead.[161]

Potential problems with the Indians prompted the settlers to build forts for their protection in the 1850s, but no major fights erupted and all returned to their homes. There was only one Tenino man killed during the Indian War, and that was near Rainier when he was bringing supplies for the militia.

The Tenino post office was established in 1860, with Stephen Hodgden as its first postmaster, and the site was called Hodgden's Station. The only available transportation was by stagecoach until Northern Pacific laid tracks from Kalama to Hodgden's Station, where it constructed a roundhouse. Tenino grew up around the railroad, beginning in 1872. Rail crews also constructed the depot and office. The final spike was driven in on October 8, 1872, and the station was named Tenino.

Unfortunately, the railroad ran into financial difficulties and completion of the tracks to Tacoma was stopped for about a year. Olympia thought it would be the terminus of the railroad, but it was completely bypassed, leaving passengers to disembark at Tenino and take horses or wagons the rest of the way to town. Finally, in 1878, a narrow-gauge railroad was completed to Olympia and called the Thurston County Railroad Construction Company. The line name was later changed to the Olympia and Chehalis Valley Railroad, then to the Port Townsend Southern Railroad Company. Northern Pacific bought the line in 1914, which was abandoned when its new line was established and went through East Olympia.[162]

Tenino became more than a railway depot after a specific

type of sandstone was found. S. W. Fenton and George VanTine were looking for building stone, and went to Olympia to secure financial backing for a stone quarry. They missed the train and stayed with a man named Sam Spurlock, where they noticed his stone fireplace. When they asked Sam about the fireplace, he told them it was built from stone taken from Tenino. They returned and found the stone outcropping and established the Tenino Stone Company. The sandstone was soft and easy to quarry, but when exposed to air it hardened. As time went on, about a half-dozen quarry companies were formed. Some of the buildings built with the sandstone were the old State Capitol and the Portland and Seattle Libraries. With the advent of concrete, the sandstone was no longer in demand.[163]

Tenino also supplied about 375,000 cubic yards of the sandstone quarried by the Hercules Company for the breakwater project at Gray's Harbor to the tune of over $1 million. The company then got a contract for rock for the Skookumchuck River Gorge Project. The project ended when funding was cut off because money was needed for harbor improvements during World War I.

After the war, Tenino went into an economic slump. Because sandstone was no longer needed with the advent of concrete, residents turned to logging and farming. When the depression hit after the bank failures, Tenino made headlines when it created "wooden money." The Tenino Chamber of Commerce came up with an idea to issue emergency scrip following failure of their local bank. The wooden money was made out of cedar and spruce, given to depositors in exchange for assignment to the Chamber of up to 25% of the depositor's bank account balance. It turned out to be somewhat profitable when more than $10,000 worth was sold to collectors, but the Chamber realized only $40.

Local folklore has it that the name Tenino came from the number on a locomotive: 1090; or because of a railroad survey staked that had marked on it, 10-9-0. There were Tenino Indians who lived along the Columbia River. Tenino is a Chinook word that could mean "meeting ground," "ford in the road," or "junction;" all of the definitions referring to the Indian trail crossings.

Not far from Tenino, off Route 507, are the Mima Mounds, which contain hundreds of dimple-like knolls that were discovered by pioneers in the early 1800s. When the Wilkes Expedition came through, Charles Wilkes dug into one of the mounds and noted that "They bear the marks of savage labor, and are such an undertaking as they would have required the united efforts of a whole tribe." While people thought they were burial mounds, they were actually naturally forming mounds. According to geologists, these mounds were what was left of blocks of frozen ground that had buckled. The irregular blocks eroded at the upper levels as the earth thawed, creating the unusual forms. But no one is really sure, and the mounds are still a mystery.

TOKELAND

Lieutenant John Meares first came this way in 1788 and called the inlet Shoalwater Bay. About sixty years later, a man of many talents as scholar and writer, James Swan, came to the region and wrote about the Indians who lived here.

Located on north Willapa Bay, Tokeland saw its first settler in 1854 when J. F. Barrows settled at what was called Toke Point. Chief Toke, who may have been of the Chehalis Tribe and was living here when the Barrows arrived, used this site as a summer home which had a wealth of food, especially shellfish. Swan said that Toke "had been a man of a great deal of importance among the Indians, but advancing years and an inordinate love of whiskey had reduced him to being regarded as an object of contempt and aversion. . ."[164]

At one time there was a lake, but it disappeared because of progress, called a landfill. George Brown moved to Toke in 1858 and lived in a tent until his home was built, then sent for his family, where they eventually claimed more than 740 acres of land and began farming.[165]

By the 1890s, news had spread about Toke Point's beautiful beach, and one of Brown's children opened the Kindred Inn. The post office was established in 1894, and the name went from Toke Point to Tokeland. Then in 1910, Brown's other daughter, Lizzie, and her husband, William Kindred, began construction of the Tokeland Hotel to accommodate the visitors. The hotel

also touted a golf course, stables, and a general store. Because
the family was friendly with the Indians, the hotel had a large
collection of their handicrafts. In 1925, the Kindred family
deeded the streets of the platted land to the county, under the
condition that they remain public highways forever.

Herbert Nelson came to Tokeland after the logging industry
went belly-up in 1929. He purchased an old boat and crab pots
and went into the crabbing business, shipping the shellfish to
Seattle in wooden crates. One year, Nelson's entire shipment
arrived spoiled and it all had to be destroyed. Nelson then started his own processing plant. One of his sons found that by putting citric acid in the canned crab, the meat would not turn
dark. Then in 1944, someone put together a basket of Nelson's
seafood and gave it as a gift. As a result, Nelson had a new side-
line called SeaTreats which were sold all over the world. Other
processing plants were established over the years, but eventually most of them were abandoned because of the extreme
weather conditions.

When William Kindred and his wife died, he left his property to his housekeeper. She in turn sold it to the Nelson Crab and
Oyster Company, which reopened the hotel and turned it into a
boardinghouse for its employees, but it closed down in 1949.
Then a year later, the hotel was sold and reopened again. The
Tokeland Hotel wasn't the only one to spring up. About 1907, a
unique hotel was built that looked like a river boat. Called the
Hotel Rustic, it didn't last because it had been built too close to
the waterline, and erosion was its "downfall," and the hotel was
washed away.

The sea was not kind to Tokeland and began to erode the
shoreline. A beach that protected the hotels washed away completely, and the stand of timber fell into the sea. The result was
some of the hotel cottages were swept into the sea when storms
hit. Residents finally got together and built a rock wall, which
helped until 1973 when a monster storm hit. The Nelson
Cannery then built a barrier that helped to stabilize the beaches. Tokeland today is mainly a resort town.

TONASKET

Sitting on the floor of the Okanogan Valley, Tonasket is an old Indian campsite where trappers also hunted in the early 1800s before any settlers arrived. The town was named for Chief Tonasket of the Okanogan Tribe, which may be a branch of the Colville Indians.

Tonasket's birth date was between 1819 and 1825. He was considered a very intelligent leader, was fair to his tribe, and his philosophy was to promote good will and peace. He owned some land near Osoyoos Lake just below the Canadian border, and in 1885 he sold it and moved east to the Republic-Curlew area. Because the winters here were not as mild, Tonasket purchased wagons and a mowing machine from Colville, which enabled him to feed his cattle so they thrived during an extremely bad winter in 1889. He also built a racetrack above Kettle River and established a trading post which supplied many of the new settlers. Tonasket died in 1891, and there are different versions of his death. One was thought to be from an eye infection that was so bad he had to have his eye removed, but that didn't help, and he died. It was also said he committed suicide in 1898, but the date does not coincide with his actual date of death. A more likely reason is that he simply died from old age when he was in his late seventies.[166]

The town got its start when Watkins Parry came to the Okanogan Valley in 1888 and called his site Parry's Landing. He first opened a trading post on the west side of the Okanogan River, then moved it at a bend of the river just south of the present town. He established a store and hotel, blacksmith and barn, and then a post office. A ferry was later used to cross the Okanogan River when it was in flood.[167] The rest of the time, the settlers forded their horses and wagons.

When word came about the possibility of a railroad, a banker named Arthur Lund decided the present site, rather than Parry's section, was the best place for a town. The railroad from Wenatchee was built in 1914. The town had already been platted in 1910 when the Bonaparte Land Company was formed, then the post office was taken from the now defunct Parry's Landing. The newspaper carried a slogan for promoting Tonasket in 1913: "All Roads Lead to Tonasket."

The town was not without its bootleggers, because it was only about twenty miles south of the Canadian border, a perfect route for rumrunners to bring in Canadian whiskey. Sheriff Bernard McCauley was one of the driving forces in the control of illegal liquor traffic. An old storage shed was rented by U.S. Customs to be used as a pseudo-garage. The smugglers could peek through the cracks of the shed and tell how many police cars were in the area (so they thought). On the other side of the wall in another office, the Feds had a false duty roster on a blackboard just for the benefit of the spies, who went back and told their superiors, really messing up their schedules.

TOPPENISH

Toppenish is thought to come from the Indian word Thappahn-ish for "People of the trail which comes from the foot of the hills." Others think the word came from qapuishlema, "people from the foot of the hills;" and yet another for a Yakama word that meant "sloping and spreading land."

This town is situated on the million-acre Yakima Indian Reservation. The tribe has in recent years adopted the original spelling of its name, Yakama, as signed on the Treaty of 1855.

The Northern Pacific Railroad laid its tracks in 1884 into the valley that connects Pasco to Yakima. Toppenish was the halfway point where a substation was established with a section house, water tank and a telegraph. This was a blessing to local cattlemen who previously had to drive their cattle to local market, and could use the railroad to ship them east. With business booming, the railroad built stockyards and laid sidetracks.

With the railroad in place, Charles Newell saw an opportunity to make money with all the wild horses in the region. Because he was fluent in the Yakama language, Newell hired the Indians to help him round up the animals. By 1885, he had more than 1,000 head of horses transported to New York. During the Boer War, British agents came to Newell and purchased horses. By the early 1900s, Newell was shipping out 6,000 head of horses by rail each year.

When Toppenish was just getting started, there was scuttlebutt that the Yakima Reservation was going to come under the allotment system. This meant pieces of land would be given to individuals rather than held in common. So members of the Yakamas took squatter's rights near Toppenish. When the Dawes Severalty Act was passed in 1887, the squatter's rights became the allotments. For more than twenty years, there would be no land sold in the town itself to protect the landowners from money-hungry developers. Shanties were quickly built along the railroad's right of way until such time as the allottees could legally sell their property.

The town grew up around the depot, with a hotel and blacksmith shop. A canal was built that meandered through the reservation, and the settlers began to grow produce and fruit. In one year, more than 1,400 railroad cars were needed to transport all the vegetables and livestock. A sugar processing plant was built in 1918, and the beets were supplied by local farmers. Unfortunately, the venture did not last long because the leaf hoppers invaded all the crops, and the company closed down. In 1931, a blight-resistant beet was developed, and a few years later another plant was established at Toppenish and operated until 1980.

Hops was another important crop, and the Indians were employed, where they erected small villages in the hop fields until the end of harvest.

Potatoes were also a good cash crop for Toppenish. When the Northern Pacific Railway began using a huge baked potato as its advertising, the town took advantage of it and came up with the slogan, "Route of the Big Baked Potato."[168]

Toppenish is the place of murals. In the 1980s, the town had kind of fallen on hard times after some of the industries relocated and farming declined. When the town was preparing to celebrate Washington's centennial year, a man named Roger McCarthy became the driving force for creating the Toppenish Mural Society. The idea was for one mural to be painted on a building each day, quite a feat, but it was accomplished with a team of artists. The town has a total of thirty-eight murals (so far) which depict Toppenish from 1850 to 1920. In 1991, the Mural Society was the recipient of the Georgie Tourism Award for having the best tourism idea.[169]

TUMWATER

Growth of this community began about 1845, in what was originally British Territory, and became the first American settlement in the Puget Sound region. Located on the Deschutes River, the town's history and economy was tied to the river.

The Indians called the Deschutes River Tum Chuk, which referred to the falls that sounded like the beating of a heart, and meant "throbbing (or noisy) water." An 1864 map shows the name TE'm-wata. First called New Market, the town's name was changed to Tumwater in 1857. The Indians were later removed to the Nisqually Reservation.[170]

Michael Simmons and George Bush, who was a black man, left Missouri with a group of pioneers and came to the Northwest looking for a place to settle. They entered Oregon, but the state had a law that would not allow blacks to own land, so the party went across the Columbia into Washington, stayed at Washougal for a while, then came to Tumwater. Simmons liked this place because the falls would give settlers the water power they needed for flour mills and saw mills. Simmons later sold his land to Clarick Crosby, who was an ancestor of famous singer, Bing Crosby.[171]

About a year after settlement, the first grist mill was built where farmers brought their wheat to have it ground into coarse flour. Sawmills followed, along with a tannery, furniture business, and breweries. An old saw was purchased from the Hudson's Bay Company, which was the beginning of the timber industry at Tumwater.

Simmons called one of the first public meetings in the state when he protested cattle grazing south of the Nisqually River by the Puget Sound Agriculture Company. Because the land was going to be opened for settlement after the British were gone, the settlers knew there would be for a fight for land possession, and Simmons was trying to keep Hudson's Bay from getting a stronghold on any more land.

Leopold Schmidt was the founder of the first brewery in Tumwater. He learned his craft in Germany and worked as a brewmaster in Montana before settling here. Years later, this brewery would be known as the Olympia Brewing Company with its famous slogan, "It's the Water." Schmidt was a fanatic about his brewery being squeaky clean. Local folklore has it that one time while he was inspecting the premises he found a rusty nail and picked it up after watching his executives ignore it. When he asked them why they didn't pick it up, they told him they were too busy. His reply to them was that by picking up rusty nails he built this brewery, and that they should "think about that."[172]

Near Tumwater is Hewitt Lake which the subject of a native legend. It seems that a young warrior was going to marry a chief's daughter. The girl went to the lake to find loon eggs because they were thought to be good luck. But she disappeared under the water, never to be seen again. The warrior searched for his love, but he also went under water, and both were later found below Tumwater Falls. If you listen carefully, you just might hear the cries of the two lovers down by the waterfalls.

TWISP

Twisp is a modification of the Indian word t-wapsp, meaning "yellow jacket." Another derivation could be from twistsp, which was supposed to be an imitation of the sound a yellow jacket makes. Others suggest the name might have been a Chinook word designating the forks of two rivers. When explorer Alexander Ross came through here in the 1850s, he noted there was an Indian village here called Chilkotahp.[173]

H. C. Glover was the first settler, called the site Gloversville, and platted the town in 1897. Later, John Risley bought Glover's land, sold the lots, and brought in a few businesses. The post office opened a year later. When a woman named Amanda Burgar purchased land adjacent to Gloversville, she built a hotel and named the section Twisp. The hotel drew more people to the town, and there was considerable development. By the turn of the century, Twisp had a doctor and dentist, and a trading company. There was also a daily stagecoach running between Twisp and the town of Brewster.[174]

One of the town's main sources of income was mining, which started in the 1890s when gold was discovered. Prospectors purchased most of their supplies at Twisp and hit the saloons on payday. When the miners left, the townspeople turned to raising livestock, dairy farming and agriculture. Because the railroad never came this way, residents had to find other means of commerce and transportation. Then a fish hatchery added to Twisp's economy. The Methow Fish Hatchery released hundreds of thousands of fry salmon into the Twisp and Methow Rivers. The town was also home to the Methow Valley Creamery which manufactured butter. Then Twisp got really modern. In 1908 the town boasted a Model T Ford taxi cab.

About 1910, the town installed a gravity flow water system that originated about two miles above the townsite on the Twisp River. Before it was in place, the residents had to haul water from the river. The year 1924 brought a devastating fire, the origin of which was believed to be an iron left on in the drugstore. It was so hot that as the fire hoses were pulled into the street, they simply burned up. Most of the business district went up in flames. The people rebuilt the town using brick instead of wood.

When the Depression hit, Twisp was greatly affected, especially because a drought came along with the economic bad times. But most of the families were pretty self-sufficient and they survived by trading for what they couldn't grow. During this period, the American Legion Posts of Twisp and Winthrop got together and built an airport which became a smoke-jumping base.

After surviving Depression and fire, what else was left but the flood of 1948. The water washed out the town's bridge, and many of the residents had to leave their homes. Many of the people went to the airport where the Red Cross provided food and bedding. Workers at the local mill brought people across the river using cables. But again, Twisp residents pulled themselves up by their bootstraps and repaired the damage.

WALLA WALLA

Founded at the end of the Indian wars of 1855-1858, Walla Walla was the place where Governor Isaac Stevens and Joel Palmer, with Indian Affairs for Oregon, held a council with many Indian tribes in 1855. There were over 5,000 Indians and only about 100 white men present. The meeting was to try and convince the Indians to move onto reservations. After about a week, Stevens had just about persuaded the Indians to relocate when Chief Looking Glass of the Nez Perce Tribe returned after being gone for some time. He was very angry and said that Stevens had sold their country. Despite opposition, Stevens did get some compromise and three treaties were signed in June.[175]

Several factors contributed to Walla Walla's growth: lifting of a ban on immigration into the territory, and construction of the Mullan Military Road. First called Steptoeville, the name was changed to Walla Walla in 1858, which is derived from a Nez Perce word, walastu, meaning either "running water," or "small, rapid streams."

With the discovery of gold in Idaho, miners flocked to Walla Walla which became a supply station. Residents were astonished when they saw some of the packtrains enter town with camels. It seems that in 1850 the U.S. Army had imported camels as pack animals in the Southwest desert. A few years later the Army sold the camels and some of the clever packers bought them. So between 1865 and 1867 the camels, who could each carry up to 500 pounds of supplies, were used between Walla Walla and Missoula, Montana. They were employed because as one old-timer said, "They would be loaded with sacks of flour until you couldn't see anything of the camels except their heads. . . . They would go up and over the mountains in the roughest and steepest places and never refuse to keep moving along in their slow, deliberate way."[176]

The miners who struck it rich returned to Walla Walla, and hotels, saloons, general stores, and stables were built. By 1862, the main street boasted more than fifty buildings. Many of the settlers were farmers. With very little irrigation in the uplands, they began to grow wheat, and with the wheat came the flour mills. H. Isaacs had received a tract of land as a military warrant in 1864 and built a flour mill. A large percentage of the flour was shipped to the Midwest and Europe. By 1878, more than 66,000 bushels of wheat had been shipped to England. More granaries and mills were constructed to handle the ever-increasing quantities of the grain. A post office was established.

In 1875, a steam railroad was built that connected Walla Walla to Wallula, thanks to Dorsey Baker and a group of men who were interested in his enterprise. They investigated financing the project by issuing bonds, which failed, so Baker decided to take on the project himself. He purchased an engine for $4,000 from Pittsburgh and had it shipped around Cape Horn. Baker began construction in 1872 after he built a sawmill to make the railroad ties. Because he couldn't afford steel rails, he had rawhide plated to the wooden rails. But that didn't work too well because when it rained the rawhide got soft so the train couldn't operate. When the rawhide dried in the spring, the train was ready to roll, and roll it did with more than 5,000 tons of freight carried the first year.

Then problems with the wolves began during an extremely cold winter and the animals were running out of food. They traveled long distances to find whatever food was available and ended up in the Walla Walla Valley, where they survived on cattle carcasses. But when that source ran out, the wolves got so hungry they started to eat the rawhide on Baker's rails. One of the local Indians ran to Dr. Baker, shouting in broken English, "Railroad—him gonum hell. Damn wolves digum out—eatum all up—Wallula to Walla Walla." Baker finally made enough money on the freight to replace the rawhide with steel rails.[177]

In 1875, two dogs named Ponto and Thor were made mascots of the "Rawhide Railroad." Their function was to be on the lookout for any cattle that might be on the tracks. They were stationed on a platform called a cowcatcher, and held their watches until they sighted a cow, then jumped off the train and chased the animal off the tracks. Because the train only traveled about two miles an hour, this posed no hazard to the dutiful dogs. Baker later sold his line to the Oregon Railway and Navigation Company and went into banking.

Walla Walla is famous for its onions. A French soldier named Peter Pieri found an Italian sweet onion seed on the Island of Corsica and brought it here. The gardeners were impressed by the onion's winter hardiness, and began harvesting the seed. Today, the Walla Walla Onion has been developed to ensure sweet jumbo onions. The town celebrates this innovation by holding the Sweet Onion Harvest Fest in July.

Courtesy Bill Coleman, Wapato, Washington
Wapato (1912). Named for Indian word, Wa pa too, which means "big potato."
Farmers grew potatoes in addition to hops.

WAPATO

In 1805, Lewis and Clark were probably the first white men through this part of the country that would eventually be called Wapato. The town started out as a blind siding for the Northern Pacific Railroad. Although settlers had arrived in 1885, it wasn't until about 1904 that the majority of businesses were established.

Wapato was located on the Yakima Indian Reservation, and Alex McCredy was appointed the Indian post trader. In 1902, he opened a general store with Indian goods, along with general supplies. He was not allowed to sell liquor or lemon and vanilla extracts to the Indians, and had to post a $10,000 bond.

First called Simcoe, the town's name was changed to Wapato about 1903 because of the confusion with mail delivery to Fort Simcoe, which was only twenty miles from town. Wapato is derived from a Chinook Indian word Wapatoo meaning "potato, or "big potato," probably referring to the Camas root the Indians dug up for their food and for trading. [178]

Until a post office was established in 1902, mail came by rural delivery from Toppenish. The first lumber company was built in 1904, followed by a cigar and confectionery store. A year later, Congress granted a patent of eighty acres for a townsite. Alex McCredy and the Wapato Development Company bought the land and developed the new community. Wapato became incorporated to solve the problem of the illegal sale of liquor. Incorporation allowed city officials to regulate liquor.

When the farmers moved here, they bought reservation land from the Yakama allotments and used the government irrigation projects for their farms. When the Northwest Development Company planted apple orchards, it needed workers, and by 1915 more than 500 Japanese people were imported as contract labor. Then in 1921, the Alien Land Acts was passed, which would not allow the Japanese to lease any of the land. But they got around that by making private agreements with the Indian landowners, and produced a great wealth of fruit and vegetables.

When World War II started, many of the Japanese residents were evicted and interred at a camp near the town of Toppenish. The Japanese were replaced by Filipinos. Later, Latinos took over the agricultural work. Today, Wapato has a diverse cultural heritage, and celebrates its Annual Cultural Unity Fair during the spring, which features ethnic food.

WASHOUGAL

American settlers led by Michael Simmons and George Bush came here about 1844, and called the site Parker's Landing. Washougal is considered the first American settlement in Washington north of the Columbia River. Although Vancouver is much older, it was settled when it was still British territory. Founded in 1844, Washougal wasn't laid out as a town until 1880.

Bush, who was a Mulatto and with the Michael Simmons party, first went to Oregon. But early settlers in the Willamette Valley were determined that Oregon should never become a slave state, and enacted laws which prohibited colored people from residing there. Bush encountered considerable prejudice and when he found out he would not be able to own land, he moved on to Washington with Michael Simmons. They later decided to visit the Puget Sound area, then returned to Washougal, packed up their families, and moved to Tumwater.

British officials investigating the conditions of their territory came upon Simmons and Bush at Tumwater. Realizing that many other Americans would soon follow, they reported to their government that the Americans were already beginning to settle in the Puget Sound area. The British later relinquished the territory.

Farming was one of Washougal's mainstays; in addition, logging camps and the copper mines in the region of Bear Prairie helped the town's economy. Christopher Columbus Simmons started the first shingle mill and traded shingles for supplies at Fort Vancouver. River boats making trips on the Columbia River to Portland and landings along its route employed many of the men from Washougal.

A pioneer named Dave Wright spoke of the town's early settlement: "My uncle, Joseph E. C. Durgin and Captain Love, a steamboat man of Portland, bought twenty acres of the Dick Ough donation land claim and started the town of Washougal. My uncle, Mr. Durgin, had it mapped and platted in the spring of 1880. He built the first house in Washougal and put up the first store here. . ."[179] The post office was established in 1880 in a general store. Once hauled by boat, the mail was later transported by horse and buggy. The post office was moved whenever a new postmaster was selected. At various times during its early existence the post office was housed in a men's shop and furniture store. When Washougal became a third-class town, postal authorities required the office have its own building. By 1908, the mail was carried to Vancouver to Washougal by train.

During the early 1900s, many of the men worked on the river boats that went between Washougal and Portland, Oregon. The Washougal Woolen Mill was established in 1910. What started with 450 head of sheep driven into the Oregon territory and sold to settlers became the home industry of making wool socks. Over a number of years, more wool goods were manufactured, and when the mill was built it provided many jobs. The fabrics were shipped to manufacturers throughout the United States. During World War I, the mill was entirely at the disposal of the government, making thousands of blankets for U.S. troops. In 1923, the mill experienced a devastating fire that took about half the company's structures, but they were replaced.

Several definitions of of the origins of the name Washougal. At one time it was called Wash-ough-ally by Alexander Ross when he came through in 1811. Folklore has it the name came about when an old Indian met a man and his daughter who were traveling upriver from Astoria. When the Indian saw the little girl whose face was very dirty, he said "wash-ou-gal" (wash you gal). Actually, it could mean "between two rivers," "laughing waters," "running water," or "land of plenty and pleasant." The most popular explanation seems to be "rushing water."[180]

WASHTUCNA

Washtucna was founded in 1878 by George W. Bassett. While touring Oregon and Washington, he liked this area so much that he stayed and settled down. He believed the wealth of bunch grass here would support cattle. Before he could build his home he had to travel to Walla Walla to get the lumber. On one of his trips to pick up his lumber, he met a sheepherder who warned him that the Indians were becoming troublesome, but nothing ever happened.[181]

The pioneers had to go clear to Walla Walla to pick up their mail until a post office was established in 1882, and George Bassett was the first postmaster. Mail was delivered to Washtucna once a week by horse. Because the town had a post office, it needed a name, so Bassett called it Washtucna for an old Indian chief. When Bassett asked an Indians what the word meant, all they would tell him was "Big Chief named Washtucna in the long ago." He was never able to find out the definition. Another theory is that Washtucna was a Palouse Indian word that means "many waters."

In 1886, the Oregon Improvement Company built a railroad from Connell to Moscow, Idaho, and Washtucna had a siding. The train schedule included stops every day at Washtucna. But some time later, they were only four times a month. Like many other small communities, Washtucna's homes were built or relocated near the tracks. The farmers began to raise wheat, but having to go the fifty miles to Walla Walla for supplies became very tiresome. So in 1894, T. C. Martin established a general store.

By 1891, Washtucna was such a large wheat-shipping station that Pacific Elevator Company built a platform for the grain. More than 30,000 bushels of wheat were purchased at a price of fifty-five cents a bushel. In the 1940s, the wheat crop was so large that thousands of bushels had to be dumped because the elevator couldn't handle all of it. Although quite prosperous, by 1902 Washtucna only had about ten houses.

In 1892, Eastern investors and businessmen from Tacoma organized the Palouse Irrigation Ditch Company. Their plan was to irrigate 400,000 acres of land between Hooper and Pasco, carrying water by flume along Washtucna Coulee for storage in Washtucna Lake. The company went under after building only twelve miles of ditch. In 1902, the Reclamation Service dammed up the Palouse River when the Newlands Act was passed, which supported the irrigation of the west.

In the 1900s, George Bassett realized the town needed a church, so he asked the residents what religious organization they would like to have in their community. The people opted for Presbyterian and Reverend Robert Cooper became the church's minister. His first sermon was in the school, as a church had not yet been built. The Board of Home Missions of the UPCNA granted the town a mortgage and in 1903 the church building was completed.

Washtucna experienced a flood in 1950 when a Chinook wind melted the snow, causing a water surge that flooded the main street and filled people's basements. It was weeks before the town was back to normal. Not wanting the same thing to happen again, the community built a ditch so the water could run off. In 1956, another Chinook wind occurred, only this time it flooded worse, but because of the ditch, not as many buildings were damaged.

An early-day real estate company put out a promotional brochure that described the town's early history. It states, "Long ere the first pathfinders of the white race had climbed the eastern slope of the Blue Mountains to their summit, and from there looking westward, had viewed the wondrous Columbia river valley; this section, on account of its mild climate its luxuriant, succulent grasses and its proximity to flowing waters was famous for the red tribes . . . The expense being nominal and profits vast, the stockmen . . . made their fortunes in the 'Fat Washtucna Land' . . ."[182]

WENATCHEE

Wenatchee sits at the foothills of the Cascade Mountains, which was a favorite spot for many of the Northwest tribes who used it as a council ground and camp. Wenatchee has a number of definitions: "robe of the rainbow," "good place," and "boiling waters." The last seems to be the accepted version.[183]

Although not settled until the 1870s, Wenatchee did have earlier visitors. Explorer Alexander Ross came this way by canoe in 1811 and met the Wenatchee Indians, spending some time with them. Three years later, Ross returned where he had earlier established a fur post upstream at a place called Fort Okanogan. Planning to canoe down the Columbia in search of more furs, he stopped here again to visit the Indians. Miners also came to the area during the Frazer River gold rush, along with Chinese placer miners working along the Columbia River.

The first settlers to establish a business near the townsite were two men named Ingraham and McBride who opened a trading post in 1867 to sell supplies to the Indians, mainly whiskey. They sold the trading post five years later because they got caught selling illegal liquor to the Indians, and were obliged to leave in haste. Then in 1888, a man named McPherson built a general store about a mile from the town. The post office was established and the mail arrived by stage twice a week.

When the Great Northern Railroad began to lay its tracks in 1892, Wenatchee was moved from its original site on the banks of the Columbia River to a point closer to the rails. The Wenatchee Development Company exchanged lots in the new site for the old lots and moved the buildings at no charge. The *Wenatchee Advance*'s June 2, 1892, edition states, ". . . butcher shops are now on the road and soon the "whole works" will be located in the town of Wenatchee on the picturesque banks of the majestic Columbia, conducting business on a substantial basis."[184] Well, maybe not so picturesque, because building of the railroad did bring in less than desirable elements into town, such as more than a dozen saloons and many transients, which caused the crime rate to go up.

On October 17, 1892, the silver spike was driven. With completion of the railroad, the transients left town and many of the saloons closed their doors. But Wenatachee was visited by another vermin. Smallpox reared its ugly head and part of the town was put under quarantine, which hurt business. It was believed the smallpox came from the railroad workers. Luckily, there were only twenty-one cases reported.

The shout of "fire!" woke Wenatchee residents on September 2, 1893. The blaze originated in a vacant building that once housed the Minnesota Mercantile Company. The wind was blowing, and in a short time most of the buildings on the west side of Wenatchee Avenue went up in smoke. The citizens concentrated their efforts trying to save the adjacent buildings. The structures that burned down were not insured and were a total loss.

Construction of the Highline Canal in 1903 brought water to the Wenatchee region. Farmers started apple orchards, and by the late 1920s, Wenatchee became one of the important apple-producing regions in the world. More than 20,000 carloads of apples were being shipped to various destinations. Also grown were cherries, apricots and peaches.

Because Wenatchee was located near the Columbia River, it saw its share of mishaps with the railroad and steamboats. In 1901, the *Irish World* caught fire and burned; the origin of the fire was never discovered. In 1902, a railroad brakeman was scalded to death by the steam engine when it had to stop because of a landslide and another train rear-ended it. Then on July 8, 1915, four steamboats owned by Captain Alexander Griggs; the *Chelan*, *North Star*, *Columbia*, and *Okanogan*, were burned to the water's edge at Wenatchee. By the time firemen arrived, it was too late to help the boats and they focused their efforts on saving the buildings on shore. The boatyard foreman had checked the vessels about 1 a.m. and found everything OK. Flames were spotted by someone at 2:20 a.m. It was never proven, but it was believed the fire was caused by arson.[185]

In 1911 Wenatchee residents got their first look at a flying machine. The pilot was flying a Curtis-Wright-Farnum aircraft powered by an engine that pushed from the rear. After one take-off, the wind began to pick up and got so bad the pilot had to find a place to land when the plane became uncontrollable. He couldn't land the plane because gusts of wind kept slewing it all over the place, and it ended up in the branches of a large tree. The pilot wasn't hurt, and Wenatchee residents got the plane out of the tree, and all had a good chuckle over the incident. In 1931, Clyde Panborn, who flew the first nonstop flight across the Pacific, made a belly landing in East Wenatchee. He was forced to do that because one of the landing gears malfunctioned, its wheel got stuck, and Clyde had to literally climb out of the plane and take it off in mid-air.[186]

Wenatchee celebrates the Wenatchee River Salmon Festival in October to celebrate the return of the salmon.

WISHRAM

This tiny town is on the Columbia River about thirty-five miles southeast from The Dalles, Oregon. Wishram means "flea" or "louse." Originally a Chinook Indian village, Lewis and Clark visited in 1806. The Chinooks lived at Nixlu'idix (an ancient Wishram village) near the Celilo Falls. They traded with the Indians from the lower Columbia River and other tribes inland.

In the 1930s, the Indians were still using a primitive method of catching salmon, as stipulated in their treaty rights. They used scaffolding that was fastened to the rocky sides of Celilo Falls, waited for the salmon to leap up, and then speared them.[187] Most of the Wishrams were relocated to the Yakima Reservation. The Indian village was situated just above Celilo Falls, which disappeared when The Dalles Dam was built in 1957. A state park now occupies the old Indian site.

F. G. Bunn was a merchandiser from The Dalles, and when he learned in 1911 that this area might be the division point for a railroad, he moved here. He purchased 160 acres and drew up a plat for a town, which he called Fallbridge. Bunn sold a portion of his land to the Spokane, Portland and Seattle Railroad which built a roundhouse and train yard. Bunn was well regarded by the residents of Wishram. During the depression he helped the people who could not afford housing or food. When the depression was over, he never asked for reimbursement and just wrote off the costs.[188]

Because Wishram was a stopover point for the trains, it became a haven for hoboes and transients looking for work. The owners of the Jungle Café carried on Bunn's practice of good will, and oftimes gave indigents free meals. Wishram experienced few problems or thefts because of its large transient population.

World War II made Wishram an important railroad yard. Trains were switched here twenty-four hours a day, and at times the yard was so full the cars had to be stored elsewhere. At one time, there were so many cars at the station that they stretched clear across the bridge, forcing the crew to walk across the top of the cars so they could go home. Until 1981, the railroad was quite stable because the employees did not move around like they do today But when the highway bridge was built, many residents did relocate to other towns.

YACOLT

Twenty miles northeast of Vancouver is the little town of Yacolt, derived from an Indian word Yolicolb that meant something akin to "haunted valley," "place abounding in evil spirits," or "valley of the demons." The Indians became fearful of this place when some of their children came to pick berries and never returned home, causing the parents to believe that a demon had taken them.[189]

One of the early settlers was a man named Garner and his family who came from Portland, and were followed by others about 1884. According to the Homestead Law, Sections 16 and 36 of every town had to be used for schools. The settlers had put up a little school, but in a different section, so the one that was originally for the school was opened for homesteading. A man named Charley Landon filed on that section, had it surveyed into lots, and it became the town of Yacolt. He also gave some of his land for a park and baseball field, and built a shed for farmers to shelter their horses when they came to town during bad weather.

A road had to be built, because the only one was about two miles from town. The community began to cut a road, which took about a month. There was no mail delivery yet, and the residents had to go to Amboy to pick it up. When the roads were passable someone delivered mail in a wagon. If the roads were bad, horses were used.

The Yacolt Burn of September, 1902 destroyed more than 250,000 acres of forest, and was the worst fire to ever hit Washington. It affected many counties. Nobody knows for sure how the fire started, but some people thought it was from sparks from logging trains or donkey engines, a common occurrence during dry summers. When the paint on the houses started to blister, the residents evacuated the town. Many people and livestock lost their lives because the fire spread so fast they could not escape. The fire was even felt as far south as Eugene, Oregon, where the ashes had been carried by the wind.

After the great fire, Weyerhaeuser came in to start clean-up operations, and the Northern Pacific extended the Vancouver-Battleground Railroad to the Yacolt Prairie a few months later. When Weyerhaeuser got ready to start salvage of the burnt forest, the operation would employ a lot of people. The *Vancouver Independent* reported that "The little town of Yacolt at the end of the Portland, Vancouver and Yakima Railroad are experiencing quite a boom. Two logging companies have recently been started nearby. Petitions for licenses for two saloons have been filed. Other metropolitan features are soon to be added."[190]

Peter Connacher became manager of the Yacolt operation, and got a group of experienced men together to grade railroad spurs and bring in the necessary equipment. It took about a year to get the operation set up, and in the fall of 1903, logging began. Yacolt had its first logging camp for the salvage operations on the edge of town. By the time the set-up work was completed, more than fifteen camps had been constructed, with each camp operating for several years.

The beautiful stands of timber were now blackened, and would take almost ten years of work to clear. The loggers had to work in ashes, and when it rained, the ground and logs were dangerous because they were so slippery. Someone said that after the loggers finished their work for the day, they looked more like coal miners than timber men. Weyerhaeuser worked the Yacolt timber operation until 1924.

YAKIMA

Because of Indian problems during 1855, Yakima was not settled until about 1858, after the Yakama Indians signed a treaty putting them on a reservation. The first permanent residents were Fielding Thorpe and his family who came from Salem, Oregon. More people came to Yakima, but it didn't really grow much until irrigation was brought to the arid valley.[191]

Yakima could mean many things. It's been defined as "big belly," "pregnant one," "runaway," or "bountiful."

By 1879, many families were living here, and four years later the Northern Pacific Railroad built its station a few miles from town. Residents were very upset about it, but officials said that because of a swamp they couldn't lay the rails through town. It may have been more likely that the town asked too high a fee for a railroad right of way at this site, so the railroad built it elsewhere and called it North Yakima. The railroad did offer free lots to anyone from Yakima who wanted to move here, and the settlement finally decided to do just that. In 1884, the entire town was moved using rollers and skids. It took a month to move the hotel on rollers by placing four-inch planks in front of the building, but the hotel still operated while on its laborious journey. The first train arrived on December 24, 1884. In 1918, the named was shortened to just Yakima.

With the coming of the railroad, the town became a wild place, with plenty of gamblers and outlaws. But that was short-lived when a town marshal was appointed. Many of the settlers raised livestock, but the late 1870s brought irrigation and the livestock was replaced with agriculture. When the Reclamation Service unified its irrigation efforts in 1902, Yakima's population tripled, and the people began to grow hops, in addition to fruit and vegetables.

The year 1907 brought an unusually cold winter and residents ran out of coal, leaving them without heat. The Northern Pacific Railroad was hauling a lot of coal to its snowbound bunkers in Montana and the Dakotas. The people of Yakima went to the railroad and asked for just one car of coal because they were freezing, but railroad officials refused their request. Desperate, the people had burned just about everything that was burnable from their homes in order to keep warm.

Someone suggested they simply rob the train. While the train was stopped, they went to the cars and pulled the levers on the bottoms and all the coal fell onto the tracks. Railroad personnel did not see this because the cars were at the tail end of the train. When the train pulled out, the coal was sitting on the tracks waiting for the residents to pick it up. The engineer finally noticed what was happening, alerted the station master, and went looking for the sheriff and mayor, who were conveniently gone.

YELM

Yelm is located on the Yelm prairie that stretches to the foothills of Mount Rainier. There was a trail on the prairie that the Hudson's Bay Company used for traveling between Fort Nisqually and Fort Vancouver. The company later established a ferry that went across the Nisqually River, and built a herding station for the cattle raised on the Yelm Prairie. After the Americans took over from the British, the trail was used as a military road.

James Longmire brought the first immigrant train over the Cascades in 1853. He wrote of their struggle coming down Summit Hill: "We spliced ropes and prepared for the steep descent. . . One end of the rope was fastened to the axles of the wagons, the other thrown around a tree and held by our men, and thus, one by one the wagons were lowered gradually. . . All the wagons were lowered safely, except the one . . . which was crushed to pieces by the breaking of one of the ropes, . . ."[192] They finally arrived at Yelm Prairie, where Longmire purchased a home, but he owned no land because the area had not yet been surveyed.

The settlers lived in relative peace until 1854 when a council meeting for treaty negotiations was scheduled at a place called Medicine Creek. The Indians were told they would be able to hold the land of their choice. But settlers were taking land wherever they pleased. Longmire had Indian friends who warned him there was going to be big trouble, so he moved his family to Olympia in 1855. It wasn't long after that when the Indians began looting the settlers' homes and driving away their livestock. Most of the people left for Olympia, except for a

Courtesy Yelm Prairie Historical Society
Main Street of Yelm (early 1900s). Located on the prairie, this site was originally an outfitting and starting point for Mount Rainier climbers.

few who stayed and built blockhouses for protection. It was more than a year before they could return to their homes.

The little settlement of Yelm began to take shape when more people moved in after trouble with the Indians was over. In 1873 the Northern Pacific Railroad reached Tacoma, and soon extended its line to this area. Businesses were established, a little log cabin that served as a school was purchased from a settler, and mail delivery began via horseback. Unfortunately, the residents of Yelm didn't benefit much from the railroad because the town was not on the train's schedule, and instead it became just a flag station. It wasn't until 1912 that Yelm finally got a train depot. When irrigation came to the area, Yelm became an agricultural community, growing and marketing cherries in addition to filbert nuts.

Yelm had a female mayor in recent times named Mrs. Coates. It was said "She operates on the philosophy that the shortest distance between two points is the truth." Apparently, she called it as she saw it, and sometimes that didn't sit too well with the *Daily Olympian* newspaper that didn't share her viewpoints. Coates made local headlines when she fired a policewoman for wearing what Coates called hotpants with her gun dangling from her waist, and didn't think the town was quite ready for that yet.[193]

The railroad first named this place Yelm Prairie, but it was later shortened to Yelm. The name may be a Salish word shelm or chelm, which described the heat waves that emanated from the ground during the hot summers. The Indians believed that it was a manifestation of their Great Spirit.[194]

Chapter one notes

[1] Federal Writers' Project, Washington: *A Guide To the Evergreen State*, Metropolitan Press, OR, 1941, p. 358 (hereafter cited as WPA WA).

[2] *An Illustrated History of Southeastern Washington*, Western Hist. Pub., 1906, pp. 692-694.

[3] Ibid., pp. 676-681.

[4] Ibid., p. 678.

[5] Ibid., p. 678.

[6] WPA WA, Op. cit., pp. 411-412.

[7] Emma G Miller, *Clatsop County, Oregon, Its History, Legends and Industries*, Binfords & Mort, 1958, p. 40.

[8] Fred Lockley, *History of the Columbia River Valley: From the Dalles to the Sea, Vol. 1*, S.J. Clark Pub., 1928, p. 96.

[9] Fritz Timmon, *Blow for the Landing: A Hundred Years of Steam Navigation on the Waters of the West*, Caxton Printers, 1973, pp. 111-112.

[10] The *Morning Astorian*, Aug. 28, 1923.

[11] Lambert Florin, *Historic Western Churches*, Superior Pub., 1969.

[12] Chehalis Community Development Program, History Report: Adventure in Co-operation, 1954, pp. 2-3, 5-7.

[13] Ibid., p. 6.

[14] James W. Phillips, *Washington State Place Names*, Univ. WA Press, 1971, p. 25

[15] Marge Davenport, *Fabulous Folks of the Old Northwest*, Paddlewheel Press, OR, 1986, pp. 173-174.

[16] Edmond S. Meany, *Origin of Washington Geographic Names*, Univ. WA Press, 1923, p. 44.

[17] Richard F. Steele, *An Illustrated History of Stevens, Ferry, Okanogan and Chelen Counties*: State of Washington, Western Heritage Pub., 1904, p. 721.

[18] Ibid., p. 724.

[19] Ella E. Clark, *Indian Legends of the Pacific Northwest*, Univ. CA Press, 1953, pp. 70-71.

[20] Elizabeth F. Riley, Still strong Beats the Heart, 1985.

[21] Walt E. Goodman, Chewelah and Vicinity Before 1971.

[22] Rev. Myron Eells, *The Twana, Chemakum, and Klallam Indians of Washington Territory*, Ye Galleon Press, 1996, p. 13.

[23] Mrs. Stephen Hall Bishop, *Early History of Chimacum Valley*. n.d.

[24] James Hermanson, "Chimacum Trading Co. was community center," *Port Townsend Jefferson County LEADER*, Jan 6, 1993, p. A7.

[25] Ruth Kirk and Carmela Alexander, *Exploring Washington's Past*, Univ. WA Press, 1990, p. 260.

[26] Rev. Myron Eells, Op. cit., p. 13.

[27] Jervis Russel, ed., *Jimmy Come Lately: History of Clallam County*, Publishers Printing, WA, 1981, pp.526-527.

[28] Gordon R. Newell, *SOS North Pacific*, Binfords & Morts, 1955, p. 101.

[29] James W. Phillips, Op. cit., p. 27.

[30] Chehalis Comm. Dev. Program, Op. cit., pp. 3-4.

[31] Cle Elum Community Development Study, History Report: Operation Cooperation, 1955.

[32] James W. Phillips, Op. cit., p. 28.

[33] Cle Elum Com. Dev. Study, Op. cit., p. 102.

[34] Ibid., p. 72.

[35] Edmond S. Meany, Op. cit., p. 55.

[36] Bruce Wilson, *Late Frontier: A History of Okanogan County, Washington*, Okanogan County Hist. Soc., 1990, p. 160.

[37] Robert Hitchman, *Place Names of Washington,* WA State Hist. Soc., 1985, p. 84.

[38] Phyllis Griffith, "The Entiat Rapids," *Entiat Valley Explorer,* Sept. 2, 1998, p. 4.

[39] Edson Dow, *Passes to the North,* Wenatchee Bindery & Printing, 1963, pp. 68-69.

[40] Lindley Hull, *A History of Central Washington,* Shaw & Borden, 1929, p. 449

[41] Phyllis Griffith, "Entiat Bachelor's Club," *Entiat Valley Explorer,* June 17, 1999.

[42] "Enumclaw," The *Buckley News Banner,* May 20, 1998.

[43] Lois R. Poppleton, *There is Only One Enumclaw,* 1985.

[44] Bill Speidel, *The Wet Side of the Mountains (or Prowling Western Washington),* Nettle Creek Pub., Seattle, 1981, p. 312.

[45] Pauline K. Capoeman, ed., *Land of the Quinault,* Continental Ptg., Inc., Seattle, 1990, p. 111.

[46] Brief Historical Sketch of Grays Harbor, Washington, incorporated from manuscript by Ed Van Sycle, Rayonier, Inc., 1942, pp. 13, 24-25.

[47] Kramer A. Adams, *Logging Railroads of the West,* Bonanza Books, NY, 1961, p. 129.

[48] *The Sou'wester,* Vol. 22, No. 4, Autumn, 1967, p. 52.

[49] Raymond J. Feagans, *The Railroad That Ran By the Tide,* Howell-North Books, 1972, p. 10.

[50] Edwin D. Culp, *Stations West,* Caxton Printers, 1972, p. 98.

[51] Raymond J. Feagans, Op. cit., p. 118.

[52] Ibid., p. 76.

[53] Harriet J. Fish, "Name Game - What to Call the City?" *The Issaquah Press,* online edition, www.isspress.com/archive/name/name/

[54] Clarence B. Bagely, *History of King County, Washington,* S.J. Clark Pub., 1929, online edition, www. issaquahhistory/or/bagley/issaquah/early history.htm

[55] Joseph Gaston, *Centennial History of Oregon,* S.J. Clark, Pub., 1912, p. 509.

[56] Phillip Swart, *Hole in the Ground: Tales of Kahlotus,* Sand Hill Books, Seattle, 1997.

[57] John Harder, M.D., letter to author, March 6, 1999.

[58] Carol Neufeld, Kapowsin, Washington, n.p.

[59] Guy Ramsey, *Postmarked Washington*: Pierce County, WA State Hist. Soc., 1981.

[60] WPA WA, Op. cit., p. 370.

[61] Kennewick Library vertical files.

[62] Aviva L. Brands, Assoc. Press, "Feds: Send Kennewick Man back to tribes," *The Mail Tribune,* Sept. 26, 1000, p. 1.

63 Jennifer Cochran, "Kittitas County History," website: www.co.kittitas.wa.us/history.htm

64 James W. Phillips, Op. cit., p. 73.

65 Kittitas County Library vertical files.

66 Joseph Gaston, Op. cit., p. 34.

67 Pete May, ed., Klickitat County Hist. Soc., *History of Klickitat County*, 1982, p. 83.

68 James. W. Phillips, Op. cit., p. 73.

69 Jonathan Edwards, *History of Spokane County*, W.H. Lever, Pub., 1900, pp. 277-278.

70 "Years Ago," The *Standard-Register*, 1953, pp. 11-12.

71 Lalia Boone, *Idaho Place Names*, Univ. Idaho Press, 1988, p. 219.

72 Jonathan Edwards, Op. cit., p. 277.

73 Lucile S. McDonald, *Making History: The People Who Shaped the San Juan Islands*, Harbor Press, WA, 1990, pp. 172-173.

74 Alfred Powers, *Little Known Tales from Oregon History, Vol. 1*, Geoff Hill, ed., Sun Pub., 1988, p. 77.

75 Pauline K. Capoeman, Op. cit., p. 143.

76 Opal McConnell, letter to Author, August, 2000.

77 Historical Building Survey, Mukilteo, Washington, prepared for City of Mukilteo, Historical Research Associates, Inc., 1994, pp. 2-7.

78 Ruth Kirk and Carmela Alexander, Op. cit., p. 260.

79 Gordon R. Newell, Op. cit., p. 119.

80 Mike Hiler, Naches in a Nutshell, Naches Basin Community History, 1988.

81 Cindy Warren, "Naches is the Town that (Painter's) Butter Built," *Yakima Valley Sun*, May 26, 1977, p. 24.

82 "Naches...A Valley Town With a Long Past," *Yakima Valley Sun*, Oct. 28, 1976, p. 28.

83 Greta Gossett, *A History of the Nile Valley in Washington State*, Ye Galleon Press, 1979, p. 477.

84 James W. Phillips, Op. cit., p. 94.

85 James Swan, *The Northwest Coast*, Intro by W.A. Katy, Ye Galleon Press, 1966, p. 30.

86 James A. Gibbs, Jr., *Shipwrecks of the Pacific Coast*, Binfords & Mort, 1957, pp. 66-67.

87 Stanton H. Patty, "Oyster port showcases history on the half shell," *The Seattle Times/Seattle Post-Intelligencer*, Jan 6, 1991, pp. J2-J3.

88 Bill Spiedel, Op. cit., p. 81.

89 First Inhabitants of Naselle, *The Sou'wester*, Vol. X, No. 1, Spring, 1975, p. 3.

90 Naselle Centennial Committee, Nasel 1878 - Naselle 1978, The Centennial Book, Pacific Printing, pp. 2-3, 6, 9.

91 Guy Ramsey, Op. cit., p. 51.

92 James W. Phillips, Op. cit., p. 95.

93 Ruby E. Hult, *The Untamed Olympics*, Binfords & Mort, 1954. pp. 45-46.

94 James Gibbs, Jr., Op. cit., pp. 85-86.

95 Makah website: www.northolympic.com/makah/

96 James W. Phillips, Op. cit., p. 96.

97 Ruth Kirk & Carmela Alexander, Op. cit., p. 239.

98 WPA WA, Op. cit., p. 456.

[99] Edmond S. Meany, Op. cit., p. 196.

[100] Bruce A. Wilson, *Late Frontier: A History of Okanogan County, Washington*, Okanogan County Hist. Soc., 1990, p. 238.

[101] Ibid., p. 308.

[102] Edmond S. Meany, Op. cit., p. 200.

[103] Alice Rushton, *The History of the Town of Orting*, Warren's Printing & Graphics, 1981, p. 43.

[104] Ibid., pp. 75, 77.

[105] Alice Rushton, conversation with author, July, 2000.

[106] Origin and Meaning of the Geographic Name Palouse, *WA Hist. Qtly.*, Vol. 24, No. 3, July, 1933, pp. 190-191.

[107] Keith C. Peterson, *Company Town: Potlatch, Idaho, and the Potlatch Lumber Company*, WA State Univ. Press, 1987, p. 51.

[108] Elgin V. Kuykendall, *History of Garfield County*, Ye Galleon Press, 1984, p. 60.

[109] W.D. Lyman, *Lyman's History of Old Walla Walla County*, S.J. Clark Pub, 1918.

[110] Puyallup Library newspaper files, n.d.

[111] Bill Spiedel, Op. cit., p. 304.

[112] Murray's People: A Collection of Essays, 1960, Tacoma Pub. Lib., online edition: www.tpl.lib.wa.us/v2nwroom/morgan/cantwell

[113] Elizabeth Bayley Willis Papers, Box 1, Manuscripts and University Archives, UW Libraries, website: www.lib.washington.edu/exhibits/

[114] Margaret Felt, *Rivers to Reckon With*, Gockerell & Fletcher, Pub., 1985,

[115] Ruth Kirk and Carmela Alexander, Op. cit., p. 481.

[116] George Wuerthner, *Olympic, A Visitor's Companion*, Stackpole Books, PA, 1999, p. 92.

[117] Robert Hitchman, Op. cit., p. 244.

[118] Jefferson County Hist. Soc., *With Pride in Heritage,* Professional Pub., 1966, pp. 164-166.

[119] Ruth Kirk and Carmela Alexander, Op. cit., p. 509.

[120] WPA WA, Op. cit., p. 545.

[121] Ivy Mitchel Hills, "Salkum," typescript, 1950's.

[122] Salkum Library newspaper files, n.d.

[123] Bill Spiedel, Op. cit., p. 379.

[124] Clarence B. Bagley, *In the Beginning, Hist. Soc. of Seattle and King County*, New Materials Copyright, 1980.

[125] James A. Gibbs, Jr., Op. cit., p. 93.

[126] Marge Davenport, Op. cit., p. 67.

[127] Bill Spiedel, Op. cit., p. 11-12.

[128] WPA WA, Op. cit., p. 548.

[129] Marge Davenport, *Best of the Old Northwest*, Paddlewheel Press, 1980, pp. 42-43.

[130] James W. Phillips, Op. cit., p. 131,

[131] John W. Butler, "Butler's Landing on the Columbia," *Skamania County Heritage*, Vol. 9, No. 2, Oct. 1980, pp. 3, 7; see also History of Skamania County, Local History Committee, 1972.

[132] Irene Martin, Skamokawa: *Sad Years, Glad Years*, 1985.

[133] Ibid., p. 6.

[134] Ibid., p. 7.

[135] "Historically Speaking," Town of Skykomish.

[136] Joann Roe, *Stevens Pass: The Story of Railroading and Recreation in the North Cascades*, The Mountaineers, Seattle. 1995, p. 160.

[137] Ibid, p. 163.

[138] Robert Hitchman, Op. cit., p. 277.

[139] *River Reflections: Snohomish City - 1859 to 1910*, Snohomish Hist. Soc., 1975, p. 6.

[140] Bill Spiedel, Op. cit., pp. 182-183.

[141] James W. Phillips, Op. cit., p. 133.

[142] WPA WA, Op. cit., p. 527.

[143] Dorothy E. Thompson Winston, *Early Spanaway*, Graphic Press, 1976, pp. 11, 15, 17.

[144] WPA WA, Op. cit. pp. 245-248.

[145] Ibid, p. 248.

[146] Gay Robertson, *Stehekin Remembered*, Pacific Northwest National Parks & Forests Assoc., 1987, p. 6.

[147] Ibid., pp. 6, 12.

[148] Richard F. Steele, Op. cit., p. 736.

[149] Gary F. Reese, *Origins of Pierce County Place Names*, R&M Press, 1989, p. 106.

[150] Paul W. Harvey, "Steilacoom Boomed Decade Before Tacoma Became Town, The *Tacoma News Tribune*, June 27, 1969.

[151] Marjorie P. Mottishaw, "Quiet, Peaceful, Old Steilacoom," *Pacific Northwest Qtly.*, Vol. 46, #1, Jan. 1955, p. 1.

[152] Marge Davenport, *Fabulous Folks of the Old Northwest*, Op. cit., p. 111-112.

[153] Roy F. Jones, *Boundary Town*, Fleet Ptg., 1958, pp. 92, 138, 297, 145.

[154] WPA WA, Op. cit., pp. 264-266.

[155] Murry & Rosa Morgan, *South on the Sound: An Illustrated History of Tacoma and Pierce County*, Windsor Pub., CA, 1984, p. 40.

[156] Richard Erdoes, *Saloons of the Old West*, Alfred A. Knopf, 1979, p. 78.

[157] WPA WA, Op. cit., p. 266.

[158] Winifred Elyea, "The History of Tatoosh Island," *WA Hist. Qtly.*, Vol. 20, No. 3, July, 1929, pp. 223-224.

[159] Gordon R. Newell, Op. cit., pp. 152-153.

[160] Ella E. Clark, Op. cit., p. 120.

[161] Art Dwelley, Tenino: *The First Hundred Years*, Tenino Independent, 1971, pp. 3-4.

[162] "History of Tenino," Tenino Chamber of Commerce.

[163] WPA WA, Op. cit., p. 489.

[164] James Swan, Op. cit., p. 33.

[165] Ruth McCausland, "Tokeland: Alive and Well," *The Sou'wester*, Vol. 12, No. 2, Summer, 1987.

[166] Elva Helm, All Roads Lead to Tonasket, *Statesman-Examiner*, ca 1985, p. 4.

[167] Bruce Wilson, Op. cit., p. 230.

[168] WPA WA, Op. cit., p. 467.

[169] Toppenish Murals, website: ww.wolfenet.com/!murals/

[170] Gayle Palmer, ed., *City of Tumwater, The River Remembers: A History of Tumwater, 1845-1995*, Donning Co., 1995.

[171] Archie Binns, *Sea in the Forest*, Doubleday & Co., 1953, pp. 119-120.

[172] Bill Spiedel, Op. cit., p. 338.

[173] Sally Portman, *The Smiling Country*, Sun Mt. Resorts, 1993, pp. 188-189.

[174] Bruce Wilson, Op. cit., p. 231.

[175] WPA WA, Op. cit., pp. 290-291.

[176] Ruth Kirk & Carmela Alexander, Op. cit., p. 182.

[177] George Estes, *The Rawhide Railroad*, George Estes' Pub., 1924, pp. 51, 53-54.

[178] *Wapato History and Heritage*, Wapato Hist. Comm., 1978, pp. 16, 17, 23.

[179] Fred Lockley, Op. cit., p. 332.

[180] Kathleen Stevenson, *History of Washougal*, WPA WA project, 1938.

[181] Adams County Hist. Soc., *A Pictorial History of Adams County, Washington*, Taylor Pub., TX, 1986, pp. 51-52.

[182] William S. Lewis, *The Story of Early Days in the Big Bend Country*, W.D. Allan, Pub, 1926; facsimile, Shorey Book Store, Seattle, 1965, p. 757.

[183] Richard F. Steele, Op. cit., pp. 711-716.

[184] Ibid., p. 714.

[185] Fritz Timmon, Op. cit., p. 76.

[186] Marge Davenport, *Fabulous Folks of the Old Northwest*, Op. cit., p. 193.

[187] WPA WA, Op. cit., p. 397.

[188] Klickitat County Hist. Soc., Op. cit., p. 89.

[189] Pat Jollota, "Naming Clark County," *Ft. Vancouver, Hist. Soc.*, p. 60.

[190] Alden H. Jones, "Yacolt," *Ft. Vancouver Hist. Soc.*, Vol. 16, 1975, pp. 59-60.

[191] WPA WA, Op. cit., p. 301.

[192] Edgar Prescott, *Early Yelm*, The Folly Press, 1979, pp. 6-8.

[193] Bill Spiedel, Op. cit., p. 327.

[194] Gayle Palmer & Shanna Stevenson, eds., *Thurston County Place Names: A Heritage Guide*, Thurston County Historic Comm., 1992, p. 97.

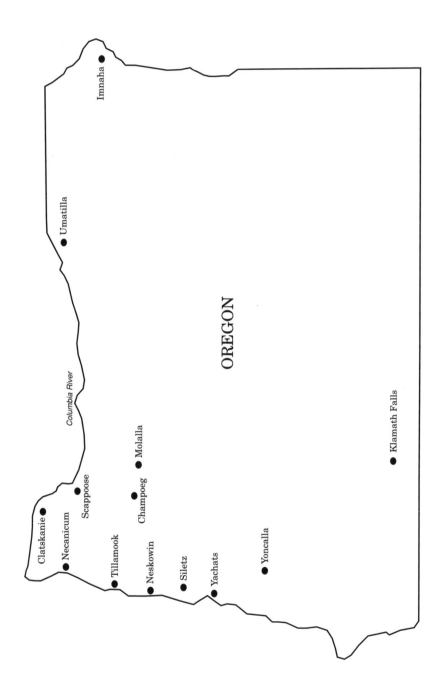

Chapter Two

OREGON

CHAMPOEG

Called the Birthplace of Oregon government, Champoeg
began to take shape when the Hudson's Bay Company established its post along the banks of the Willamette River in 1821.
The company selected this place because it was right in the
middle of larger settlements, and had easy river transportation.
This region was part of the Kalapooian Indian territory, a place
where the Indians came to trade.

Chief Factor John McLoughlin expanded the company's
operations by growing grain in the region. Champoeg later
became one of the major settlements after trappers who had
retired from the Hudson's Bay Company moved here with their
Indian wives. It wasn't long before more people arrived. One of
them was Willard Rees who built his home in the 1840s and
said that "Champoeg was the principal Indian village between
Chemeketa (Salem) and Willamette Falls and the home of
Champoeg chieftains from time immemorial."

During the Hudson's Bay era, this site was called
"Campment de Sauble." The name Champoeg was thought to be
derived from Cham-poo-ick, which was the name for some type
of edible plant. Another source defines the word as "place of the
camp," designating the prairie that extended to the river bank.[1]

In 1843, Champoeg was selected as a meeting place to form the first provisional government in the territory. Apparently, a mountain man named Joe Meek broke a deadlock by asking, "Who's for a divide? All for the report of the committee and an organization follow me." He drew a line in the dirt, and fifty French Canadians and Hudson's Bay Company men went on one side, and fifty-two Americans and French Canadians stepped on the other side of the line. Shortly thereafter, a provisional government was set up and its officers were elected.[2]

Fires and major floods took their toll. In 1892, a terrible flood destroyed the town. The site was turned into a state park about 1901. Joseph Buchtel devoted much of his time trying to acquire land to honor the provisional government. He said that "No event in the history of the Northwest was so important as the convention at Champoeg in 1843, which saved all this country to the United States. . ."[3] Unfortunately it didn't save the town itself.

When Anna Pittman married Methodist Jason Lee at his mission, she was given a rose bush near Champoeg. It was the first rose to be planted in the Northwest. Today, descendants of that rose are still growing in Portland at the Pioneer Rose Garden.

CLATSKANIE

There is little authentic data about the Klatskani Tribe, but its members may have been here as recently as 2,000 years ago—relatively new compared to other tribes. The name was spelled in a variety of ways: Klats-kani, Tlatskani, Klaatshan, and Klatskanine. According to one theory, the name referred to a place in the hills where two rivers originated. Others believed it meant "round head," "swift running water," or an unknown Chinookan proper name.[4]

Tales of white men coming across a band of Tlatskani Indians who turned out to be quite formidable and warlike contradict articles written in the newspaper, the *Clatskanie Chief*. The first mention of the Indians may have been a report given by Alexander Kennedy of the Hudson's Bay Company in 1825. He noted that the Clatskaneyes lived on the upper part of the Chilwitz River. Tlhuckwa was their chief and there were about

175 people in the tribe. The majority of Clatskanies died in the 1830s due to a malaria (or smallpox) epidemic.

Clatskanie Chief Chewaman and what was left of his tribe moved here, with the first white people arriving in 1852 because of the Land Donation Act. The Indians were friendly to the new settlers, trading and visiting with them. A woman named Ruth Thomas wrote in 1931 that "In 1867, this chief [Chewaman] died, and was missed a great deal by the people to whom he had been so kind."[5]

The town of Bryantville was founded in 1852, and later became part of Clatskanie when Columbia County was formed. W. K. Tichenor built the first general store. Enoch Conyers was one of the first settlers and it is believed his home was the first built in town. The place became a stopover for many travelers. It wasn't until 1871 that Clatskanie got a post office, with Conyers as postmaster. He also was owner of the steamboat *Novelty*, which was the main mode of transportation, hauling mail, supplies and passengers. The *Clatskanie Chief* was founded in 1891 by E. C. Blackford (the paper is still in business today). A mill that was purchased by Myron Woodard many years earlier (1810) was upgraded and brought power to Clatskanie and other surrounding villages.

Travel became easier in 1898 when the Astoria-Portland Railroad was built, and also opened the area for more settlement. On May 16, the train made its first run and stopped at Clatskanie to add fuel (wood). With an influx of new residents, lumber became a mainstay, as did farming and the sawmills.

In 1851, the Clatskanies signed a peace treaty with the white man's government, that included a promise of goods and money, which never were received. Today their descendants are still trying to get recognition from the government.

Courtesy Janie Tippett, Joseph, Oregon
Imnaha (2000). Nestled between the mountains, Imnaha has remained a very small community. It boasts a store, café, and gas station.

IMNAHA

The early 1800s brought Imnaha its first settler, Jack Johnson, followed by A. B. Findley and his family. Johnson staked out his claim and began his life here as a farmer, raising alfalfa and sugar cane. He constructed a mill that crushed the sugar cane, which was later made into sorghum and molasses. Findley became an orchardist and raised the first fruit grown in the Imnaha Valley. He also built a dryer for fruits and vegetables, and later became postmaster.

The Nez Perce Indians spent their winters at Imnaha, near the eastern boundary of present day Oregon. When white surveyors came across the Indians in 1865, they learned the chief's name was Imna. The surveyors adopted the name and changed it to Imnaha, which was translated to "land where the Imna dwell (or rule over)."[6]

It wasn't until 1902 that the first general store was built a few miles from town, established by Jasper Simmons. About two years later, one was built in town. Cattle ranching was lucrative for a while, but then sheep were introduced and replaced the cattle in the early 1900s. Findley later sold his land, which was converted from orchards to hay fields to feed the sheep. By the Depression, the sheep ranchers lost their money. Shortly thereafter, beef prices went up and cattle were once again the chief livestock.

There were no decent roads built to Imnaha until about 1935. Before that time, getting in and out of town was hazardous at best, because the trip entailed climbing a steep canyon road for about ten miles. A section of the road was called "the Devil's Elbow," because oftimes the cars had to have their wheels blocked to keep them from plunging down the canyon. During the winters, one can only imagine what the road was like. Imnaha didn't get electricity until the 1960s because it was so isolated.[7]

The Imnaha Grange was established in 1926, and was known for the many services it provided to the community. It was also instrumental in getting the Idaho Power Company and Pacific Power and Light to bring electricity to town.

KLAMATH FALLS

There was no settlement here until 1867 due to the hostility of the Klamath Indians. John Fremont came through Klamath in 1846 and was attacked, losing three men. An immigrant train was attacked in 1850 and most of the people were killed. The area became known as the "dark and bloody ground of the Pacific."

The Klamath Indians were a Lutuamian tribe and called themselves Eukshikni or Auksni, which was thought to mean "people of the lake." They, along with the Modocs, ceded their land in 1864.[8]

The first settler was George Nurse, who originally had his trading post at Fort Klamath. He moved it to the Link River anticipating abundant trade with travelers going down the river. He platted the site, established a post office, and named the place Linkville. Because the Indians had been removed to the Klamath Reservation, by 1867 many settlers had moved here thinking it was safe. That feeling was short-lived when the

Courtesy Klamath County Museum
Early photo of Klamath Falls (undated).

Modoc Indians refused to stay on the reservation. A band of Indians, led by Chief Keintpoos (Captain Jack) attacked some cavalry troopers, and started the bloody Modoc War in 1872. Keintpoos and the other Modoc leaders were finally captured and executed.

After the war, the town's economy was stimulated by the construction of mills and building of a branch line of the Southern Pacific Railroad that came from Weed, California. The community became a shipping point for lumber. The Natron Cutoff between Klamath Falls and Chemult was finished in the 1920s. Weyerhaeuser Timber Company planned to build a sawmill at Klamath Falls, but had a problem. They needed to get enough ties for the railroad to lay its tracks here before the mill could be constructed. So Weyerhaeuser built a portable sawmill on a railroad flatcar in 1927 and cut the ties for a 100-mile stretch of railroad. When the railroad was completed, the company built its sawmill where it could run the larger operation.[9]

In 1893, the town's name was changed to Klamath Falls

because the people wanted a name that better described the water power from the falls. When the first electric power dam was constructed, the falls disappeared. Today, the town's main economy is in agriculture, where the farmers produce potatoes, sugar beets, and algae. Cattle ranching comprises about one-third of farm income.

MOLALLA

The Molalla Indians lived off the land, hunting and fishing. They did not grow agricultural products, but foraged for their food. They used the Indian trails to visit the Klamath Indians where they traded. Molalla has been defined as "deer" and "berries" ('mo' for deer and 'allie' for berries).[10] It was during the 1840s that the white settlers came into Molalla territory.

When homesteaders appeared, they either cut off some of the Indian trails or used them as wagon roads. The people came to this part of the country because of its prairie land and the lush forests at the foothills. As a rule, the settlers got along well with the Molallas and traded with them. About 1848, there was some trouble with a few renegade Molallas, but for the most part, they were a peaceful tribe.

The first settlers to arrive were William and James Russell, who told other people of the beautiful area. Before the Donation Law went into effect in 1850, claims were often irregular, causing a lot of heartburn for later surveyors. The community was first known as Four Corners, because this was where the first four settlers' claims met. William Barlow, famous for the Barlow Road, preempted one of the corners in 1845. He later sold it to a man named Sweigle. The Molalla post office was established in 1850 near the community of Libby, but was moved into town five years later. During this same time frame, the school and Rock Creek Methodist Church were built. A few years later, the first general store was opened by the Engle family, which was most welcome, because the settlers had to travel to Oregon City to get their supplies. A stagecoach stop was established at the Vonder Ahe home midway between Molalla and Oregon City. By 1856, Molalla was a thriving community. The early 1900s brought in the timber companies, followed by sawmills, which made Molalla an important trading center. A number of years later the railroads came through.[11]

Harvey Gorden came to Mollala in 1846 and worked as a surveyor. He later went to California to try his luck in the gold fields, and returned with his pockets full of cash. When the Constitutional Convention met in 1857, it appointed a committee to come up with a seal for the state. Gorden submitted his design to the committee, and it was adopted as the Oregon Seal.

NECANICUM

Necanicum was settled about 1886, and is located some ten miles southeast of Seaside. Herman Ahlers came from Germany and may have been its first permanent resident, for whom the community was originally named. Ahlers established the first post office in his home on January 10, 1896. Three years later he changed the name to Push because he thought it would expand fast and become quite the industrious town. In 1906, the name was once again changed to Necanicum for the nearby river. Ahlers noted the word meant "gap" for the gap in the mountains. But the name may have been derived from Ne-hay-ne-hum, describing an Indian lodge.[12] When Lewis and Clark came through, they called the Necanicum River the Clatsop.

In addition to his job as postmaster, Herman Ahlers also raised bees, and became known as the "Bee King of Clatsop County." He was "perhaps the best known apiarist and honey producer in Clatsop County." Ahlers sold the honey that was "a most pure white fireweed honey on local markets as fast as it could be produced."[13] Fireweed was a plant that sprang up and thrived after a looper infestation destroyed most of the hemlock and spruce trees in 1890. Ahlers died on February 13, 1944, at Astoria.

There doesn't seem to be much early history written about the early settlement of Necanicum. Herman Ahlers was postmaster through all three name changes, and helped get a bridge built and the road modernized (now Highway 26) from Necanicum to Seaside. Until this improvement occurred in the early 1900s, John Gerritse, who had a mail contract between the two towns, traveled by horseback on the Necanicum River

Courtesy Seaside Museum & Historical Society

Mary Gerritse (left of woman with flowers) delivered mail between Necanicum, Oregon, (then called Push) and Seaside in the early 1900s. She was born in 1872 and died in 1957.

trail and had to ford the river several times on his route. In 1905, the *Seaside Signal* wrote, ". . . converting the old pack trail to a road that wagons could pass over, thus lightening the hardships of the settlers living in the interior who have been obliged to pack their provisions over the tortuous mountain trail. . ."[14] That same year the newspaper also wrote, "John Gerritse informs the editor that he will run a hack on the mail route to Push this season (And now will some sage please state how such a name as that ever became attached to one of Uncle Sam's post office?)"[15] The paper noted that Push claimed to be a "settlement," although there was only one family living there (probably the Ahlers).

In 1898, John used his team of horses to drag a cannon that was found at Cannon Beach. It was washed ashore in 1846 when the U.S. Survey Schooner, *Shark*, sank at the mouth of the Columbia River.

John's wife, Mary, also carried the mail by horseback twice a week between Seaside and Push. Occasionally, she would stop at the Necanicum River to go fishing, with the mail sack strapped onto her back. When the Necanicum post office closed its doors in 1916, Necanicum became part of the Star Route (rural delivery).

There was a small local railroad that eventually became part of the Astoria and Columbia River Railroad. The company was thinking about extending a line from Portland to Tillamook by way of Seaside. In 1906, the *Signal* wrote, "President Hammond, Gen. Manager Talbott, Supt. McGuire and Secretary McLeod of A and C Railroad company went to Hug Point and to the surveyors' camp on the Necanicum."[16] Just past the Necanicum post office was a railroad engineer camp ready to lay the tracks, but the plan proved to be not viable, and the railroad was never established.

NESKOWIN

Located in southern Tillamook County, this was home to the Nestucca band of Tillamook Indians. The Indians lived by hunting and fishing, and were thought to be cruel and thoughtless people. They were known to beat their wives, and at times traded them for other women. In 1855, the Nestucca country was set aside as an Indian reservation until 1876 when it was opened for white settlement.

First known as Slab Creek, the community was settled in the 1880s. When the first homes were built, some of the wood came from old Indian canoes that had been used as burial containers which were hung between trees. The settlers took the canoes down and dumped the bones out on the ground.

Henry Page and his family homesteaded the site and built a small house on the beach. Because it was so close to the water, the home was constantly threatened by high tides, so Page built another structure in 1895 that later became the Neskowin Hotel. A rocky promontory was blasted out to make room for the building. Wealthy people visited Slab Creek and used the site as their exclusive campground, and the place became a tent town. The creek got its name because of the slabs of lumber that came off of a wrecked ship, that may have belonged to the Hudson's Bay Company.[17]

Because there were no roads until 1886, residents used the beach for access. It wasn't until the 1920s that a highway was built that went from Neskowin over the Cascade Head to the town of Otis.

Some of the settlers fished in the river or bay for their living, and sold their product in the Willamette Valley. A few of the families went there to pick hops during the summer, and others sold mutton at the camp grounds. There was no store at Neskowin and the people had to travel to Grand Ronde for their supplies.

The post office was opened on December 4, 1886, and Mrs. Page became postmaster the next year. She saw an Indian pointing to the creek one day, saying, "Neskowin, Neskowin." When she asked him what it meant, he said, "plenty fish, plenty fish."[18] In 1925, Slab Creek was changed to Neskowin, the name Mrs. Page requested on the postal application.

A salmon cannery was built in 1887 on the east side of Nestucca Bay by Linewebber and Brown, and as a result other supporting businesses were built in the surrounding towns. Another small business established in the area around 1898 was a cheese factory, which was located between Neskowin and Oretown. In 1912, the factory was consolidated with a cheese company in Oretown. A few years later a cranberry marsh was planted, but it failed. Salt water from the high tides may have led to its demise.

At one time the Neskowin Hotel suffered damage when what residents called a tidal wave hit. The road was washed out and the steps to the hotel were destroyed; the kitchen was also washed away. One of the homes situated on the beach was taken out to sea by the waves. In 1925, a road was blasted out on the promontory behind the building, and the hotel was improved.

In 1886, a full-rigged British ship named the *Carmarthen Castle* got stranded near Neskowin in a gale storm. She was on her way from San Pedro, California, to Portland. Because he was running on dead reckoning, the captain thought the ship was thirty miles offshore when it ran aground. It turned out the ship's compass was defective. Luckily, all crew members escaped and no lives were lost. After they got ashore, the men didn't know where to go for help until they were found by the Indians, who notified the settlers. Some of them brought horses for the crew to ride, and after the men were taken to one of the resident's homes, the captain allegedly said, "If I ever lose another ship, I'll walk to the nearest shelter if it's a thousand miles away." Apparently, he'd never been on a horse.[19]

NETARTS

Archaeological studies indicate the Tillamook Indians inhabited the Netarts region as early as the 1400s. This community once extended from Cape Lookout to Cape Meares. The Tillamook Indians called this place Ne Ta At, which is defined as "near the water." The name was later spelled Netarts.[20]

This site was parceled out by a government surveyor named Snowden in 1855. The Indians who were still here were removed to the Siletz and Grand Ronde Reservations about 1859. Three years later, the first Donation Land claim was filed on the Netarts Spit, which occurred when the Federal Homestead Act was passed.

The settlers began to claim land and the first home was built by Tom Goodale in 1867 on Netarts Bay. Many of the residents went into the oyster business. Schooners came from San Francisco to load the product and the residents were paid fifty cents a bushel. The post office was established in 1871, with Edward Bunnell as postmaster.

In 1875, the Glassock family took up a homestead at Netarts. One of the family members once wrote, "when the boat failed to come, the little settlement would run short of food except that furnished by the gardens, the forest and the sea." He also wrote, "The forest furnished elk, deer and bear in abundance. Wild hogs were plentiful, but as they ate the dead fish that were thrown up on the waves, they were unfit for food. There were even wild cattle, small, runty, red mullies, that were said to be the descendants of stock that had come ashore from a Spanish ship that had been wrecked on Cape Lookout on some unnamed date in the long ago."[21] These were contradictory statements, because although the supply boat would miss Netarts from time to time, there were still plenty of natural resources available.

As the community prospered with oystering, it brought in a ferry business and the timber industry, followed by a large sawmill. Unfortunately, when one of the ships loaded with lumber never arrived at San Francisco, the sawmill shut down because it failed to meet its contract.

Consistent with early towns, Netarts' roads were the pits. About the only time they could be used was during the summer when they were dry. Road travel was improved during the 1920s.

Just north of Netarts is the Octupus Tree, located at Cape Meares State Park. Mystery surrounds its shape. Some believe the wind fashioned the tree into its interesting shape, but the tree leans in the opposite direction of the prevailing winds. Folklore says it's a burial tree that was shaped when it was young to hold canoes of dead Indians, which was their traditional burial practice in this region. The Octopus tree spans more than fifty feet at its base. Until the tree's rings are counted, no one will never know its age. Some believe the tree was planted around the time of Christ.[22]

SCAPPOOSE

The Scappoose Plains area was once used by the Chinook Indians for their potlatches (ceremonial gatherings). In 1828, Tom McKay with the Hudson's Bay Company was sent to look for more land to grow hay for the company's ever-increasing livestock. McKay found the Scappoose Plains had everything that was needed: light, gravelly soil; silt from the winter and spring freshets that acted as fertilizer; and large stands of timber. (Another source cites a different year for McKay with the company, ". . . He started to work for Doctor McLoughlin, chief factor of the Hudson's Bay Company in 1841. In 1843 and '44 he was located at Linnton, buying wheat for the Hudson's Bay Company. . ."[23])

In 1828, a Boston trader named Captain Dominus brought his ship, the *Oywhee*, into Scappoose Bay. The Chinooks traded their furs for merchandise Dominus had brought with him. He may have left behind more than just merchandise. Soon after Domimus left, many of the Indians got sick and most of them were wiped out, probably from smallpox.

When Methodist missionaries led by Jason Lee were looking for a place to establish their mission, McKay was asked to find a suitable site. He selected Scappoose, but Lee decided this site was too far away from the settlements that were being established in the Willamette Valley.

After passage of the Donation Land Claim Act in 1850, some of the first settlers took land that was once the old Indian village. David A. Cloninger took a claim just north of the future town, and went into land dealing. S. T. Gosa built a boat dock, store, and post office in 1870, which he called Gosa's Landing. L. Armstrong and E. Gilmore built two brick kilns on Scappoose Bay. A sawmill was constructed in 1852, from where the settlers hauled their cut lumber to a fringe road and then on to Gosa's Landing. A cooperage plant was then established, which cut ash timber into staves and made barrels which was a thriving business, because the homesteaders needed barrels for salting their meats and vegetables. The barrels also were used for shipping salted salmon.[24]

James McKay talked about his father and the town's early settlement: "In about 1850 father took up a place at Scappoose . . . He built a sawmill on Scappoose Creek in 1850. The first store at Scappoose was owned by W. W. West. J. G. Watts was the first mayor. Before they started a post office at Scappoose, we got our mail at Gosas Landing on Willamette Slough, three miles from the present town of Scappoose."[25]

During 1855, the residents were in fear of their lives when the Indians began talking about killing the whites before they took all their land. A blockhouse was built in Scappoose, although it was never used because the Indian uprising didn't get down this far.

A man named William West said he would donate some land to the railroad in 1883 if it would build the town a depot and switching yard, and requested the town be called Scappoose. Ten years later, West built up the business district that encompassed seven blocks. The town had many trains that came through in a single day, but when the Northern Pacific Railroad constructed a bridge in 1898 over the Columbia River, Scappoose had less rail traffic. But it didn't dampen the town's economy because there were still enough trains coming through and picking up thousands of carloads of lumber.

The post office was moved from Gosa's Landing in 1872 and

renamed Johnson's Landing. It was later changed to Scappoose, which means "gravelly plains."

SILETZ

This settlement was originally developed as the administrative headquarters for the Siletz Indian Reservation, established in 1856. It was composed of twenty-seven bands of Indians who resided from the southern portion of Washington State down to Northern California, and became known as the Confederated Tribes of Siletz. The name may be derived from a Rogue River Indian word, silis, which one source says means "black bear." The native interpretation is "crooked rope (or water)," referring to the Siletz River which is one of the snakiest rivers in the state. When an agent asked the Indians their name, they said "Se-La-Gees." Because the agent could not pronounce the word, he called them Siletz.[26]

When gold was discovered in the Rogue River area of Southern Oregon, the Indians were forcibly removed by the government in 1856 to a reservation that had been established under various treaties. Many of the Indians died from illness and starvation after they were removed. The Indians were told they would be provided for, and had to leave all their belongings behind. When they arrived at the Siletz Reservation, all they found were empty promises, because nothing was there for them. The Indian agent did all he could for them with his limited funding.

One of the reservation superintendents stated, "They [the Indians] have acquired all the vices of the white man without any of his virtues; and while the last fifteen years have witnessed the most frightfull diminution in the numbers, their deterioration, morally, physically, and intellectually has been equally rapid. Starvation, disease, and bad whiskey combined is rapidly decimating their numbers, and will soon relieve the government of their charge."[27]

But the Indians did survive, and learned how to farm and log the region. Timber development began on the Siletz River drainage by U.S. Spruce Production Corporation. Today, the stands of old growth timber are gone from the area. The reservation headquarters also is gone, and the reservation itself was dissolved in 1956. Siletz is now a bedroom community and most residents are employed in the towns of Toledo and Newport.

On September 14, 2000, The Siletz Indians went on their annual 200-mile Run to the Rogue Relay race, which took about three days to complete. It commemorated their forced march in 1856. One of the members said, "We're honoring our ancestors and all the hardships they went through."[28]

TILLAMOOK

Tillamook, the "land of cheese, trees and ocean breeze," was first called Hoquarten, an Indian name of unknown definition. The first homesteader was Joseph Champion who arrived in 1851, and his first home was in the hollow of a big tree. An old Indian fighter, Thomas Stillwell, came in 1861, purchased a 320-acre farm, and laid out a town he called Lincoln. Another early settler was Elbridge Trask who became a blacksmith by day and a school teacher at night.[29]

Stillwell started the first general store. When the post office was established in 1866, the name Lincoln was submitted, but postal officials turned it down because there was already a town by that name in the state. So Tillamook was selected, which means "land of many waters," a very descriptive name, because there are seventy miles of coastline and many bays and rivers in the region. It was the first town to be settled in the county.

As the settlement grew, more stores came in, and some of them had their fronts facing the water to better serve the water traffic. One enterprising gent had his store on a barge, so when business got slow, he could move to a place where business was more brisk.

Because the area had rich grassland in addition to the mild climate, Tillamook became dairy country. Henry Wilson was thought to have brought in the first cows into the Tillamook area. The settlers made butter that was some of the finest in the country and much of it was shipped to Portland. Transportation was sporadic, so the farmers had to come up with a product that could be stored for long periods. Peter McIntosh came from Canada in 1894 and brought with him the

Courtesy Tillamook County Historical Pioneer Museum
These two photos show the growth of Tillamook between 1875 and 1911.

art of cheese-making. From there, the dairymen got together and began building small cheese factories, and Tillamook became world-famous for its high-quality cheese.

When the settlers first arrived, timber was considered a bother rather than an asset. The forests hindered farm development. While clearing their land, the farmers either burned the trees or cut them down and threw them into the tidelands to be washed out to sea. Eventually, however, logging became one of the main industries in the county.

The loggers who came into town were met with signs that said "No caulked boots allowed," because the sharp spikes on their boots damaged the restaurant and hotel floors. Some of the businesses provided the loggers with shingles to put on their boots, and they would then slide across the floors.[30]

When prohibition went into effect, some Tillamook area residents found a way around it. One of the farmers buried his hooch in a pile of manure; another farmer who always seemed to be building fences put a bottle of booze under each post. One restaurant even had booze to go. After the food was ordered, if the customer wanted some liquid refreshment, the cook would check to see if the coast was clear. He would then tap on a pipe, and down would come a bottle attached to a string through a hole in the ceiling.

In 1933, Tillamook County experienced one of the worst fires of the century, the "Tillamook Burn." More than 311,000 acres were burned, including the largest remaining stand of Douglas fir in the state. The fire started on August 14 near Gales Creek at a lumber camp, and it took more than 1,000 firefighters to bring it under control by August 26. The loss was estimated to be more than $600 million.

A few miles south of Tillamook are remnants of old wooden hangars that housed blimps during World War II. They were used to patrol the Pacific waters for enemy ships. One of the blimps was destroyed by high winds, and another fell into the sea with no fatalities. The hangars were listed in the *Guiness World Book of Records* as the largest structures of this type.

UMATILLA

The Indians of the Blue Mountains of eastern Oregon roamed the region more than 300 years before Lewis and Clark came on the scene. Founded as Umatilla Landing in 1863 or 1864, the community sprang up almost overnight as an important trade and shipping center during the gold rush. It was here that Lewis and Clark entered Oregon Territory. The community was surveyed by Timothy K. Davenport in 1863 and was first known as Columbia. It was later changed to Umatilla, thought to mean "water rippling over sand."

The landing became a shipping point for the Powder River, Owyhee, and Idaho mines. At least a dozen buildings were constructed in four days. Within six months, the town boasted more than 100 structures, and one-quarter of them supplied the prospectors and residents. There was no real property ownership at that time. If someone claimed a lot and built on it, then left for a short while, he could come back and find that someone else had staked a claim on it, as the *Oregonian* reported in 1863, "Very little regard is paid to the pretended title of the proprietor . . . as anyone who wishes a lot just naturally jumps it." In 1865, town became the county seat until 1868, when Pendleton got it.[31]

River traffic also increased during the period. More than twenty-five steamboats were plying the Columbia River by 1888. Stage lines were established between Umatilla and Boise City. During the gold rush days, Umatilla's medium of exchange was gold dust, and every store had a gold scale. Many Chinese were imported to work in the gold fields, and they had a camp a few miles from town. With the gold came the saloons. During the winter when the Columbia River froze, many packers and prospectors stayed in town, adding to Umatilla's prosperity.

The town also became a shipping point for grain that came from Eastern Oregon farms that was loaded on river steamers and shipped to various destinations. But when construction of Oregon Railway and Navigation Company was completed, it took a lot of Umatilla's trade. The economy picked up in 1940, when work began on the McNary Dam hydroelectric project.

Umatilla had the distinction of being managed by a group of women in 1916. The incumbents, confident they would be reelected, were shocked when five women were elected by the residents. They managed Umatilla's affairs for about five years. The mayor stated that "There has been a great deal said about the so-called petticoat government and many wild speculations made as to how we would manage the city affairs, being mere women. . ." In addition to a competent administration, the "Petticoat Council" brought in a new library, repaired street lights and gave the town fire protection. After five years, satisfied they had done their job well, they left the political scene.[32]

YACHATS

Yachats is located in Lincoln County along the Pacific Coast. Captain Cook was probably one of the first white man to see the area in 1778. There was not much written history of the town until the Alsea Indian Agency was established in 1855 just north of Yachats. Many of the Indians died in 1852 from smallpox and pneumonia. They tried to get rid of their high fevers by plunging into the icy waters, and more often than not died from the shock.

The Alsea Indian Agency was a "substation" of the Siletz Indian Agency. Sam Case became agent in 1869 or 1870, and tried to get the government to provide better living conditions for the inhabitants. The agent's pay was minimal and the Indians' living conditions were worse than poor. A few years later, the government finally sent tools and equipment to the agency, and the Indians began to learn how to farm by growing potatoes and corn.[33]

The government opened up the area for homesteading in 1875. Farmers and cattle ranchers claimed most of the land because it was very suitable for their livestock. When the post office was established in 1877, it was named Ocean View. In 1916, the name was changed to Yachats, which could mean many things and was spelled many different ways: Youitts, Yawhuck, Hauuts, Yahatc, to name just a few. Some definitions were "at the foot of the mountain," "dark water between timbered hills," "silent waters," "little river with big mouth," and many others. The syllable YA in the language of the Alsea Indians is "water." Whatever its definition, it became Yachats.[34]

Many people who came here had summer cottages. A warehouse was built in 1905, and five years later it was renovated and became the Yachats Hotel. The first general store was established in 1900, and a man named "Dunk" Dunkelerger opened a blacksmith shop and served the logging outfits. One day a transient came by looking for work. Not wanting to have much to do with the man, Dunk told him he could have the job if he could make a "three-way weld," an impossible task. Dunk then left to go to lunch, and when he came back he found his tongs were welded together around the horn of an anvil in a perfect three-way weld. It took Dunk two days to get the tongs off his anvil.[35]

When the settlers first arrived, they were surprised to see large shellfish mounds on the beach, reputed to be the largest in the world at about forty feet high. No one knows how old the mounds are, but when a large spruce tree stump was dug out of a county road near Yachats, there was a shell mound underneath. The Indians apparently had lived in the area for thousands of years.

Roads arrived in the 1930s, and had to be blasted out because Cape Perpetua was solid rock. Some of the rock was blasted using hand fuses and caps. The powder would be placed during the day and exploded at night, which left the neighbors less than happy when it woke them up. One time, a powder "expert" overloaded the shot with the result that he blew out the quarry near town, and much of the rock fell into the river, damming it up.

Bill Brubaker, famous barnstormer in the 1920s, lived near Yachats. He was granted a government contract to take aerial photographs of the Northwest. Then during World War II, he photographed the Oregon coastline for the government, checking for signs of saboteurs.

The Little Log Church By The Sea was built in 1930 in the shape of a cross, and its bell was donated by the First Evangelical Church of Portland. By 1986, the church was deteriorating, and some people wanted it torn down and replaced with a parking lot. But volunteers stepped up and began restoring the little church. Many of the volunteers were elderly people. The church restoration was completed in 1993. The Little Log Church is now a museum and open to the public.[36]

YONCALLA

When botanist David Douglas was traveling through the region for a horticultural society, he met the Yoncalla Indians. His notes may be the earliest accounts of the tribe. Very little was written about them, but it is known they were a dialectic group of the Kalapuya Indians. It was believed most of the Yoncallas died out during the epidemics that ravaged the region in the 1830s.

Jesse Applegate, famous for blazing the Applegate Trail, came to Yoncalla in 1849, took up a homestead, and opened a general store a few years later. He also operated a cattle ranch. Applegate was involved in politics, and probably wrote more letters to the editor than any other person in the state, which earned him the moniker, "Sage of Yoncalla." When George Burt arrived in 1872, he offered the O&C Railroad some of his land if it would build a depot on his property. Years later, he also donated part of his land to build a courthouse and school. When the post office was established, Robert Booth was its first postmaster. He also established a sawmill in 1882. The O&C then gave him a contract to cut timber the railroad would need for its bridges and tunnel shoring. The *Independent* newspaper operated for a short while, but it folded.[37]

In the 1850s, an Indian shaman named Chemocchot told the

story of how the tribe of Yoncallas began: "In the beginning was a mountain, and on the mountain top was a table of stone. On this table was a deposit of some kind of matter, jelly-like in consistence . . . and out of this . . . grew a living being in the form of . . . a woman. She held in her arms a male child, and when she was fully grown she descended, carrying the child on her bosom, to the base of the mountain, where the two were joined by a wolf. . ." The Yoncalla called these three figures Snowats, Iswukaw, and Quartux.[38]

When the post office was established, it was called Yoncalla. The word may be derived from yonk (eagle) and colla (mountain), "eagle mountain," or yonc-alla-alla, meaning "eagles nest on top."

Roselle Applegate wrote in 1852, ". . . what is Yoncalla . . . now it is not a town nor a place of man's creation nor of a white man's naming . . . but it is a hill round and high and beautiful; a splendid representative of hills in general . . . it is ten miles in circumference and one and half in height. . . The hill is called after a chief who with a numerous tribe once inhabited these valleys-among the few remaining survivors of this tribe that occasionally came to beg a crust of bread or an old garment that is getting worse for the wear—there are some old ones who remember the chief, say that he was a great physician and skilled in witchcraft."[39]

Chapter two notes

[1] Joe Gaston, *Centennial History of Oregon*, S.J. Clark, Pub., Chicago, 1912, p. 444.

[2] Connie H Battaile, *The Oregon Book*, Saddle Mountain Press, 1998, p. 89.

[3] Joe Gaston, Op. cit., p. 205.

[4] John Todd, "History of Clatskanie Indians Discussed," *The Clatskanie Chief*, Dec. 30, 1999, p. 9.

[5] Clark Mallory, "Little Known About Native Americans Who Gave Name to Clatskanie," *The Clatskanie Chief*, Nov. 25, 1999, p. 11.

[6] Irene Barklow, History of the Post Offices of Wallowa County, 1982, p. 66.

[7] Wallowa County Museum Board, *The History of Wallowa County, Oregon*, Taylor Pub., Texas, 1983, pp. 21-22.

[8] Robert Ruby & John A Brown, *Indians of the Pacific Northwest*, Univ. OK Press, 1981, p. 53.

[9] Federal Writers' Project, *Oregon: End of the Trail*, Binfords & Mort, 1940, p. 184 (hereafter cited as WPA Oregon).

[10] "Come to the Molalla River," Mollala Area Historical Society.

[11] The First Inhabitants, the Molallas, webpage, ww.molalla.net/community/

[12] Lewis L. McArthur, *Oregon Geographic Names*, Oregon Historical Soc., 1974, p. 531.

[13] Jack Fosmark, email to author, Dec. 2000. Fosmark wrote for the *Seaside Signal* and about 1991 did a seven-part series titled "Herman Ahlers, Fireweed Honey Man of Push."

[14] Ibid, from *Seaside Signal*, April 1, 1905.

[15] Ibid; Sept. 16, 1905.

[16] Inez Hanson, *Life on Clatsop*, Astoria Ptg., 1977, p.84.

[17] Mrs. Hardy (Alexandria) Rock, *Short History of the Little Nestucca River Valley*, 1949.

[18] Lewis A. McArthur, Oregon Geographic Names, *Oregon Historical Quarterly.*, v. 27, No. 4, 1926, p. 423.

[19] James Gibbs, Jr., *Shipwrecks of the Pacific Coast*, Bindfords & Mort, 1957, pp. 133-134.

[20] General History of the Town of Netarts, Netarts Steering Committee.

[21] Ibid.

[22] "Legend of the Octopus Tree," Tillamook Chamber of Commerce.

[23] Fred Lockley, *History of the Columbia River: From the Dalles to the Sea*, Vol. 1, 1928, S.J. Clark Pub., Chicago, p. 335.

[24] Jim Watts, History of Scappoose, manuscript dated 1979.

[25] Fred Lockley, Op. cit., pp. 335-336.

[26] Marjorie H. Hays, *The Land That Kept Its Promise: A History of South Lincoln County*, Lincoln County Hist. Soc., 1976, p. 35.

[27] *The Catholic Encyclopedia*, "Siletz Indians," *Vol. 12*, Robert Appleton Company, 1912, pp. 791-792.

[28] Associated Press, "Run to the Rogue recalls Indians' forced march," *The Mail Tribune* (Medford, Oregon), Sept. 16, 2000, p. 3A.

[29] Kathleen Wiederhold, *Exploring Oregon's Historic Courthouses*, Oregon State

University Press, 1998, pp. 104-105.

[30] WPA Oregon, Op. cit., p. 371.

[31] Ibid., pp. 259, 263.

[32] Umatilla website: www.ccrh.org/comm/umatilla/women.htm

[33] Marjorie H. Hays, Op. cit., p 36.

[34] Ruth Harrison, "Ever wonder where 'Yachats' got its name?" South Lincoln News, n.d.

[35] WPA Oregon, Op. cit., p. 317.

[36] Ruth Harrison, "The Little Log Church By the Sea," Yachats Museum, 1994.

[37] Betty Gibson, letter to author, first draft of "Yoncalla Yesterday," Jan. 30, 1999.

[38] Stephen D. Beckham, *Land of the Umpqua: A History of Douglas County, Oregon*, Douglas County Commissioners, 1986, p. 32.

[39] WPA Oregon, Op. cit., pp. 317-318.

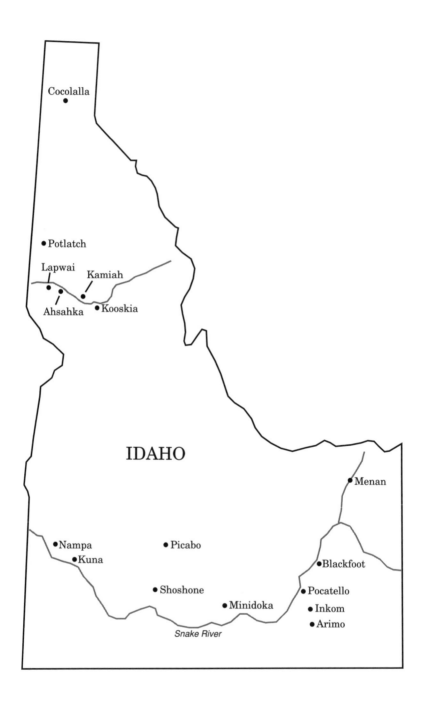

Cocolalla

Potlatch

Lapwai
Kamiah

Ahsahka Kooskia

IDAHO

Menan

Nampa Picabo

Kuna

Blackfoot

Shoshone

Pocatello

Minidoka

Inkom

Arimo

Snake River

Chapter Three

IDAHO

AHSAHKA

Located on the north fork of the Clearwater River about three miles southwest of Orofino, Idaho, Ahsahka is a Nez Perce word that could mean "the spot where the two rivers meet," or "forks of a river."[1] A Nez Perce Indian named Sam Watters believed it meant "box canyon," and another definition was "brushy country," from a Salish Indian word. The community owes its existence to the Northern Pacific Railroad.[2]

When the McLean brothers settled at Ahsahka, they built a sawmill and employed many workers on the river, who put out more than 20,000 board feet per day. The post office was established in 1898. The following year, A. M. Pierce moved in and opened a general mercantile store. When the Hotel Ahsahka was erected, it was quite small and built up off the ground with its foundation sitting on short, sturdy, logs. All the tillable land in the area was owned by the Indians.

When the Northern Pacific Railroad finished construction in September 1899, the tracks went up the Clearwater River to Orofino, which became the railroad's division headquarters. Ahsahka became one of the places the train passed through on its way up the river.

Presbyterian missionaries came to Ahsahka and founded a

Courtesy Clearwater Historical Society
Ahsahka (undated). The Hotel Ahsahka was built on short stilts.

mission in 1884. The first Indian church was built in the 1800s, and was replaced in 1903 after the Nez Perce Indians collected money for new construction. William Wheeler helped by supplying lumber he received when he traded one of his bulls for the wood. He also supervised construction of the church, which happened to be near the place where the Indians helped Lewis and Clark build their canoes in 1806. A load of lumber used to build the church was brought down by raft, and when it reached its destination it was tied up because there was no one available at the time to take off the logs. In the meantime, a large ice floe broke loose upstream and came tearing down the river, hit the tie and broke it. The raft was hurled down the river. It ended up on the bank and all the logs fell off, much to the Indians' delight because they didn't have to haul out the timber.[3]

Dworshak Dam, the largest concrete dam ever built by the U.S. Army Corps of Engineers, was constructed in the 1960s. Then in 1968, the Ahsahka Fish Hatchery was completed, which was the world's largest steelhead hatchery. This was an asset for the Nez Perce who were very anxious to save the fish industry. In 1969, Reverend Walter Moffett, who was Chairman of the Nez Perce Tribal Executive Council, stated, "And so, for a while, the decline of our steelhead was certainly a cause for alarm. This kind of rebirth is essential. It can mean new jobs. It can mean more and better food to the hungry people of our area . . ."[4] In the fall of 1968, the first migrating adult trout were held for spawn-taking. The fish were stripped of milt (sperm) and eggs in April of 1969, and the first smolts (year-lings) were released the following year.

Each state was requested to contribute historic earth to Philadelphia to commemorate the 150th anniversary of the signing of the Declaration of Independence. Idaho's contribution was one pound of historic earth that was taken near Ahsahka where the Lewis and Clark Expedition camped in 1805. These historic mounds of earth provided the soil to grow a special tree in Philadelphia. The site near Ahsahka is marked by a stone cairn.[5]

ARIMO

This eastern Idaho town was originally called Oneida. One of the first settlers claimed his land in 1868 a few miles from today's site; his home also served as a stagecoach stop, which was called Ruddy's Station. As more settlers moved in, their supplies were brought in by an Army captain from Fort Hall because there were no stores established as yet at Arimo.

In 1878, the Utah & Northern Railroad built a narrow-gauge track through Oneida, which became a freighting point until the railroad was completed to Lima, Montana. When the railroad moved to higher ground, the town followed to be near the tracks. The post office was established the same year, and its name was changed in 1912. An engineer suggested Arimo because the settlement was the old campsite of Shoshone Chief Arimo, where marriages were performed and councils were held. As leader of a Shoshone band, Arimo was admired by his followers and the white people. His Indian name was So-Yo-Ghuent. One definition of Arimo name was thought to be "the uncle bawls like a cow."[6]

A trading post was established south of Arimo. A freighter named Fast Freight Bill hauled salt from Utah to Montana for the settlers' cattle, and would stop at Arimo to sell and trade his goods. The town began to show growth with stores, hotels, about ten saloons and blacksmiths. C. D. Watson established a relay station in 1881 that supplied food and fodder for the stagecoach station. It was later used as a barn when the Henderson family acquired the property and went into the dairy business. This historical site was torn down when Interstate 15 was built.

Typical of many western towns, Arimo was a tough one where the law was a man's gun. No wonder, with all the saloons and gambling halls in town. It was not unknown for cowboys to shoot through the kitchen of a restaurant if the cook was too slow with their orders, or amuse themselves by shooting at some poor man's feet.[7]

Sheep were the main economy of this town in the early days, but later grain and other crops replaced them. Water had to be brought in manually to the flat, dry land until the first canal was built in 1889. Completed in 1912, it went into operation the next year.

BLACKFOOT

The name Blackfoot was taken from Indians who lived farther north in Montana and Canada. Blackfoot was applied to this tribe after some of its members traveled through an area that had suffered from a great prairie fire. They walked through the burnt prairie with the result their moccasins became black with the ashes. They came upon a band of Crow Indians who called them siksika, meaning "black foot."[8]

Wilson Price Hunt may have been the first white man to see what would become the town of Blackfoot. He and his party

Courtesy Grace Sandberg Collection, Bingham County Historical Society
Downtown Blackfoot (July 3, 1909). Bridge Street. The people were celebrating Idaho's Statehood, which occurred on July 3, 1890.

came down the Snake River from Fort Henry in 1811 to American Falls. Some historians think the Missouri Fur Company was also at the site to hold a meeting with the Indians in 1830.[9]

In 1864, a ferry was built just below Blackfoot when gold was discovered at Alder Gulch in southwestern Montana. Two other ferries followed; one farther upstream from Blackfoot and one at a place called Eagle Rock. The first year the Eagle Rock ferry owner took in about $30,000 worth of passenger fare in the form of gold dust. Eagle Rock later became Idaho Falls.

In the 1870s, a geological party came through and wrote in

their field notes this region would become very important in agriculture. A few years later, a man named Peter Kelley tried growing potatoes and cabbage and found them to be very successful crops. It was only a few years earlier that an Army captain had described this country as only a sage-covered valley, and was so desolate that even an Indian cayuse would have a hard time finding a living. Indeed the future Blackfoot was nothing but sagebrush.

In 1877, the Utah and Northern Railroad went to the Montana Legislature and offered to build a narrow-gauge railroad. Its route would go from Franklin to the Big Hole Country in Montana. But the Legislature suggested a different route, one that would run from Fort Hall to Helena. Part of the railroad was constructed through Marsh Valley and Pocatello to the Snake River at Blackfoot.

Because this town had access to the railroad in 1880, it became an outfitting center for the gold mines in the county, and was the nearest railway point to the mining districts where prospectors could get supplies. Stagecoaches and freight wagons also made daily trips to the Custer County gold mines. Saloons and gambling establishments came to town with the miners, as was the norm for the West.

Blackfoot became the county seat in 1885, and county commissioners were authorized to build a courthouse and jail. A Doctor Britton quoted in the *Salt Lake City Press*, "One is almost tempted to think that the Idaho Legislature perpetrated a huge burlesque when they made this settlement the capital of the newly organized county. . . If the saloons, gambling halls and bawdy houses were removed the town would be so insignificantly small that it would require a keen eye to find even a single building remaining." [10]

The first newspaper was started in 1880 by William Wheeler, and called the *Idaho Falls Register*. It was followed in 1887 by another paper, the *Blackfoot News*, with Byrd Frego as editor. At one time, someone tried to get the capitol moved to Blackfoot from Boise. The *Boise Idaho Republication* wrote, "Blackfoot is several degrees nearer hell than any other town in Idaho."[11] In 1886, the State Asylum was also constructed.

Before its establishment, patients had to go to Salem, Oregon, for treatment.

In 1879, a group of men from Dillon and Eagle Rock got together and made plans to build an irrigation canal. The American Falls Canal Company built the main ditch which ran about fifty-six miles. Farmers then began growing sugar beets, which brought in the first sugar mill. Originally created as an experiment, the mill turned out to be one of the best industrial resources in the area. The largest alfalfa seed farm was also established here. And of course, the Idaho potato was grown, with over one million bushels taken in 1915.

Blackfoot was once known as the "Grove City" because some-one planted many poplar trees around the courthouse in 1886, which had a ditch around it in order to irrigate the trees. Because they were the first trees in the Snake River Valley, people came from many distances just to see them. They had to be removed about 1912 when all the treetops died off.

Some people believe there may be about $40,000 of gold hidden near town. A freighter named Blackie robbed a stagecoach headed for Blackfoot, took the cash box, and then buried it in the lava fields along the road somewhere. When he returned the next day to get his loot, he was met by lawmen who shot him, and nobody ever knew where the strongbox was hidden.

COCOLALLA

The name of this north Idaho community and valley may have been derived from a Coeur d'Alene word meaning "very cold."[12] An early map shows the name Chocolala. The Indians came to the Cocollala Valley during the summer to gather huckleberries. Flathead Indians from Montana also came here during the summer and used it as their hunting ground.

There were very few white men here until the gold rush in British Columbia and Montana. The Northern Pacific Railroad extended its line through the Cocolalla Valley in 1881. Sawmills were established when lumber companies came into the area to harvest the trees. But in 1898, a fire came through and destroyed many of the mills. Hundreds of men were hired to harvest the trees that had burned before sap rot and worms got the rest of the timber.[13]

Ice harvesting seems to be Cocolalla's claim to fame. During the early 1900s, Cocolalla Lake had an ice house so big that ten railroad cars could fit inside. The ice house, which also had bunkhouses and a kitchen, employed more than 300 men during the winter. Teams of horses were driven over the frozen lake and the snow was plowed aside so the lake would freeze deeper. Blacksmiths had to make spiked shoes for the horses so they wouldn't slip on the ice while they pulled out the cut blocks of ice.

The *Daily Bulletin* wrote in 1922, "The big ice harvest is on at full blast at Cocolalla Lake, where the finest ice of recent years is being stored away that the passengers of the Northern Pacific may have pure ice water next summer as they journey across the Rockies and over the Cascades, and that the fruit which goes from the northwestern points to the eastern markets may also be kept from perishing at berry and fruit times next season."[14]

The ice house had the capacity of 22,000 tons. More than ten cars were loaded daily and shipped to Northern Pacific's ice stations at Yakima, Ellensburg, Toppenish, Walla Walla and Spokane.

INKOM

Inkom is located about twelve miles southeast of Pocatello in Bannock County, and began with the land rush of 1902. There were approximately 418,000 acres open for settlement, and more than 2,000 people went to Pocatello where the rush started.

Inkom was originally part of the Fort Hall Indian Reservation. After homesteading their plots of land, the settlers had to go to Blackfoot to file their claims. By 1889, a railroad was built after the Indians agreed to let the railroad have some land. The train depot and a water tower were also constructed and painted red.

Inkom may be derived from the Shoshone word eggakabni, meaning "red structure." An Indian family named Jackson told the story of the name's origin. Apparently a rock formation that now looks like a bulldog after lightening struck it many years ago once had ears and resembled a red rabbit. An Indian word for red rabbit was Inkapuppie, later shortened to Inkom for the town. Another version is that it is a Shoshoni word Ingacom which also means "red rabbit."[15]

The land that is now Inkom was originally settled by an Indian family named Nocese and Annie SoRelle. Nocese was of French-Indian descent who came from Wyoming, and Annie was from Montana. While living here, they met one of the first settlers. The Dameron family arrived in the fall, had no house to live in, and with winter not far away, the SoRelle family took them in until they could get settled. SoRelle later sold part of his property to a man named Theodore H. Gathe who then developed the townsite.

The Indians were friendly to the whites. When new settlers came to the land, they had to live in tents or dugouts until they could build their homes. The Indians helped them select the right trees for their homes and taught them how to dry game meat so it wouldn't spoil. In turn, the newcomers taught the Indians how to farm and fix their implements.

Nocese started a dairy business which he called "Idle Hour." Starting with about twenty head of milk cows, he expanded his business to Pocatello selling milk to stores and restaurants. In the fall of 1902, the first school was built. Horses had to drag the logs for for the school through heavy snow. When the school opened, there were six students. Two years later, a post office was established in a resident's home, which also housed a little store. A sawmill was built and the Latter-day-Saints ward was organized.

Nocese sold part of his land in 1912 to a man named Theodore H. Gathe who, along with H. A. Witthoft, platted the town. When they put the lots up for sale for $100 each, an ad stated, "Get choice location, secure your lot now, only $5.00 cash down, balance $1.25 per week, no interest."

In 1918, many of the residents of Inkom died in the influenza epidemic. There was no mortuary at that time, and the townspeople had to take care of laying out the dead and the men made their caskets.

By 1928, a Portland cement factory was built. It was owned by J. Simons and J. B. Maxfield, who bought property that

Courtesy Lillian Pethtel, Kamiah, Idaho
Kamiah, Idaho (1908) from a panoramic photo. Businesses in the photo included the Red Front Livery and the Kamiah Hotel.

contained limestone and silica. This became one of the largest producing cement companies in the state of Idaho.

KAMIAH

Kamiah (Kam-ee-eye) is situated on the banks of the Clearwater River, and is the birthplace of the Nez Perce Indians who called themselves Nee-me-poo, meaning "the chosen ones." During the winter they stayed in what was called a long house. There, they braided ropes from the Cannabis hemp and made baskets for use during the summer.

Historians believe the name Kamiah means "tattered ends of hemp." It may also be derived from what was called the kame hemp (or dogbane). Another definition was "the place of many rope litters." The Indians lived off the land, traded with other tribes, and traveled to the plains to get the buffalo. The Nez Perce were great horsemen, and developed the Appaloosa as a war horse.

When Lewis and Clark returned here in 1806 from their expedition to the Pacific Coast, they were forced to stay for a month until the snow melted in the Bitterroot Range. Lewis wrote in his journal, "The Spurs of the Rocky Mountains were perfectly covered with snow. The Indians inform us that the

Courtesy Martin Stadius, Dreamers: On the Trail of the Nez Perce
The "Heart of the Monster" near Kamiah. According to Nez Perce legend, this
mound was the heart of a monster whose destruction created the Indian tribes
of the West.

snow is yet so deep that we shall not be able to pass them until
the next full moon; others set the time at still a more distant
period. this is unwelcom inteligence to men confined to a diet of
horsebeef and roots; and who are as anxious as we are to return
to the fat plains of the Missouri."[16] A man named Biddle who
was with the expedition noted in his journal, ". . . this district
affords many advantages to settlers, and if properly cultivated,
would yield every object necessary for the subsistence and com-
fort of civilized man . . ."[17] During their stay, Lewis and Clark
had a bit of difficulty in language, and had to have their words
translated. First they spoke in English, which was translated
into French for Charboneau, who repeated the message to
Sacajawea in her language to a Shoshone Indian, who then
spoke to the Nez Perce in their tongue.

Asa B. Smith and his wife came to Kamiah in 1838 and
established a mission. They stayed only two years, working
under the supervision of Presbyterian missionary Henry
Spalding from Lapwai. The first Presbyterian church was
established in East Kamiah in 1870, as was the post office. It
was closed in 1877 due to the Indian war, and it wasn't until
1894 that another post office was established at Kamiah.[18]

During 1877, malcontents among the non-Christian Nez Perce, who were reluctantly moving to the reservation inhabited primarily by Christian Nez Perce, killed some settlers along the lower Salmon River. Soldiers pursued the hostiles who passed through Kamiah as they fled toward Montana. An Indian agent sent a telegram his superiors: "The non-treaty Indians commenced hostilities on the 14th inst. Up to date, 29 settlers are reported murdered . . . The reservation Indians are true to the government. A company is formed under the head chief, and are protecting Kamiah and employees. . ."[19]

The region was opened up for homesteading in 1890 and people came in droves, many of them seeking gold. Town merchants had to negotiate with the government and Indian tribes to purchase the townsite because it was on Indian land.

One of the legends of the creation of the Nez Perce involves a volcanic rock formation near east Kamiah called Heart of the Monster. The Indians thought this was where Coyote killed a monster that had eaten many of the animals. He cut the monster into pieces and scattered them to the wind. An Indian tribe was born where each piece landed. From the drops of blood from the monster's heart, the Nez Perce Tribe was born.[20]

KOOSKIA

When the Nez Perce lands were opened for settlement in 1895, a number of patents were applied for. Frank McGrane was one of the first residents to take up some land and build a shingle mill. While preparing to cut cedar bolts that would make up more than one million shingles, something happened and his mill burned down.

Kooskia (Koos-key) first started out as a trading center, and when the Northern Pacific Railroad was completed in 1899 the town rapidly expanded. First named Stuart for a Nez Perce Indian named James Stuart, the name was officially changed to Kooskia in 1909.

George Rowton filed an application with the U.S. government to set aside 104 acres of land for a new townsite. As soon as it was approved, businesses were rapidly established. When the railroad laid its line four miles farther, the town of Stites became its terminal, and Kooskia was designated as one of the stations. The railroad renamed the town Kooskia because there was another station called Stuart on its line.

The *Idaho County Free Press* carried a news item on December 2, 1898: "Final proof was made Saturday before U.S. Commissioner DeHaven of the Stuart townsite. From all appearances Stuart will be the first town in Idaho County to get the railroad." Someone else wrote, "Stuart enjoyed a genuine boom. March 13, 1899 was a day of jubilee in Stuart, for upon this date the people celebrated the arrival of the iron horse, which it was thought would go no farther for several years. The people were doomed for disappointment, as the rails were laid another four miles and a half and Stites became the terminal . . ." [21]

The early 1900s brought in a flour mill and a new telephone line from Winona. Kooskia was also known as the home of the Decker saddle. A blacksmith named Oliver Robinett moved here in 1906 and developed the saddle. He also designed a mattock axe that became standard equipment for forest fighters. In 1935, Kooskia became an outfitting town for hunters, and also served as a trading post for lumbermen, farmers and ranchers.

Kooskia was thought to be a contraction of a Nez Perce word for the Clearwater or "Kooskooskee." Frank T. Gilbert wrote in 1882: "The name Koos-koos-kee erroneously supposed to be a Nez Perce word meaning Clearwater, was given to it. P. B. Whitman, the interpreter for the Nez Perce agency, accounts for this error in the following way: The Nez Perces probably, in try-ing to explain to Lewis and Clark that there were two large streams running through their country, the smaller of which was the one they saw, and the larger one now called Snake, repeated the words "Koots-koots-kee" and pointed to the visible stream, meaning "This is the smaller," from which the whites inferred that this was its Indian name. Kaih-kaih-koosh is the Nez Perce word signifying "clear water." Literally translated, the word meant "water see."[22]

Passengers wait for a train at the Kuna Depot. The depot was located across
Indian Creek, south of town. It was demolished about 1960.

KUNA

Describing the end of the railroad line, this southwest Idaho
town was called Kuna, an Indian word meaning "the end."
Some believed the word meant "snow" in Shoshoni,[23] or "good
to smoke," the first explanation seems to be the one accepted.

Kuna was established along the Oregon Short Line Railroad,
near a freight road to Silver City. A construction camp was
located at Kuna during building of the railroad, and after its
completion in 1882 the camp was closed down. There were also
many graves left behind because of a diphtheria epidemic that
hit the camp. The town experienced very little growth until
establishment of the Desert Land Act of 1877 and the
Reclamation Act of 1902.[24]

Kuna was along the Silver Trail, where freighters passed
between Silver City and Boise, the only road in the area for
many years. The wagon ruts were quite deep because of the
vast numbers of freighters who used the route. On one occasion,
a stamp mill was hauled through that required a team of more
than twenty horses, which did nothing to improve the already
bad road.

After the railroad was completed, Kuna had no depot, so
freight and mail were simply dropped on the ground as the
train passed by. If anyone wanted to take the train, they had to
signal it with something the engineer could see or the train just

Edith Cornell photo collection
One of the early buildings in Kuna. It housed the offices of the local newspaper for more than thirty years.

kept going. A boxcar was finally put along the tracks for shelter and eventually a train depot was built. Until a spur line was built to Boise, passengers from that town had to take a stage to Kuna to board a train.

The settlers were forced to get their water from a well that had previously been dug and used by sheepmen. The well was full of sulfur and sometimes had an odor of sheep dip, but the people had no choice as it was the only water in the area until canals were built. For drinking water, the residents had to travel to the Snake River, which was quite a distance away, and haul it back in barrels.

F. H. Teed filed a claim for this site in November 1904, and became the first postmaster in 1907. When reporting to the postal service his quarterly receipts, he sent in his records showing a gross of sixteen cents. The total year's receipts came to a grand total of $3.16. In addition to his postmaster duties, Teed was also manager of the Coast Lumber Company, which was built in the early 1900s.

In 1911 construction of Arrowrock Dam began and canals

were dug that would bring water for agricultural use. Unfortunately, some of the settlers had their homes above the canal and either had to move into town or settle elsewhere. The dam officially opened in 1915. The canal was not without its problems, however. When the floods came, parts of the canal were washed out. And when there was no rain, the settlers were without water again.

In 1909, the Teed homesite became the town of Kuna after a lottery sale, which was an interesting process. A special train brought people from Nampa, Boise, and other surrounding towns who were interested in buying the property. After the lots were drawn, the new owners were asked to bid what they thought the land was worth. Others were then allowed to bid on the same lots, and high bidder got the land even though someone else had won the draw. After the lots were sold, the town became a tent city until homes were constructed.

Kuna expanded somewhat when a general store was opened by F. B. Fiss who came from Iowa. A school was built and the first commencement had one graduate in 1914. The first Sunday school was born in a tent. Because there was only a Methodist missionary in the area, it was decided that the church built was to be Methodist, because a majority of three Methodists were present at the day of its organization. D. R. Hubbard, who was instrumental in promoting getting water to Kuna, along with Gus Carlson, later opened a blacksmith shop.

Agriculture in the area consisted mainly of apple orchards as the climate was exceptionally good for them. Most of the orchards were established between 1909 and 1911. The fruit became a large cash crop and boosted Kuna's economy.

Kuna was described by Mary Hallock Foote in the 1800s when she wrote, "I wish I could make you feel a place like Kuna. It is a place where silence closes about you after the bustle of the train, where a soft, dry wind from great distances hums through the telephone wires and a stage road goes out of sight in one direction and a new railroad track in another. There is not a tree, nothing but sage. . . Hawks sail far up in the blue, magpies fly along ahead, coming back now and then like ranging dogs to make sure you are not lost. . ."[25]

Rumor has it that there may be some gold buried in Kuna

Cave, left over from a "gent" who robbed a stage. According to the legend, the strongbox he was carrying was so heavy he shot the lock off and carried as much money as he could and hid it in the cave.[26]

LAPWAI

Presbyterian missionary Henry Spalding settled on the Clearwater River in 1836 and built a mission, which he named Lapwai (Lap-way). It is a Nez Perce word that means "butterfly," and referred to the butterflies that gathered at a millpond.

One of the first Indians to embrace Christianity was Tu-eka-kas. Spalding gave him the Christian name of Joseph (father of Chief Joseph). The Nez Perce Indians were eager to aid the missionaries. They helped with construction of the mission and brought food to the Spaldings, who in turn taught them how to farm. By 1838, quite a number of the Indians had become self-sufficient practicing agriculture. But Old Joseph renounced the religion because he believed the missionaries did not practice what they preached, and the intention was to enslave the Indians, not to free them.[27]

Lapwai saw its first printing press in 1839, and Mrs. Spalding published a children's book in the Nez Perce language, which was the first book printed in the Pacific Northwest. Spalding also built a flour mill. Prior to the construction of the mill, they were paying more than $25 for a barrel of flour.

Elias Pierce, who was a trader with the Nez Perce at Lapwai, took some of the Indians with him to look for gold. He found enough of the ore in 1860 to make him believe there was much more in the area. So he told council members he was going to bring more white men to prospect. The Indian agent told the Indians they should not allow the white man to intrude on their reservation. But Pierce and a few men did manage to make a find on Orofino Creek and the gold rush was on.[28]

When two Nez Perce women took their allotments under the 1877 Allotment Act, it was situated where the town of Lapwai would be formed. The general store was built in 1895, but it wasn't until the early 1900s that the majority of the business district was established. During this time the Nez Perce were making money off timber sales, in addition to money received from land they rented. Because they did not trust the banks, they kept their cash hidden. Finally, in 1909, three Nez Perce and two white men incorporated a bank. Nez Perce stockholders put up the initial capital, and by 1918 the bank had substantial cash resources.[29]

Fort Lapwai was established just south of town in 1862. Its purpose was to keep the white man from encroaching on the Nez Perce reservation. In 1877, the Army told the Nez Perce they would all have to remove to the Lapwai Reservation. Young Chief Joseph tried to reason with officials, saying the land still belonged to the Indians. He eventually agreed to move to the reservation. But after some young men from Joseph's band killed settlers on the Salmon River and the Camas Prairie, a general war erupted. The non-treaty Nez Perce fled toward Canada. But after an 1,100-mile chase, they were surrounded by troops and forced to surrender.

The Nez Perce are renowned horsemen and breeders of Appaloosas. Meriwether Lewis wrote in 1806, "The horses appear to be of an excellent race. They are lofty, elegantly formed, active and durable . . ." The Nez Perce are in the process of developing a new breed of horse by crossing the Appaloosa with a Central Asian horse called the akhal-teke. More than thirty-five colts have been born since 1995. A newspaper article stated, "The Nez Perce aren't ready to brag yet, because the first of the strain are barely five years old. . ."[30]

Today, Lapwai is the center of the Idaho Nez Perce culture. Most of the members of the tribe who participated in the 1877 war did not return to Lapwai. Many of their descendents live in eastern Washington.

MENAN

Located on an island about eighteen miles north of Idaho Falls, in Eastern Idaho, Menan was originally known as the "Island." A man named Israel Heald brought his cattle here to graze in 1870, and other cattlemen followed. The Indians also used this place to hunt and fish. The island is about twenty miles long and four miles wide, and the town lies in the western part the island near the Menan Buttes. The geography

Courtesy Elaine Poole, Menan, Idaho

Menan Flour Mill (undated) began operating in 1894. The mill burned down in 1901, but was rebuilt using rock quarried from the Menan Buttes. Today, the site is occupied by a house.

was created by the Snake River on the east, north and west sides, and the Dry Bed is on the south, which runs into the Snake River.[31]

A man named Alexander Stephens was able to speak the Indian language and heard many tales from an old Indian man, who told him of the time when there were large herds of buffalo roaming the country. That was years ago, but a big winter killed them all. There is a place called Buffalo Wallows, on the west end of the Island, where many buffalo heads and bones were found.

When the Utah & Northern Railroad started laying its tracks in 1878, a railroad grading contractor named John R. Poole was employed by the railroad. During the winter, he and his sons camped on the west bank of the river. After grading work was closed for the season, Poole sent his children back to Ogden to attend school.

During the winter, Poole, a Mormon, hunted deer which came down to the area for the lush blue grass. He became fond of the island and decided to bring his three wives and twenty-two children, but first had to build a suitable home for them. Because the winter of 1878-1879 was an unusually mild one,

Courtesy Elaine Poole, Menan, Idaho
Inside of the Menan LDS Church (1935). Along the back wall are choir chairs, and just below the rostrum is the organ.

Poole had his sons and other young men return to the camp in February to resume work. He told them of the country east of the river which he had explored and said he wanted to locate there. Poole went by train to Ogden and reported his purpose to leaders of the LDS Church, which met with approval. Approximately twenty settlers located on what was known as the Island during that year. They got their supplies, equipment, and stock together and came to Menan on July 2, 1879. During the summer of 1879 Poole continued to work for the railroad.

In June, Poole moved one of his wives and her family to Idaho. They stayed at a railroad camp until completion of the cabins on the Island. In November he moved two more of his families and his stock to the Island. The Fisher family loaded their possessions into their wagon and started out north to find a new home in the vast wilderness of Idaho. They selected a place called Willow Creek and stayed through the winter. That fall they went out to the island and liked it so much they returned in the spring to stay permanently. Other families came to the Island between 1879-1880. Their stock was fed during the winter with the wild hay that grew in the region.

The winter of 1880 was so severe that in the spring, when a warm wind melted the snow, it almost flooded everything out. The H. S. Cattle Company had turned several hundred head of its cattle loose during the winter, and spring found most of the water holes full of dead cattle. The following year brought another bad winter and the farmland that was planted with wheat froze, but the setters were able to save their oats.

John Poole purchased a self-binder in the 1880s and brought it into the Snake River Valley. He also bought a threshing machine, and some of the young men of the settlement went to the Cache Valley, Utah, to engage in threshing. The money they earned fed their families. Through John Pool's efforts and influence, an entire section of fertile land on the island was reserved for townsite purposes. Under his leadership the town was surveyed in 1883. When the settlers started to come to the Island, it was called Poole's Island.

The same year, Robert Tarter had a ranch on the banks of the North Fork of the Snake River, that became a stopping place for people using this route to and from a train station located at Market Lake. A band of rustlers also stopped by from time to time, and it was found out later that Tarter was one of its members.

By 1884, one of the settlers had planted fifty apple trees and thirty plum trees, but because of frost they took a long time to bear fruit. Other families began to clear their ground of willows and sagebrush that were so dense it was difficult to see the neighbors' homes. They had the foresight to plow furrows around their entire farms so when they burned the sagebrush it would not spread to the timber or their homes. Early settlers of Menan spent long, tedious hours of hard labor clearing the land of sagebrush and willows to raise crops and build their homes.

The Utah & Northern Railroad was completed to Camas in 1880. It also carried the mail to Market Lake, and residents from Menan had to travel there to pick it up. When the post office was established in 1885, the mail was brought to Menan via the river and boated across.

It wasn't until 1886 that Menan got its first general store, followed by a grist mill a few years later. When Tom Caldwell built a ferry across the river by the Buttes, the settlers were able to cross the river with their grain. In 1881 a branch of the Mormon Church was organized and the town was renamed Cedar Buttes. In the spring of 1891, work began on the Rock Church which was completed in 1899. The rock was taken from Menan Butte and brought across the Snake River in boats. When the river froze, a bridge was built across it in 1892 to make transportation of the rock easier. The flour mill began operating in 1894, but burned down in 1901. It was rebuilt with black rock quarried from the Menan Buttes. The mill was three stories high and powered by a waterwheel. John Poole died the day the mill opened.

Residents of Menan had to deal with huge mosquitoes. One of the settlers said the insects were so big they trampled the underbrush. Someone else said that in mosquito time he could swing a pint cup one around his head and fill it with mosquitoes every time. The women did their laundry before the sun came up to avoid the bugs. The insects nearly drove the animals wild.

Menan went through many name changes. First called Island, Heald's Island, and Poole's Island, it was renamed Cedar Buttes after a Mormon church was organized. When the post office was established, it was named Menan, which could mean "island," or "surrounded by water," or "many waters."

During a conversation with Mrs. Elaine Poole, she spoke about the difference in Menan today, "Things have changed. The train depot was taken away. Orchards have been cut down, and homes have been built in their place. Many go away from Menan to work."

MINIDOKA

Located in a place where only the sagebrush grew and the dust blew, the Oregon Short Line Railroad laid a siding here in 1884, which was the beginning of Minidoka. About the only thing here was a railway station, which was later followed by settlers who established a general store and hotel.[32]

Courtesy Minidoka County Historical Society
Minidoka (1904). Now a very small community, during the early 1900s, the town had more than 1,000 residents.

In 1875, the Sears family joined an emigrant train that was heading for Oregon. But they decided to stay at Minidoka, where they built the Sears Hotel. Some of the family members became sheepmen, other cattle ranchers. A stagecoach began its route in 1887 between Minidoka and Albion, and a ferry was later built.

When the mail run started, it was hazardous at times. Muddy roads caused hardship on the horses, and crossing the Snake River was dangerous for the ferry, especially during the winter because of the slush buildup. Occasionally, the mail had to be carried across by a cable. A dog named Carlo was used in extreme conditions because he was light enough to cross the river on thin ice with the mail.

The lava flows made the soil rich for agriculture, but because of very little rainfall and winds, the settlers had very short growing seasons. They didn't realize what obstacles they would be up against. Horrid dust storms permeated their homes and livestock feed was swept away by the wind. Hundreds of thousands of jack rabbits didn't help matters, and it was all but impossible to get rid of them. Many of the settlers were unable to beat the elements and sold their land.

The Minidoka and Southwestern Railroad tracks were laid from Minidoka to the town of Buhl, followed a year later by the construction of a roundhouse. In 1902, President Teddy Roosevelt signed the New Reclamation Act which opened the doors for irrigation. Two years later, work on the Minidoka Dam began, which brought prosperity to the town with an influx of people, some of them workers on the dam, and others to farm the land. The reclamation project brought the needed water to the farmers.

As work progressed, the *Rupert Record* wrote, "Thruout the land the name of Minidoka is known, but all do not know what wonderfull possibilities this country affords, . . . for there are here no fields of grain, no meadows, no orchards, no lawns, no trees to greet him; only vast stretches of sage brush. . . And the water is coming. . . Great construction crews, working on the canals, are strewn out all over the land, and every day marks the finishing of some part of the great canals. . . It is a land of promise, a land of sunshine, whose possibilites are almost unbounded. . . To the home seeker seeking a home; to the businessman hunting for a location; to the manufacturer looking for cheap power; to the capitalists desiring safe investments, we say come, here is the place for you, . . ."[33]

A construction worker's wife once wrote, "My father helped Grandfather Smith stretch the cable across the Snake River to start building the Minidoka Dam. Men shoveled the dirt in a wagon, then the wagons were pulled by a team of horses to the dam site. . . While at the dam we lived in tents walled up with boards. It was awful cold. It got as low a 40 degrees below. They burned sagebrush for fuel." A local newspaper wrote in 1905, "New people are coming so fast we'll soon have no other place for them then to stick 'em up against the wall. Where do they all come from?" It wasn't easy to build the dam. One of the men had the dangerous job of hanging from a suspension rope above the river so he could hand tools to the workers. The dam was completed in 1906 and the first water arrived to the land in 1907. It was not without its pitfalls. Some crops were lost over the years because of sporadic water delivery. Construction of the American Falls Dam proved more successful.[34]

By the 1940s, Minidoka lost its status as a railroad terminal when the branch lines went elsewhere. The 1950s brought construction of an underground aquifer which turned all the sagebrush land into farming areas.

E. P. Vining from Massachusetts was assigned to give station names for the Oregon Short Line in 1880 for sites west of American Falls. He used the Dakota dictionary when selecting Minidoka. A man named Stephen R. Riggs deciphered the word, which he said meant "fountain" or "spring of water." Minidoka was also thought to be a Shoshone word for "broad expanse," but new information came to light challenging the definition.

Professor Carrie Shomer, a Dakota Indian Language Instructor at the University of Minnesota, stated that the "mini" sound in Minnesota is the same word as in "Mini"doka, and that "doka" sounded like the Dakotas word "dokahum," meaning "without any," "gone," or "not there." So Minidoka would mean a "place with little or no water," which certainly makes more sense as this was a very dry, arid land. But there is the unanswered question of why the town got a Dakota name. It was theorized that either a Sioux scout or railroad worker might have named the site. Then there's the big question: how did anyone know a Sioux named the site in the first place?[35]

During World War II, Minidoka was selected by the federal government as a relocation area for Japanese-American families. Coming from Camp Harmony at Puyallup, Washington, almost 7,000 people were "housed" at the Minidoka Relocation Area until the war was over. Conditions were poor at best; families had to find scrap lumber to make their tables and shelves, and had only rough-hewn furniture. Only twenty-five percent of the soil was suitable for agriculture because of the extensive lava beds.[36] The "inmates" were required to have lights out at 10 p.m., and were restricted on their movements. Seems like the government treated these people much the same way they "honored" the Native Americans' treaties.

Nampa's Dewey Palace Hotel.

NAMPA

In the summer of 1883, the Oregon Short Line Railroad laid its tracks through the future southwest Idaho town, and later built a section house and pump station for its engines. Alexander Duffes filed a land claim that straddled the train tracks, then built his store and hotel. A townsite company was organized, which began promoting the little community, and within a year more than twenty-five homes had been built. The post office was established in 1887, with Duffes as postmaster. Until the town got a depot, he had to go to the train tracks and grab the mail sack as it was thrown off the train.

The Boise and Nampa Canal Company was established in 1887 for the purpose of bringing water to the Nampa area from the Boise River. One of the residents had trees brought in from Nebraska and watered them by hand until water was piped in. Agriculture began with the completion of canals and ditches.

By 1890, the town could boast a number of businesses: lumber yard, bank, church, and a school. But Nampa didn't really begin to expand until Colonel W. H. Dewey purchased part of the townsite and built the Dewey Palace Hotel in 1902, which became the focal point of Nampa. The Dewey Palace was so luxurious that travelers who had business in Boise came to Nampa just to stay at the hotel.

Dewey ended up in Nampa because he was angry with Boise businessmen. They had reneged on an agreement where they would provide him with a right of way and give him land so he could build a hotel. He had also planned to build a railroad to the mines at Silver City. Dewey vowed he would make cheatgrass grow in Boise's streets and moved his fortune to Nampa.[37]

A devastating fire burned down tmost of Nampa's business district on July 3, 1909. Its cause was premature fireworks. Unfortunately, the city was having its wooden water mains replaced at the time and had no water to fight the fire. A pumper had to be shipped by railroad from Boise to save the rest of the town. When the train arrived, there was a team of horses waiting at the tracks to grab the pumper and take it to the fire.

Nampa was named for a legendary Shoshoni Indian named Nampuh, which means "big foot." Local folklore says the Indian's foot measured about seventeen inches long and six inches wide. Some historians believe the word may mean "moccasin print." A Nez Perce woman said this story originated because one time the Shoshones stuffed extra-large moccasins and made huge footprints to scare the settlers to keep them away.[38]

PICABO

The Kilpatrick brothers made their living grading roadbeds for rails and train stations in the West, building more than 5,000 miles of track. They came to Picabo from Beatrice, Nebraska, in 1882 while building a railroad spur. In a letter from Bud Purdy he mentioned that William Kilpatrick (his grandfather) and his three brothers built the railroad for the Oregon Shortline in 1883.[39] It was at times difficult in areas because part of the track crossed the lava beds, and explosives had to be used.

They homesteaded three sections (640 acres each) at Picabo and proved up the land in 1889. Because they were so busy building railroad, they didn't actually live on the ranch but

Courtesy Leonard "Bud" Purdy, Picabo, Idaho
Picabo train depot (1917).

hired managers to run it for them. The town was platted by
Kilpatrick about 1900, who also built the first store. Later, the
depot and grain elevator were constructed, in addition to a feed
mill, water tower and lumber business.

In 1917, the land was subdivided and put up for sale by the
Picabo Land Company, with lots starting at $50 an acre.
Advertisements went out boasting that the value of the land
would double because of good water in the region. The
Kilpatricks got most of the land back when the Depression hit.

Kilpatrick Ranch crews cut ice from the pond, which the railroad used in its refrigeration cars. At one time, more than 5,000
tons of ice were shipped to Canada on the refrigerator cars.
Picabo was the site where Marlboro took photographs for their
cigarette ads, and it became "Marlboro Country." Starting out
with about 1,700 acres, today the ranch is comprised of about
12,000 acres, which surrounds the town.

Ernest Hemingway came to Picabo in the late 1930s for duck
hunting. Purdy once said, "Ernie was always getting everyone
charged up . . . It wasn't just getting the ducks. He just liked to
get out and walk and walk and hunt. The excitement of the
hunt." Hemingway once wrote a letter to his son, "You'll love it
here. . . Saw more big trout rising than have ever seen. . . We'll
fish it together next year. . ."[40]

Concerned with the environment, in 1982 the Purdys built more than twenty-five dams because of overflow from Copper Creek which caused flooding. When that didn't work, they brought in a number of beavers so they could build dams, which was successful. By 1985, the beavers had built more than fifty dams. Because of their environmental work, the Purdys received a National Riparian Award in 1991.[41]

Picabo is located on the plains, and although quite windy at times, it was still a fertile place to live. Picabo could mean "come in," or possibly from the Shoshone word "friend." The most popular definition is "shining water."

POCATELLO

The early history of Pocatello is centered around the Utah & Northern and Oregon Short Line Railroads. These lines were organized by the Union Pacific with the intent to operate a railroad from its main overland route through Southern Idaho to Oregon. The line reached this region in 1882. With the railroads came the settlers.

The town began with tents and box cars, and the main inhabitants were construction workers. A freight depot was built, and in 1883 the railroad established the Pacific Hotel. As more people moved to what was called Pocatello Junction, they began encroaching on more reservation land while the railroad looked the other way.

Until 1887, the only buildings in Pocatello were the hotel and a trading post. But the town grew when the railroad repair shops were brought in from Idaho Falls and hundreds of rail workers relocated their families to Pocatello, which was part of the Fort Hall Reservation. The *Pocatello Tribune* wrote in 1893, . . . over 100 freight cars per week have found their way to the shops for repairs during the last six weeks. This indicates a pretty heavy traffic."[42]

Because of the railroad, more businesses and homes were established. An Indian agent wrote to the Commissioner of Indian Affairs in 1885 that Pocatello had "grown into an important point of transfer of through freight and of storage of merchandise for distribution by dealers to local territory, east, west, and north of that point."[43]

In 1902, President Teddy Roosevelt signed a proclamation that opened the land for sale, the rush was on, and the settlers gobbled up most of the Indian land. The *Pocatello Tribune* described the event: "Pocatello is already for the great rush for reservation lands and mines at noon tomorrow . . . The race when it starts will be a mad one . . . Every horse in this city has been engaged for this rush and if some of the horses are not run to death it will be a matter of the greatest surprise to everyone."[44] The Bannock and Shoshone Indians were now crowded onto a smaller reservation. The town expanded when more industry arrived, which included bakeries, brick makers, and beverage manufacturers.

This town was a wild, wide-open place in its youth, with prostitutes and drifters, whiskey and fights. As one traveler said, Pocatello was a place with "all the activity, wickedness, and glaring freedom of an awakening metropolis."[45] It became a bit more quiet when a formal government was established.

Chief Pocatello was a leader of a band of Northern Shoshoni Indians who roamed southest Idaho and northern Utah. After resisting white encroachment for years Chief Pocatello agreed to move his people to the Fort Hall Reservation. He helped secure tribal consent for a railroad right of way across the reservation.[46] His name may be an obscure Shoshone word, Paughatello, which was thought to mean "he does not follow the road." Folklore has it that when Pocatello died, he was weighted down with his personal possessions and dropped into a spring which the Indians thought was bottomless. A number of his horses were also killed and thrown in after Pocatello. The spring disappeared when the American Falls Dam was built.

Pocatello is called the "U.S. Smile Capital." This came about when the city fathers passed an ordinance in 1948 that made it illegal not to smile in town. This law went into effect because of an unusually bad winter, and residents' spirits were at their lowest. In 1987, city staff discovered the ordinance which was still on the books. Community leaders organized Smile Days, an annual week-long event in September.

POTLATCH

Before this site became a company town, it was a campground for the Nez Perce Indians, who foraged for camas roots
and berries, and also held potlatches. Potlatch is similar to our
English word "convention." It was a ceremonial gathering of one
or more tribes that was held in the spring. Potlatches consisted
of horse racing, archery, and the Indians' artistry was displayed
in the form of beads and baskets. At the end of the potlatch,
gifts would be exchanged.[47]

Potlatch began in 1906 with the establishment of the first
lumber mill. The towns of Palouse, Washington, and Moscow,
Idaho, wanted the mill, but William Dreary, general manager,
selected Potlatch. When someone insisted on Moscow, Dreary
piped up and said, "Gintilmen, Moscow doesn't have enough
water to be baptizin' a bastard. The mill will be here."[48]

An architect from Spokane, Clarence White, was hired to
design homes for the workers. When he arrived at Potlatch, he
found that more than twenty-five homes had already been constructed along mud-filled streets. He was told by a company
official, "You had better bring a good pair of stout high rubbers
that will stick to your feet unless you want to stick fast in our
mud and stay here." [49] By 1906, there were enough homes built
to house about 1,500 people. Although company officials wanted their town to be a "family" town, many of the lumber companies attracted single men who went from camp to camp as work
was available. So bachelor quarters were also constructed. In
their haste to build all these houses, many of them were built
with green lumber, so as time went on, doors and windows had
to be reset, and gaps had to be plugged.

The company provided employees and their families with a
store, church, and school. It also had a hotel, hospital and jail.
No alcohol was allowed in town. The company also had a railroad built that linked with transcontinental lines. It was called
the Washington, Idaho & Montana Railroad, which started at
Palouse, Washington

Potlatch Lumber had purchased the Palouse sawmill, and
with the railroad beginning there, Palouse believed it was really going to boom. But by 1906, the company had pulled up

stakes and left Palouse high and dry. The *Palouse Republic* wrote, "After God had finished making the rattlesnake, the toad and the vampire he had some awful substance left from which he made the knocker,"[50] referring to Potlatch Lumber.

Potlatch lasted almost fifty years as a company town, but it is gone now. Its railroad did open up more remote areas for settlement. While college students were hired to survey the railroad's right of way, they named the stops Harvard, Princeton, Cornell, Vassar, etc. The *New Yorker* magazine made a list of these stops in its 1946 issue, with the headline: "Dept of Higher Education (Choo Choo Division)."[51]

SHOSHONE

This town began in 1882 when it was anticipated that the Union Pacific Railroad's short line would go from Ogden to Portland. General L. F. Cartee, along with other investors, formed the Shoshone Town Company and applied for a patent. In October 1882, the post office was established and called Naples. It was later changed to Shoshone, which was thought to mean "great spirit." The railroad line was completed in 1883.

Shoshone is located at the confluence of the Big and Little Wood rivers. The region was called Soggy Bottoms and Big Bog because the Little Wood River flooded in the spring. It was also called Kilpatrick's Camp and Junction City. The Kilpatrick brothers built a rail line to the Wood River Valley mines. It must have been really rough country, as shown by someone who wrote a poem about his arrival:

> . . . *Next morning I started out for Kilpatrick's camp*
> *And thought myself quite fortunate, like any other tramp,*
> *But When I struck the wretched spot, my hear was filled with woe,*
> *For it was a dirty, lousy camp – the worst in Idaho.*[52]

Because the town's occupants were mainly railroad men and miners, Shoshone was a pretty wild place. It was not unknown to have at least fifteen arrests every day. There was no jail building, so the violators were stuck in a hole in the ground.

Early Shoshone was one of the wildest towns in the west, and also boasted the widest main street (undated).

With no bars to hold the prisoners, guards stood by the hole with their rifles and had orders to shoot if they saw a head pop up.

Prostitution was legal until the 1950s, and the Hotel Shoshone was home to the town's last madam, "Whispering Ted," a nickname she got because she never spoke above a whisper. Rumor has it that the mayor's wife had prostitution abolished while he was out of town.

This place became a railhead for sheep when Frank Gooding brought in the first band of animals, and other sheep and cattle men followed. In 1886, the first load of sheep was transported to Chicago. The year 1889 brought a terrible snow storm, and with little fodder many of the livestock died. One of the ranchers had over 10,000 head of sheep, and when the storm was over, he was left with less than 1,500.[53]

Shoshone had flourished as a transportation center, but after the snow storm, the people realized they needed a good irrigation system in order to grow feed for their animals. In 1900, a Shoshone Indian named Ira Perrine came up with a plan to divert the water from the Snake River, and within ten years the Milner and Magic dams were in place. Shoshone was called the center of the "Best Dam Country," and became an agricultural community.

The town became the county seat, but lost it to Bellevue in 1890. The *Shoshone Journal* wrote in 1896, "Then comes Shoshone, the county seat of Lincoln County. The railroad division was there once, but the immence shop buildings are now deserted, and the good old boys won't break the windows. The division will return to Shoshone when the Pocatello reservation opens, when the Minnie Moore Mine at Bellevue is pumped out, when Hailey people don't want any county lines changed, when Boise barracks are moved. Still, there are men in Shoshone today who believe the division is coming back almost any day."[54]

In 1886, the first church services were held. About three years earlier, a Presbyterian minister named Reverend Renshaw tried to form a church, but didn't have any luck, so he left. It wasn't until 1902 that a church building was constructed. In the 1890s, the United Methodist Church was established. A donation of $75 was put into the building fund and the church was built between 1890 and 1903; no one is sure of the date.

This town is the land of lava rock and one of the few places in the world to have that distinction. An early explorer, Peter Skene Ogden, described his experience: "We had certainly a most hilly road this day, and I may safely add, without exaggeration, a most stoney one; stones as sharp as flints, and our tracks could be followed by the blood from the horses' feet, . . . A more wretched country was never seen."[55]

The Basques who lived here used the stone for building material. Their method is a lost art, and even today modern architects have not learned how to recreate load-bearing walls of lava rock.

While the owner of one of the hotels was drilling for water, he lost his tools at a depth of twenty feet. It was discovered there was a huge subterranean chamber under the town. It was thought to be bottomless because when a rock was thrown down, no sound ever came back. The hotel then used the cavern for its sewage, but nobody ever knew where the heck it went.

About fifteen miles north of town are the Shoshone Ice Caves, located in a section of a lava tube that was formed when Black Butte Crater erupted. It may have been the 1880s when the caves were discovered. A phenomenon of the cave forms ice by the natural refrigeration action of a delicate balance of moisture and airflow in the lava tube.[56] The town had a permanent ice source, and tradition has it that this was the only stop on the railroad between Denver and San Francisco where one could get an ice-cold beer.

Chapter three notes

[1] Federal Writers' Project, *The Idaho Encyclopedia*, The Caxton Printers, Ltd., 1983, p. 347.

[2] Bernice Pullen, letter to author, Feb. 6, 1999.

[3] Herb Ashlock, Herb, "North Fork Presbyterian Church for Indians Holds 75th Anniversary at Ahsahka Today," *Lewiston Morning Tribune*, July 26, 1959.

[4] "Indian Leader Lauds Hatchery," *The Spokesman-Review*, Aug. 24, 1969, p. 34.

[5] "Historic Soil From Ahsahka Camp of Lewis and Clark is Sent to Philadelphia for Memorial Tree," *Lewiston Morning Tribune*, n.d.

[6] Federal Writers' Project, *Idaho: A Guide in Word and Picture*. The Caxton Printers, Ltd., 1937, p. 279 (hereafter cited as WPA Idaho).

[7] Brief History of Arimo, Pocatello library files, n.d.

[8] Lalila Boone, *Idaho Place Names*, University of Idaho Press, 1988, p. 37

[9] Herma G. Albertson, History of Blackfoot and Vicinity, Univ. of ID term paper, 1923.

[10] Betty Derig, *Roadside History of Idaho*, Mountain Press Pub., 1996, p. 30.

[11] Ibid., p. 29.

[12] Lalila Boone, Op. cit., p. 84.

[13] Grace R. Pratt, "history of the beautiful cocolalla valley; part one," *Sandpoint News-Bulletin*, July 20, 1968.

[14] Bonner County Hist. Comm., *Beautiful Bonner: The History of Bonner County, Idaho*, Curtis Media Corporation, Texas, 1991, p. 24.

[15] Marcell Wanner and Julie Miller, comp., *Ingacom: A History of the Inkom Area*, Mike Boyce, Pub., 1989, pp. iii & 11.

[16] Gerald W. Olmsted, *Fielding's Lewis and Clark Trail*, Fielding Travel Books, NY, 1986, p. 217.

[17] Ibid., p. 218.

[18] Lillian Pethtel, letter to author, March, 2000.

[19] Floyd R. Barber and Dan W. Martin, *Idaho in the Pacific Northwest*, The Caxton Printers, Ltd., 1956, p. 120.

[20] Betty Derig, Op. cit., p. 284.

[21] Sister M. Alfreda Elsensohn, *Pioneer Days in Idaho County, Vol. 1*, The Idaho Corporation of Benedictine Sisters, Cottonwood, IR, 1978, p. 396.

[22] Ibid., p. 398.

[23] Cort Conley, *Idaho For the Curious*, Backeddy Books, 1982, p. 315.

[24] *The Settlement of the Kuna Region, 1900-1925*, Kuna Joint School District No. 3, The Caxton Printers, Ltd. 1983.

[25] Clay Morgan and Steve Mitchell. *Idaho unBound*. West Bound Books. Ketchum, ID. 1995, p. 204.

[26] WPA Idaho, Op. cit., p. 258.

[27] Ralph Friedman, *Tracking Down Oregon*, The Caxton Printers, Ltd., 1978, p. 284.

[28] William S. Greever, *Bonanza West: The Story of the Western Mining Rushes, 1848-1900*, University of Idaho Press, 1963, pp. 257-258.

[29] Cort Conley, Op. cit., p. 631.

[30] Associated Press, "Tribe's dream horse is on horizon," *The Mail Tribune* (Medford, OR), Aug. 6, 2000, p. 5B.

[31] Elaine Poole and Gwen Fellmore, Menan: 1879-1986; letters to the author, March & April, 1999.

[32] Minidoka County Hist. Soc., *A History of Minidoka County and Its People,* 1985., pp. 22-23.

[33] "Land of Sunshine, Land of Promise," *Rupert Record,* Sept. 28, 1905.

[34] Clay Morgan and Steve Mitchell, Op. cit., p. 70.

[35] Joan Falkner, DeMary Memorial Library, letter to author, March 11, 1999.

[36] Relocation Communities for Wartime Evacuees, Washington, D.C., War Relocation Authority, Sep. 1942, p. 9., Manuscripts 7 University Archives, UW Libraries, website: www.lib.washington.edu/exhibits/

[37] Cort Conley, Op. cit., p. 391.

[38] Betty Derig, Op. cit., p. 222.

[39] Bud Purdy, letter to author, Sept. 13, 2000.

[40] Paula Rock, "The Next Chapter," *Pacific Northwest,* Nov. 30, 1997, p. 31.

[41] Heather S. Thomas, "The Ultimate Enviro," *Range,* Winter 1992, p.42.

[42] Robert L. Wrigley, Jr., "The Early History of Pocatello, Idaho," *Pacific Northwest Quarterly,* Vol. 34, No. 4, Oct. 1943, p. 362.

[43] Ibid., p. 368.

[44] Ibid., p. 365.

[45] Betty Derig, Op. cit., p. 21.

[46] WPA Idaho, Op. cit., p. 154.

[47] Lalia Boone, Op. cit., p. 302.

[48] Betty Derig, Op. cit., p. 301.

[49] Keith C. Peterson, *Company Town: Potlatch, Idaho, and the Potlatch Lumber Company,* WA State Univ., 1987, p. 90

[50] Ibid., p. 104.

[51] Betty Derig, Op. cit., p. 302.

[52] Idaho State Hist. Soc., 18th Biennial Report, 1940, p. 72.

[53] Shoshone Historic Walking Tour, Gem Community Action Team.

[54] From *Shoshone Journal,* Dec. 4, 1896.

[55] Peter Skene Ogden, *Ogden's Snake Country Journals,* Hudson Bay Record Soc., 1971.

[56] WPA Idaho, Op. cit., p. 196.

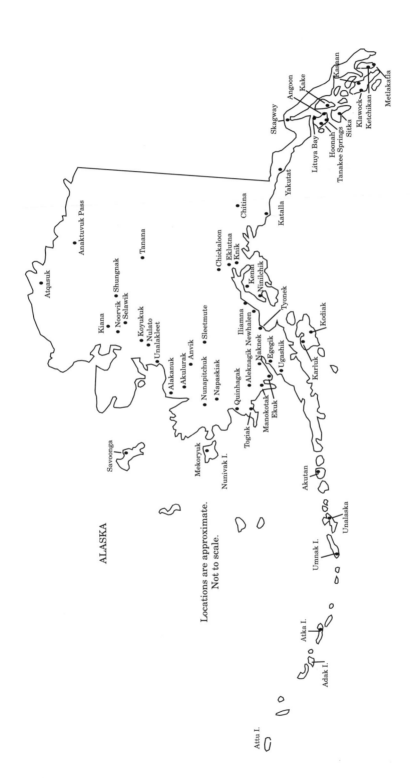

Chapter Four

ALASKA

ADAK

Adak is located on the Andreanof Islands in the Aleutian Chain and has been called the "birthplace of the winds." Because it is situated in the maritime climate zone, the weather is consistently overcast and quite windy, and it is not unknown to have 100 mile-per-hour winds when storms arise. The island is mainly tundra with no trees except for about thirty Sitka spruce that were transplanted from Kodiak in 1944, but they only stand about twelve feet high. Adak comes from the Aleut word adaq, which means "father."[1]

Adak was historically occupied by Aleuts. When the Russian ship *Sv. Pavel* arrived in the late 1700s, it was met by the Aleuts in their bidarkas (kayaks). The Russians began trade with the natives, but many of the Aleuts turned down the blankets and trinkets offered them; instead, they preferred to barter for knives and axes. Most of the villages were abandoned in the 1800s when the Russians moved their fur trade further east and the Aleut hunters followed them. However, they did return occasionally to hunt and fish until World War II. The U.S. military then moved in and restricted access to the island.[2]

In 1933, a Geodetic Survey group mapped the island for the prospect of using it as a U.S. military harbor. The only other facility available to the Navy at that time was Dutch Harbor in the Fox Islands, and when World War II started, Adak became a factor in American defense. Because the Japanese had taken possession of Kiska and Attu, it took too long for Navy planes to fly from Dutch Harbor and try to stop their movement. So on August 28, 1942, a commando unit checked out Atka and found it to be free of Japanese troops, whereupon U.S. forces came and took possession of the island, and it became an advance base for attacks against Kiska and Attu.[3]

After the war, Adak became a naval air station and was used for submarine surveillance during the Cold War. It was located on the northern part of the island near Sweeper Cove. The air station was decommissioned in 1997.

AKULURAK

This village's history revolves around the mission that was established in the 1890s. About all that's left is the cemetery. Akulurak is located southeast of Alakanuk near the Yukon River and means "in between."

In the 1890s, Jesuits were looking for a place to build a boarding school in Eskimo territory. They first attempted to establish one at Tununak, but were unsuccessful, and went to the village of Akulurak. In 1894, the sisters of St. Ann's (founded in 1850 at Quebec) went to Akulurak which was a rough trip. They had to take a barge on the Yukon River that was towed part of the way, then the Jesuits had to pole the rest of the way, which was hazardous because the river was full of sand bars. The sisters had another shock waiting for them. The house that was built for them was mostly windowless. The winds were so fierce it blew right through the house. The Eskimos fared much better because they lived in subterranean sod houses.[4]

The school officially opened on December 11, 1894, and was called the St. Joseph Mission. It was difficult for the sisters because of the difference in cultural customs. They insisted the children dress in mission clothes, and tried to dissuade them from wearing nose pendants and tattoos. Problems began when the local shamans did not want the children to attend school, and when spring came, the students did not return. There were still boarders from some of the other villages, and the sisters

Courtesy Sisters of St. Ann's, Victoria, B.C.
Old Akulurak (undated). The Sisters of St. Ann's opened a school in 1893.
After its demise, the children were sent to St. Mary's.

were able to teach them how to speak English, and read and write.

Food was scarce and vegetables were almost nonexistent. As a result, three of the sisters got scurvy. They had attempted agriculture, but because the land was tundra, dirt had to be transported in from Holy Cross. Long winters and early freeze-ups often prevented cultivation of gardens and at times the food had to be rationed.

By 1896, the mission had only a few boarders. There was talk of closing the mission and sending the sisters to Unalaska or Forty Mile. When the gold rush began in the Klondike, the Jesuits decided there was a need at Dawson, where massive numbers of prospectors were congregating and a typhoid epidemic was making inroads. It was announced that Akulurak would close down in summer of 1898.

The sisters were upset that Akulurak was being deserted in favor of Dawson. In the spring of 1898, the children were sent home. The mission was closed for seven years. In 1905, Father Joseph R. Crimont took over and asked the sisters to return. He was able to get the Ursaline Sisters, who reopened Akulurak, and the school continued to prosper for about thirty-five years.

By the 1940s, the permafrost had melted under the buildings because of the school's heaters, and the structures began to shift. On top of that, silt had built up at the mouth of the Yukon and it became almost impossible for a barge to deliver supplies. The buildings were finally torn down in 1949. The mission children were relocated to St. Mary's in the 1950s, which today is an Eskimo community that maintains a fishing and subsistence lifestyle.

AKUTAN

Akutan is located on the east coast of Akutan Island, about thirty-five miles east of Unalaska. The name could mean "I made a mistake," or "behind the salmonberry bushes." Nearly treeless, the island does have willows and berry bushes in certain areas. The land is mountainous and mainly tundra with lichens and other types of vascular plants.

In 1878, the Western Fur & Trading Company built a trading post and fur storage facility. Hugh McGlashan, one of the company's agents, assisted in establishing a commercial cod fishing and processing business which brought residents from nearby villages to the area. The same year a school and Russian Orthodox church were built.[5]

The Aleuts had been whaling here long before any white man arrived, and it wasn't until about 1849 that the Russians ventured into the business. Later, Norwegian entrepreneurs invested in a whaling endeavor, along with some American capital. Because the Norwegians were known for decimating whales in the Atlantic, the Americans didn't want anyone to know they invested money in the business, and gave the whaling outfit an American name, the Alaska Whaling Company, formed in the early 1900s.

Hunting activity began with two whaling boats. However, there were no profits because Novarupta Volcano erupted across the Shelikoff Strait on the Aleutian Peninsula in 1912 and destroyed much of the whales' feeding ground. In addition, the equipment that was shipped in (slicers, steamers and collection systems) cost the company much more than expected, further depleting its profits. As a result, the station was sold to North Pacific Sea Products in 1913.

By 1939, the whaling plant closed down and it was then leased to the U.S. Navy, which turned it into a refueling station for the Russians. This station gave relief to Dutch Harbor's limited facilities where the Russians fueled their vessels. It also kept them away from major American facilities and gun batteries during World War II. The Norwegians who had worked at the whaling plant returned to their homeland when the war began. U.S. Seabees were assigned to rebuild the station which was in bad disrepair because of the elements and poor maintenance. When the property was returned after the war, nothing was left of the structures because they had all burned down. In recent years, Trident Seafoods operated one of the largest processing plants just west of Akutan, and employed mainly transient fish-processing workers.

During World War II, Akutan residents were evacuated to Ketchikan by the federal government when the Japanese attacked the neighboring island of Unalaska. Many of the natives never returned.

A traditional Aleut village, commercial fishing is the base of Akutan's economy, and local residents are seasonally employed. They also subsist on hunting and fishing.

ALAKANUK

Alakanuk is located on a maze of waterways, and is a Yup'ik word that means "wrong way" or "mistaken village." The people who were looking for their summer camp would miss it and end up in one of a myriad of sloughs by mistake. Located about fifteen miles from the Bering Sea, Alakanuk is part of the Yukon Delta National Wildlife Refuge. The village differed from other communities in that it was spread out on both sides of the slough over a three-mile area.

This village was called Alerneq by the first man to settle here, an Eskimo shaman named Anguksuar. In 1899, the name was reported by the U.S. Geodetic Survey. It wasn't until 1946 that the community got a post office and was named Alakanuk, which was the English spelling of Alerneq. By 1959, Alakanuk's population decreased when a Catholic mission in the region was closed. The Bureau of Indian Affairs (BIA) had a school built this same year, but it closed because of its proximity to the spring floods. Trailers were then brought in by the BIA that served as a school, and in 1982 the State took over.

One of the Elders voiced his concerns about the welfare of the children. He wanted to make sure they got the proper education while still retaining their culture. He noted that "Through the years, I notice that more and more of the young adults are not willing to help the elders or family unless they are paid. It's saddening to see that . . . If the young people learn to respect the law of nature, man and the meaning of education, life would be better for everyone."[6]

The community met to talk about the problems they were facing with their children and the fact they were growing farther apart from their traditional values. Mike Hull, the principal of the Alakanuk School, wrote about how the people took matters into their own hands by taking on the responsibility of solving their own problems. As a result, the teachers integrated subsistence activities into the curriculum. In 1997, students from sixth through twelfth grade practiced subsistence activities at three different camps. These included hunting, fishing, and gathering berries. In 1999, the school was planning to hold a culture camp for the students so they could learn their traditional lifestyles. It was hoped that this new program would bridge the generation gap and bring better understanding.

The residents subsist on commercial fishing that is conducted between June and August. Many of them also belong to the Alakanuk Native Corporation, which owns a processing boat called the *Yup'ik Star*. A number of the shareholders are employed on the boat. No roads connect Alakanuk with any other village and transportation is by plane or boat.

ALEKNAGIK

Known as the Gateway to Wood-Tikchik State Park, this little village is located where the Wood River flows out of Lake Aleknagik, about 300 miles west of Anchorage. Aleknagik is defined as "wrong way home." While canoeing on the Nushagak River on their way home from fishing trips, the natives often encountered fog and got lost. They would be swept into the

Wood River with the tide, and end up at Lake Aleknagik instead of their village.

The 1918 flu epidemic wiped out many of the villages in the area, and the people who were left moved out of the region. They returned when a Seventh-Day Adventist colony was established on part of Lake Aleknagik that is known as Mosquito Point. In 1937, there were enough people living at the village that a post office was warranted, and it was established with Mabel Smith as the postmaster. Prior to this, the residents had to wait until each spring when the boat *Star* would bring the mail and other news from the outside world.[7] A territorial school was built three years later on the south shore of Aleknagik, bringing even more people into the area. In the early 1950s, the Adventist colony itself declined, but a Seventh-Day Adventist mission was built, in addition to the Moravian and Russian Orthodox churches, and the community's population further increased.

The territorial school that was built in 1940 went out of existence. In more recent years, the children were transported across the lake by a Hovercraft to go to another school. That proved too expensive to operate, and today the children are taken by bus to a school in the town of Dillingham. The normal mode of transportation is either boat or snow machines, depending on the seasons.

The state of Alaska built a twenty-three-mile gravel road that connected Aleknagik with Dillingham, which was only passable during the summer months and four-wheel-drive vehicles were necessary on portions of the trail. Many times it had to be closed after the rains because the road was impassable until the road was upgraded in the 1980s. When Lake Aleknagik freezes over during the winter, small trees are strung out and used as markers where the ice is safe to support snow machines and cars.

Aleknagik natives are involved in commercial fishing on Bristol Bay during the summer months. Some of the residents are engaged working at the Togiak herring fisheries, and the rest of the year they subsist on fish and game. Supplies are barged in to Aleknagik.

ANAKTUVUK PASS

This community is situated on the divide between the Anaktuvuk and John Rivers, and is the last remaining settlement of the semi-nomadic Nunamiuts (inland northern Inupiat Eskimo). For centuries, the natives depended on the caribou for their survival, but when the caribou population dropped drastically in the 1920s, many of the Nunamiut families moved to other areas. During the 1940s, they moved to Anaktuvuk Pass which was a caribou crossing, and means "the place of caribou droppings." The natives stayed here because of the meat supply and the willows that grew abundantly, providing them with fuel for heat. The people respected the caribou and took them only when necessary for food and clothing. Some of the natives walked to the coast to trade their caribou skins for seal oil.

Because there was no timber in the area, the residents lived in sod houses. Some of the people had plywood shipped in to build their homes, but they weren't sure if these structures would keep the families warm, especially because the winds could reach eighty to 100 miles per hour in the winter. The cost of shipping the wood was so expensive, the majority of the people continued to live in the sod homes.

The post office was established in 1950, and Anaktuvuk Pass was incorporated in 1959, allowing the residents to institute local laws to keep liquor from being sold there. A Presbyterian church was established in the early 1950s. Generations of Nunamiut passed down a legend that a deliverer called Ataanik would come to them when the tundra was littered with containers (fifty-gallon oil drums were left behind when the U.S. Navy explored the Brooks Range for oil). When a Presbyterian missionary named Reverend William Wartes arrived, the natives asked him, "What took you so long?"[8] At first the services were held outside until a church was built, and in the winter time, the minister preached inside sod huts.

During the 1966 election when the villagers were preparing to vote, Sam Wright asked the people their views about the election. One of the residents said, "Everyone wants to be elected. They say what they will do for the villages but it is just wind." Another spoke up and said, "No matter who I vote for nothing changes in Anaktuvuk, . . ." The village had no formal voting apparatus; the ballot box was a paper bag and the ballot stubs were inserted into an empty crayon box. Wright took with him the villagers philosophy: "Only in solitude, say the Eskimos, can a person find wisdom. Only in solitude can wisdom be found." They called it kaviashuktok, which means "time and place of joy in the present moment."[9]

Because of Anaktuvuk's isolation, today's economic and employment opportunities are scarce. The residents subsist on caribou hunting. Some of them make caribou skin masks and carvings for sale. Because there are no roads to the village, cargo is brought via "cat trains" from the Trans-Alaska's pipeline road during winter. It's interesting that at one time one of the natives said that until the white man told them, they didn't know that they were poor people.

ANGOON & KILLISNOO

Predominately a Tlingit native community, Angoon is located on the southwest side of Admiralty Island, and the only permanent village on the island. The natives who lived here were very powerful, and tolerated no invasion by other tribes. The Tlingits called the island Kootznahoo, which meant "fortress of the bears." The natives lived along the coast where the sea dominated their lives, and provided them with plentiful salmon and fur-bearing sea mammals. They did not, however, travel too far inland to hunt because of the bears that threatened them.

It's believed that the Tlingits settled here after tracking beaver and liked the area so well they stayed. Between the late 1700s and early 1800s, they established their village here and in the Killisnoo area because of better fishing and hunting, and the climate was mild. It is known that Russian trappers, traders, and explorers were also here during this time. With the development of the fishing industry, many natives left Angoon and went to Killisnoo.[10]

The Northwest Trading Company built a trading post at the village of Killisnoo in 1878 in addition to a whaling station. This station didn't last long because the company couldn't find experienced people and there was no regular supply of whales. A few years later, the company built a reduction plant for rendering whale oil, which may have been the first such type of operation on the Pacific Coast. It was later changed to rendering herring oil. Fishermen made about a dollar a day for their hard work. Alaska Oil and Guano Company also established itself at Killisnoo, and began extracting oil from herring and converting the refuse into guano. Pacific Coast Steamship Company's fleet used Killisnoo as a regular port of call.[11]

This site was once a village just south of Angoon and had a post office, chapel and school. Killisnoo may be a corruption of Kootsnahoo (also spelled Kootznahoo). Tlingit natives thought the Island was shaped like a bear, and indeed there were many bears on the island.

During a whale hunt on one of Northwest's boats, a native Shaman was killed when his harpoon exploded. The natives demanded compensation in the form of 200 blankets, but the company refused. The natives then captured two local men and held them for ransom, again demanding the blankets. The hostages were released when the revenue cutter, *Corwin*, came to rescue the men.

Captain Merriman made some of the chiefs come aboard the cutter and wanted to know what happened. He then told them it was an accident, that they had no right to take the men, and demanded that the natives pay *him* 400 blankets for taking the men. Because the village was so poor, they could only find fifty blankets, and when they delivered them the captain threw the blankets overboard. He then told the natives they better leave their village because he was going to destroy it, which he did, bombing all the buildings and canoes. The federal government eventually compensated the natives in the 1970s, which amounted to approximately $90,000. Some think that the actual settlement came to only $6,000.[12]

Killisnoo prospered until about 1894 when it experienced a bad fishing season and the school was destroyed by fire. Many of the natives returned to Angoon. In 1928, another fire nearly destroyed Killisnoo and more villagers relocated to Angoon rather than rebuild their community.

Angoon residents are engaged in commercial fishing. In recent years, a shellfish farm was started with state and federal grants. Subsistence consists of occasional logging at Prince of Wales Island in addition to hunting. The village is accessible only by float plane because the residents refused to allow an airport built on the island. There is a monthly barge service out of Seattle.

ANVIK

Part of Anvik's history is centered around the Anvik Mission, which was established in 1887. But one of the tribal Elders said that Anvik has been here "since story beginning."[13] According to Hrdlika, the people at Anvik were the first Yukon natives seen by white men in 1834.[14]

Anvik is a small Athabaskan village situated on the Yukon River, just below the mouth of the Anvik River, approximately thirty-four miles from Holy Cross. In 1834, Russian explorer Andre Glazunov became the first white man to see these people. Following Glazunov, the village was visited by other explorers. When a Captain Raymond of the steamer *Yukon* passed Anvik in 1869, there was already a trading post in place.

The most significant event in the history of Anvik was the arrival of Reverends Octavious Parker and John W. Chapman, who were under commission of the Domestic and Foreign Missionary Society of the American Episcopal Church. The Church had been called upon by the captain of a government revenue cutter to send men to the "rescue and defense" of the native people. Chapman and Parker bought an old boat, then hired a steamboat to tow them upriver to Anvik. The natives thought the men were reincarnations of their deceased ancestors who had lost their way, because they believed that after death their souls went to the village of the dead located in the mountains.

Parker left the mission in 1889, and Chapman took over the task of learning their language with the help of a native named Isaac Fisher. Chapman also began to translate the legends and stories told to him by the natives. He then rendered into English the native language for school primers, and much of the scripture was translated so services could be held in the native tongue. During 1889, a small house and school were in place. When a sawmill was given to the village about 1902, Dr. Chapman asked that "anyone who could drive a nail and saw a board straight" to help out at the mission. A carpenter named

William Chase came from Paimute and stayed as mission carpenter for about fifty years. The post office was established in 1898, with Chapman as its first postmaster.

Unfortunately, the boarding school that was built to teach the children was closed in 1935. Because of funding problems and not enough manpower, the mission was forced to close it down. Chapman left Anvik in 1930 and his son ran the mission for the next eighteen years. When he left, the territory of Alaska took over. The mission was never again the center of activity, and now very little remains of it. What is left of the structures of the Christ Church Mission have been listed on the National Register of Historic Places.

The natives originally called this place Gitr'ingithchagg, which means "at the mouth of the long, skinny river." Conflicting stories arise as to the origin of the name Anvik. It might have come from a Siberian Yup'ik word meaning "that place where we come out." It has been perpetuated that the name came from ingalik, meaning "louse eggs" or "lousy." According to the Anvik Historical Society, this definition is incorrect, that ingalik was used as a derogatory term used for the upriver Indians by the Eskimo people.[15]

ATKA

Located on Atka Island in the Aleutian Chain within the Alaska Maritime National Wildlife Refuge, the Aleuts occupied the community of Atka for at least 2,000 years. Their main economy was trapping sea otters until the late 1800s, when the otter population was almost wiped out by the Russians. The origin of the name is unknown; it may have been derived from an Aleut word defined as either "atchu" or "atghka".[16]

In 1747, Atka became an important trading post for the Russians. It was also a safe harbor for vessels during storms in the rough Bering Sea and Pacific Ocean. The Russians enslaved some of the natives in 1787, took them to the Pribilof Islands, and forced them work at the fur seal harvest. Defenseless, the Aleuts were at the mercy of the Russians, who raped and murdered many of the people.[17]

A man named Harold Bowman established the Kanaga Ranch for the purpose of fox farming, and some of the natives were employed there. In one year, the ranch harvested over 2,500 fox pelts. The natives also went in with Bowman and became partners in a general store, and for a while it was an excellent source of income for the residents.

Then, in 1930, a schoolteacher became concerned about the welfare of the natives and complained to the Departments of agriculture and interior. She believed the natives were being mistreated, and that Bowman was mismanaging the natives' share in the store's business. She also thought one of their chief's was in on the deal. After a two-year investigation, the accusations were found to be true. Unfortunately, the bureaucracy could not file any charges because Bowman covered his tracks quite well. He also sold the natives a boat called the *Iskum*, for which they paid almost $50,000. Twenty-four hours later the boat sank when it hit a rock, and the helmsman just happened to be one of Bowman's men.

The naval air facility was based here, and used for fighter and bombing operations when the island of Kiska was under attack by the Japanese. In 1942, the federal government evacuated Atka and residents were sent to Ketchikan, as were the people from Akutan. To prevent advancement of the Japanese, U.S. forces burned Atka to the ground, including a church that housed many historic Russian treasures dating back almost 200 years. Villagers came back in 1944 and the U.S. Navy rebuilt the town for them. There were many natives from Attu who spent time in Japanese prison camps, and when those lucky enough to survive were released, they relocated to Atka after the government refused to allow them to return to their homeland. In recent years, there were only four Attu natives in Atka.

ATQASUK

Traditionally hunted and fished by the Inupiats, Atqasuk is situated next to the Meade River, approximately sixty miles southwest of Barrow on the North Slope. Atqasuk means "the place to dig the rock that burns," which referred to the coal located in the area. After World War II, the name was changed to Meade River, but reverted back to Atqasuk in the 1970s.

Bituminous coal was mined during World War II, freighted to Barrow, and used by the hospital, schools, and government.

When natural gas was developed in the Barrow region, the demand for coal diminished. Coal was used occasionally by the natives.

During the 1960s, many natives moved awa. About ten years later, some former residents who were living in Barrow returned, reestablished the village and called it Atqasuk.

The village has a health clinic that is available twenty-four hours a day for emergencies. Many years before any clinic or doctor came to the community, the people used their own home remedies, as one Elder stated, "The only sickness we have is from people who come from way far," speaking about the white man's diseases. If the person got sick, "you had to stay at home and rub seal oil all over your body."[18]

Subsistence for the natives includes fishing for a variety of seafood, walrus and whale, plus hunting of caribou. They also trap and sell furs to supplement their income. There is a village company called the Atqasuk Corporation that owns the grocery store. Year-round access is available only by plane. Snow machines, boats, and dog sleds are used for transportation. During the winter, freight is brought in from Barrow by "cat trains."

ATTU

Vitus Bering may have been the first white person to see Attu Island, but in 1741 it was officially discovered by a Russian Lieutenant named Alexei Chirikov, who named the place Saint Theodore. The Aleuts migrated to the Aleutians from Asia and have been here for at least 8,000 years. Of unknown meaning, Attu is an Aleut word. At the end of the Aleutian chain, Attu is encompassed by the Bering Sea and the Pacific Ocean. It's been called "the lonesomest spot this side of hell."[19]

The village of Attu was sheltered by Chichagof Harbor, and whalers and traders used it as a refuge in the 1800s during severe storms. Early Japanese were in the region too, as records show two of their vessels wrecked on Attu: one in September 1862, and another in 1871.[20]

The island was the scene of bitter fighting during World War II. Japanese invaded the island in June 1942 and captured the

Courtesy Chad McNeill, U.S. Coast Guard.

Attu (1999). Islands guarding Chicagof Inlet where the
Aleut village was located.

village of Attu. One of the residents was schoolteacher Charles Jones. He tried to radio for help as the enemy swarmed all over the village. Jones died after being shot by the Japanese, although they never admitted it and said he committed suicide. After rounding up all the inhabitants (which numbered about forty), the Japanese shipped them by freighter to concentration camps where many of them died, including Attu's Chief, Mike Hodikoff.[21]

America's leaders knew Japanese strength here would put the whole Aleutian Chain in danger. In May 1943, U.S. forces were sent to take control of Attu, and the invasion was led by General Albert Brown. It was a bloody

Courtesy Chad McNeill, U.S. Coast Guard.
Attu (1999). From World War II, a Japanese 105MM shell found near Attu Village.

encounter, but American troops prevailed. More than 500 Americans were killed, and the Japanese lost about 2,300 men.

A few years ago, writer Stewart O'Nan wrote a condensed 'history' of Attu: "First there was only sea and sky and wildlife. Next came Aleuts, and Russians, and Americans, and Japanese. And a horrifically bloody battle, and scientists, and birders. And, on rare occasion, tourists. And finally - very soon - there'll be only sea and sky and wildlife."[22]

CHICKALOON

About twenty-five miles from Palmer, in the Talkeetna Mountains, is the small community of Chickaloon. This village was called Nay'Dini'aa Na by the Ahtna Athabascans, which means "log that crosses over the flowing water." Chickaloon is derived from an Athabascan Indian named Chief Chiklu.

High-grade coal was discovered in the Talkeetna Mountains in 1899. Chickaloon was established in 1916 when the Alaska Railroad made the village its terminus of the Matanuska Branch, which was used in order to obtain the coal for its locomotives. In 1920, the Navy built a coal mining operation. The discovery of the ore brought in miners and settlers. The impact on the population was devastating, bringing disease and alcohol, and many of the natives perished. By the 1920s, the tailings runoff from the mines caused so much pollution in the Chickaloon River that most of the salmon died, which was the main food supply for the residents. It wasn't until recent years that the salmon made a comeback. The Navy's coal mine was shut down because the ore could not be mined economically.

During World War II, the coal was used for the ships that patrolled the Aleutian Islands. By the time the coal mines closed down after the war, there were very few natives left because of disease, and Chickaloon became a village of mostly non-native people.

Chickaloon natives refused to accept the Alaska Native Claims Settlement Act in 1971, stating that it was invalid and was without the people's consent. They believe most of Alaska was taken from the tribal governments, and the land was given to so-called native corporations created by the act. Chicaloon residents saw it as termination legislation.[23]

Employment for residents is mainly through local retail businesses and government offices. Chicaloon is located near a major highway, and supplies are brought in from Palmer or Anchorage. Chickaloon holds its annual Pow-Wow on Memorial Day weekend.

CHITINA

The tiny village of Chitina sits on the outside boundary of Wrangell-St. Elias National Park. It is surrounded by mountains, except for a gap on the southwest end where Spirit Mountain can be seen. The natives believed the mountain was a place where a great spirit dwelled. The name Chitina comes from two Indian words, chiti and na, meaning "copper river."

The Athabascan Indians are believed to have resided here for the past 5,000 years, and there are many archaeological sites in the area. Russians were never able to subdue the natives because whenever they pursued them, the natives just hid in the nearby mountains. But as occurred with so many villages, the population was eventually decimated by disease.

With copper easily available here, the natives became experts at tempering the ore, and using copper tools they hammered copper nuggets into plates and used them to barter with the Tlingits. The more plates a native had, the more he was worth. The only thing they did not use their copper tools for was hammering their fishing stakes on the river, but rather used stones. They believed that using copper would anger the river, and when they tried to cross it, they would drown.[24]

When high-grade copper was discovered by white men, Chitina became a supply center that outfitted railroad workers and miners headed for the Wrangell Range. The town was established about 1909 as the terminus of the Copper River & Northwestern Railway (CR&NW), which served the Kennecott Copper mines owned by the Guggenheim family. This railroad was called by skeptics the "Can't Run and Never Will," but it did. Employees of the railroad said it was built on snoose (snuff), overalls, whiskey and snowballs. When the workers were lagging behind, a man named Mike Heney put a case of whiskey at the end of the line and told the workers whoever got there first had dibs on the whiskey. It didn't take long for them

Courtesy Anchorage, Alaska Museum of History and Art
Chitina (1930s). The community is surrounded by mountains. Far to the south
of town (not shown) is Spirit Mountain.

to complete their work. Heney also brought in a carload of snuff
for the men.

Prospectors and homesteaders made a beeline here and the
town flourished with hotels, tinsmiths, bars, dance halls, and
general stores. Chitina was also an important station for passengers traveling by coach to the interior via the Richardson
Highway. By 1914, the railroad had enabled Chitina to become
a thriving community and many businesses were established

Today, there are about fifty residents who live on subsistence
activities all year. They receive extra income during the summer when Chitina receives an influx of tourists and fishermen.
There is little employment except for the general store, gas station, liquor store and bar.

EGEGIK

More than 300 miles southwest of Anchorage, Egegik is
located on the Alaska Peninsula. This is tundra country where
trees do not grow because of the high winds throughout the

year. Persistent sixty-seventy mph winds during winter are a common occurrence. The Yup'ik Eskimos and Athabascan Indians were the first people in the region more than 6,000 years ago, but the first contact with the natives wasn't until around 1818 when the Russians arrived.

Egegik began as a fishing camp in the 1870s, and the village was centered around a cannery and a Russian Orthodox church. Unfortunately, erosion caused undermining of the church's foundation and a number of graves at the church cemetery were unearthed, so another church was built farther inland. By 1895, the Alaska Packers Association had been established and was operating a salmon saltery and employed about thirty-five people, but only six of them were natives.

During a flu epidemic in 1919, many natives from villages across the river came to Egegik to isolate themselves from the devastating disease. Archaeologist and anthropologist Ales Hrdlicka wrote in his diary of the surrounding villages, ". . . The last of these, remembered by several, was depopulated by the flu in 1919. There were so many dead lying here-about at that time that they had to be gathered and burnt by Coast Guard Sailors."25

The name went through many transitions: Ugaguk, Egegak, Igagik and Egegik to name a few. Egegik means "neck" (from the word Igagik), probably pertaining to the location of the village on the Egegik River. Another possible origin comes from an Aleut word meaning "swift river,"26 because of the river flowing into Bristol Bay. This place was called Ugaguk according to a Russian map of 1861, and was apparently changed to Egegik in the early 1920s.

The housing environment in the 1960s was poor. Badly constructed wood houses, usually only two rooms for a family, were built so close together that if a fire broke out, the whole village would have gone up in smoke, especially since there was no firefighting equipment. Fresh fruit and vegetables were hard to obtain because they had to be transported from the village of Naknek, and the prices were quite prohibitive.

Roads weren't much better. An unpaved, dusty, unmaintained road meandered from town and ended up nowhere. The only other road was from the cannery to the small airstrip. When it rained, the roads became incredibly thick with mud.

Summer in Egegik is bedlam when the Sockeye salmon return to Bristol Bay. More than 1,000 boats arrive for the annual salmon run, and tempers run short. It is not unknown for guns to be pulled as the boats jockey for position to get a good fishing spot. Normally quiet during winter, only one store is open, and shopping by mail is the village's main source for merchandise.

EKLUTNA

More than 800 years ago, this region was home to many Athabascan Indians. Descendants of the Tanaina Tribe still live here. Eklutna is situated at the head of Knik Arm in the Cook Inlet, about twenty-five miles northeast of Anchorage. Eklutna is derived from the word eydlytnu, which means "by several objects river."[27]

This location was probably a winter camp for the natives until the 1800s when it became a permanent village. It was located near a number of Indian trails which were later used by prospectors when gold was discovered. During the Russian fur-trading days, Eklutna natives were used as go-betweens with the hostile Ahtna Indians. While the Alaska Railroad was being constructed from Seward to Fairbanks, a train depot and section houses were built at Eklutna.

St. Nicholas Church was established in the late 1800s. It was thought that the church was originally built near the village of Knik and physically moved here, but no one is really sure. In any case, Father Nicholas would send a notice to the village on his time of arrival, and services would be held in a canvas church that he carried with him. Father Nicholas also vaccinated the natives against smallpox[28]

In 1924, the Department of Interior had an orphan home built for the surviving children of the flu epidemic that hit in 1918. It was later turned into a boarding school called the Eklutna Industrial School, and run by the Bureau of Indian Affairs. The children were taught academics the first half of the day, and the rest of their time was spent learning industrial work. There was also a program for the blind children, where, in addition to regular studies, Braille was taught. During the summer when the salmon were running, the boys went fishing with their fathers, and the girls went berry-picking with their mothers for their winter food.

Eklutna is known for its vibrantly colorful spirit houses behind the old church, which may have originated in Asia. One of the Orthodox priests wrote in his diary in 1859, "They burn their dead because, as they say, the relatives are ashamed to leave the bodies as food for worms."[29] There was a mourning period of forty days before a spirit house was constructed; this was the time the spirit of the dead wandered over the earth. As soon as the person was buried, a blanket was placed over them as a sign of respect. The spirit house was placed over the grave and painted bright colors that may have been clan colors. Sometimes during the mourning period, food was put into the houses. Today there about eighty spirit houses at Eklutna.

EKUK

The farthest community south on Nughagak Bay, Ekuk means "the last village down," and was believed to have been an Eskimo village in prehistoric times. Located about seventeen miles south of Dillingham, the community is situated on a gravel spit that is two miles long.

The Russians visited this site in 1824 and 1828, and called the village at one time Ekouk and Seleniye Ikuk. When the Russians were preparing to navigate Nushagak Bay to a trading post at Aleksandrovsk (now called Nushagak), they hired the Ekuk natives as guides on their boats.

Before the North Alaska Salmon Company established a cannery here in 1903, many of the natives had moved to a Moravian mission north of Nushagak because the shore of Ekuk had severe erosion and was prone to constant flooding. Others moved upriver where hunting was better, and only came back to Ekuk during the fishing season. With the addition of more canneries across the bay, other Ekuk residents moved to these sites, leaving the village almost deserted. The people who stayed had their homes moved a considerable distance from the shoreline to keep them from flooding. In 1917, a Russian

Orthodox chapel called St. Nicholas was built, and is now on the National Register of Historic Places.

During the summer, Ekuk teems with cannery workers and fishermen. The Columbia Ward Fisheries employs about 200 workers. There is really not much in the village, no stores, health services or schools, and therefore it has no economic base. There are about three people who live year-round at Ekuk, and the only housing consists of bunkhouses for the cannery workers provided by the company. What is left of the native homes are substandard cabins.

A former watchman for the cannery (Peter Heyano) built Ekuk's airstrip in 1954. The gravel roads in the village were eventually built, but never maintained, so the beach is used as a road by the set netters between the cannery and Etolin Point, a distance of about fifteen miles. A barge brings in supplies.

HOONAH

Hoonah is located on Chichagof Island, and is the largest Tlingit settlement in the southeast, about forty miles west of Juneau. The first village was called Huna, meaning "place where the north wind doesn't blow." Occupied since prehistory times, legend tells the story of how the Huna Indians made their home here. They originally lived in the Glacier Bay/Icy Strait area, but moved because a glacier they called Sit-e-tee-gee was moving. It was believed that when a girl reached maturity she was considered ritually unclean, and confined to a hut in isolation for three months and occasionally up to one year. Only the girl's mother was permitted to come near her daughter. There were two girls who were secluded in this manner, but one of them left the hut in rebellion and called to the glacier to come down on the village. Tradition says when the glacier began moving in on them, natives left to find another location.

Seeking the ideal place to reestablish their village, the Hunas finally settled in what was first called Brown Bear Bay because of its many otters and abundant berries and creeks. They called this place Ku S'eil after a slave girl who was drowned by a tribe called the Chookaneidee. Hoonah was also known by many other names: Gaud'ah'kan, Hoonyah, and Kantukan, just to name a few. When the post office was established in 1901 in back of a store, it was named Hoonah, which means "village by the cliff." Another definition recorded was from the word hooniah, interpreted as "cold lake."[30]

The Hoonah natives excelled in seal and sea otter hunting, and had many profitable fur-trading years. In 1880, the first store was built by the Northwest Trading Company where the natives took their trade goods. Two years earlier, a missionary named S. Hall came to what was then called Koudekan, found the natives very receptive, and suggested Hoonah become one of its mission stations. By 1881, the Presbyterian Home Mission was built. Hall noted, "We next visited Kowdekan, the largest village of the Hoonya tribe. . . They are a simple hearted, primitive people. The women are comparatively unpolluted and the children numerous. . . We should make this one of our chain of mission stations among the Tlingit-speaking people." He added later, "We found the Hoonahs the most receptive of all the Alaskans; and this was the beginning of what has been one of the finest and largest of our Alaska missions."[31]

The populace seems to have fared better than some of the other villages in Alaska. The main economy is fishing and there is full-time employment through summer. Local employment is also provided by fish-packing companies, a cold storage, and a timber facility.

IGIUGIG

Igiugig is located about 350 miles southwest of Anchorage, and sits on the banks of the Kvichak River. The name means "like a throat that swallows the lake water." Another report says the name came from kigusig, a word for "volcano," and referred to the volcanoes in Katmai National Park. The Kiatagmuit Eskimos who lived in a village called Kaskanak originally used this site as a summer fishing camp, then settled here permanently in the early 1900s. In 1934, a post office was established and closed down twenty years later. Nearby Kukaklek Lake became a reindeer station where the natives herded them between Igiugig and the station. Place names are still left over from early days, such as Reindeer Bay and Reindeer Island.

Because of the Alaska Native Claims Settlement Act, Igiugig

was entitled to about 69,000 acres of land. The Igiugig Village Corporation runs a land use program that controls the number of hunting and fishing lodges allowed to use the corporation's land. Permits are only issued to responsible lodge owners who guide hunters and fishermen. It also dictates the care of the village's subsistence. It banned berry picking on the land because the plants were being destroyed by careless pickers.

Residents rely on subsistence fishing and hunting. Many of them travel to Naknek on Bristol Bay to fish for the red salmon during the summer months, and some of them work in the canneries.

ILIAMNA

Founded in 1800 by Athabascan Indians who came from the Cook Inlet area, old Iliamna was located near the mouth of the Iliamna River. It was relocated about forty miles from the first site and retained its original name, which means "big ice" or "big lake."

The village was an early Russian settlement. An Orthodox church was built, but it was used just a few times a year because the priests only visited occasionally. Although the church was not used often, its cemetery certainly was when many of the inhabitants died from smallpox and tuberculosis in the late 1800s.

A man named Alex Flyum may have been the first white settler in the area around 1892, and within a few years Iliamna had grown to three general stores.[32] In the early 1900s the post office was established with Fred J. Roehl, Sr. as its postmaster. The natives hunted seals and walrus and made their bidarkas covered with the animals' intestines. The vessels were so well constructed that if need be, they could travel distances up to 700 miles.

The 1900s brought prospectors to the area for gold, silver, and copper. The possibility of this potential created interest in building a railroad. A geological survey was conducted on behalf of a railroad to map a route from the head of Iliamna Bay, past old Iliamna to the Chulitna Valley and onto the Yukon. The Trans-Alaska Company tried to carry mail and passengers over this route, but the venture did not succeed.

Lake Iliamna was one of the most significant places for salmon spawning in the world, and the largest contributor to the Bristol Bay fishery. The lake is designated as the Trophy Fishing Region by the Alaska Department of Fish and Game, the only waters in Alaska to receive this distinction. Some of the largest rainbow trout in the world can be found here.

Residents subsist in fishing and hunting activities. The village is connected by one road to the community of Newhalen, and under construction is another road that will connect with the town of Nondalton. A barge delivers supplies by way of the Kvichak River.

KAKE

The early Kake Tribe of the Tlingits was known as one of the most aggressive and fiercest people. They lived at this place they called Klu-ou-klukwan ("the ancient village that never sleeps"[33]). They even terrorized Captain Vancouver during his explorations. Kake is situated along the Keku Strait on the northwest coast of Kupreanof Island, ninety-five air miles south of Juneau.

The important trade routes between the Kuiu and Kupreanof Islands were dictated by the Kakes. Periodic clashes occurred with other local tribes over fishing, hunting, and trading rights. In 1857, while visiting Puget Sound, some of the natives canoed down to Port Townsend and got into a peck of trouble, with the result that one of their chiefs was killed. The next year the Kakes canoed to Whitbys Island in Washington with revenge on their minds and beheaded a former U.S. Customs officer.

Problems erupted again in 1869 when two Sitka traders were murdered by the Kakes in retaliation after a Sitka sentry shot one of the Kake people, and started what was called the "Kake War." The commander of U.S. troops stationed in Sitka, General Jefferson Davis, ordered Kake homes destroyed for killing two white men, and three of the villages were torn apart when the *U.S.S. Saginaw* took vengeance against the natives. What the ship's men couldn't destroy with guns, they broke into pieces by hand. The natives escaped and went to live with other tribes after they barely survived that winter in hiding.

The Kakes returned to the present site in 1890 and rebuilt their village. It had a school, store, and a Society of Friends mission by 1891, followed in a few years with the opening of a post office. A new cannery was built near Kake in 1912, and the village bought it in the late 1940s. The addition of timber harvesting and processing also began during this time period.

Kake's economy is the seafood industry. Kake Tribal Corporation owns Ocean Fresh Seafoods and a cold storage, and there is periodic employment in logging and longshoring. Kake Tribal Logging and Timber is the third largest timber company in Alaska. There are more than 120 miles of logging roads, but none of them connect to any other village.

On January 6 of each year, the village celebrates a ceremony that began in 1912, called Kake Day. Tradition has villagers drive in a silver stake to shut out witchcraft, superstitions, and other dark things.

KARLUK

Karluk is located on the west coast of Kodiak Island. This village may have been occupied for more than 7,000 years, as many archaeological sites are located here. The Russians established a trading post in 1786, and the Orthodox chapel was built in 1888. The name may come from the native word kunakakhvak, the meaning of which is unknown.

The late 1700s were the beginning of salteries, canneries, and tanneries established at Karluk. In fact, the village had the largest salmon cannery in the world, employing more than 1,100 people at one time. Over 200,000 tins of salmon were canned—more than 3,000,000 fish each year. There were so many fish in the river the people could barely move their skiffs. Many of the workers were Chinese.

The Alaska Improvement Company built a cannery in 1888, but it closed for about a year after the loss at sea of its ship, the *Julia Ford*. On July 7, 1895, after loading 7,000 cases of salmon at Karluk Harbor and getting ready to sail to San Francisco, the *Raphael* got caught in a gale, was swept ashore, and destroyed. Then in 1907, the bark *Servie* went aground at a point near Karluk Harbor. Its cables had snapped during a gale and severe snowstorm. The ship gave up 40,000 cases of salmon to the sea and three men lost their lives. The bark *Merom* was driven ashore during a gale in October 1900 and was totally destroyed. More than 12,000 cases of salmon were lost and all but one of the crew members survived.[34]

There were two parts to Karluk because of a sandbar and spit that separated the town. The people called the place that had the trading store the "spit" and the rest of the village was called Old Karluk. In 1892, the post office was established, and the 1900's brought the Alaska Packers Association to Karluk, and even more canneries were built. [35]

Once a place of one of the greatest wealth of salmon, by the 1930s the area was so over-fished the canneries closed down. Then, due to a devastating storm in 1978, village officials decided to move the community to another site, which was upstream on the south side of a lagoon. With the help of HUD, houses were built at the new village.

The residents subsist on fishing and hunting. The village corporation owns shares in a cannery with the Larsen Bay and Old Harbor Corporations, but operations have been idle in recent years. There is no dock at Karluk, so barges bring in supplies twice a month from Kodiak, where they are lightered to shore.

KASAAN

This was once the territory of the Tlingits until the Haida Indians migrated here from Queen Charlotte Islands in British Columbia. They were formerly known as Kaigani, the name of their first village on Dall Island. When the Haida arrived at Prince of Wales Island, tradition says they selected the village of Kasaan because it was the only place that looked good. It was also thought that perhaps the Haidas came here because one of them murdered a chief, and the perpetrators and their families were removed from British Columbia. Kasaan is a Tlingit word that means "pretty (or beautiful) town." The natives built their houses about 700 hundred feet along the shore, with some of them immediately above high tide.[36]

About twelve miles from the village, copper was discovered and in 1892 the Copper Queen Mine opened. Kasaan's site was then abandoned and the people moved their community closer to the mine, but retained the original village's name. The copper played out after about four years. A general store, cannery, post office, and sawmill were established in the early 1900s, in addition to a salmon saltery. The cannery burned down three times, but the company kept rebuilding it, until it finally closed the doors in 1953.

Unemployment is high at Kasaan and most of the natives participate in subsistence, harvesting deer, fishing for salmon and crab, and trapping mink and marten. Access to Kasaan is by float plane or boat. There is a dock and small boat harbor. The community was trying to acquire funding in order to construct a breakwater, and a road to Thorne Bay is in the process of being constructed.

KATALLA

This community is located on Controller Bay, about fifty miles southeast of Cordova, and not much is left of it except ghosts of the oil industry. Katalla is an Indian word defined as "bay." In 1894, some oil was found but there was no development at this time. It wasn't until 1902 that the Alaska Development Company actually drilled for oil. Katalla then became a supply station in 1903 for the oil fields.

When the town was established, it was called Catalla when the post office opened, but the spelling was later changed to Katalla. Three railroads were built that connected to the town. One of them, the Copper River & Northwestern Railway, was going to extend its line to the Kennecott copper mines and the coal fields. But when a tremendous storm hit in the fall of 1907, the breakwater was destroyed. The railroad went to Cordova.

Within a period of about three years, Katalla went from a boom town of more than 5,000 people down to about eighty. This was a result of the government withdrawing the land from private enterprises and restricting mineral development. There was a small refinery that produced heating oil until 1933 when most of the plant burned down. In all, the Katalla oil field produced more than 150,000 barrels of oil. In 1920, when a new land leasing law was passed, Katalla again turned into a prosperous town. More than twenty oil wells were producing paraffin oil which was refined into kerosene.[37]

In 1885, the steamship *Haytian Republic* was seized when it was found she was carrying ammunition to Haiti. The boat was again apprehended in 1889 for smuggling opium. The government sold the ship, had it remodeled and refitted, and rechristened her *Portland*. On November 12, 1910, the steamer *Portland* was carrying supplies to Katalla when it ran into a heavy blizzard and struck an uncharted rock near the entrance to Controller Bay. It then ran onshore while all the crew escaped, and was left abandoned.

KENAI

Originally established as Fort Nicholas, Kenai is located on the west coast of Kenai Peninsula, on the boundary of the Kenai National Wildlife Refuge. The name comes from the Kenatize Indians who were the first people to settle here. Or it may be from 'Knaiakhotana,' derived by the Russians for an Athabascan word that meant "non-Eskimo people."

Before Kenai became a Russian settlement, it was a Dena'ina Athabascan village called Skitok ("where we slide down"). The Russians first arrived in 1741, and fifty years later they built Fort St. Nicholas, which was the second permanent village in Alaska. The Russian American Company became headquarters for the Cook Inlet Region which conducted fish and fur trading activities. The U.S. military also built a trading post here in 1869, but it was closed down a year later.

Most Alaskan villages were heavily influenced by the Russian Orthodox Church, but it wasn't until almost a hundred years after the first Russians arrived that the Holy Assumption Russian Orthodox Church was built at Kenai.

In 1868, the Alaska Commercial Company bought out the Russian American Company and continued conducting fur trading. Years later, the first cannery was established by the Northern Packing Company. It was followed by two more canneries, the last in 1912. Each spring the ships came to Kenai to be loaded with processed salmon packs.[38]

Oil was discovered near Kenai in 1957, and its population increased with more homesteaders. Then in 1965, oil was found offshore and the town became a service center for the oil drilling industry and land exploration for more oil resources. Since 1991, more oil and gas deposits have been found in the Inlet.

Many of the residents work in oil-related industries, in addition to the timber and agriculture sectors. Tourism is Kenai's largest resource.

KETCHIKAN

Scrunched between the mountains and sea with its distinct geographical character, Ketchikan began as a Tlingit fishing camp which the natives called Kitschk-him. White settlers were attracted to the area because of good fishing and timber resources. There may have been a salmon saltery here as early as 1883.

In 1885, Mike Martin was sent here by a Portland fishing interest to check out the potential for canneries. He purchased 160 acres of land at what is now Ketchikan's waterfront property. Martin then built a salmon saltery and trading post, which operated for about eight years.

The town was laid out in an unusual manner because of the lay of the land. Homes were clustered up on hillsides, similar to the architectural style of the Norwegians. The steep hillside went down to the water, and many buildings were strung out along the shoreline. The town sprouted up with the construction of canneries, sawmills, hotels, and homes. In 1886, the Tongass Packing Company built a cannery, but it burned down a year later. Dominated by more fish-processing plants, other support businesses were established. The canneries packed more than 5,000 cases of salmon the first year, and the industry grew with the establishment of about a dozen more canneries. Ketchikan later earned the name "Salmon Capital of the World" by processing more than 1.5 million cases of salmon a year. During the 1940s, the fisheries began to decline and by 1970, it had all but collapsed from over-fishing. However, the industry did recover.[39]

What really put Ketchikan on the map was the gold rush. Gold was discovered in the area about 1899 and Ketchikan became a mining and outfitting town. Copper was also found on Prince of Wales Island, and Ketchikan was a popular rendezvous for the prospectors.

The origin of the name Ketchikan is derived from a Tlingit word Kitschk-hin, which means a creek of the "thundering wings of an eagle." Another version ascribes the name to a Tlingit chief named Kats'kan. Yet another translation is "spread wings of a prostrate eagle," referring to the rocks that divide the waters midstream of Ketchikan Creek.[40]

Ketchikan has the largest collection of totem poles in the world, numbering approximately 113. They can be seen at Saxman Indian Village and Totem Bight State Park.

KIANA

Kiana was once a central village of the Kowagmiut Inupiat Eskimos. It became a supply depot and transfer point about 1909 for placer mining camps up on the Squirrel River. Located on the north bank of the Kobuk River and about fifty-five miles east of Selewik, Kiana means "a place where three rivers meet." When the gold rush began in the Kobuk Valley, it also brought many traders to the area, most of them coming for fur. The natives traded their pelts for metal knives, axes, and guns. The climate was pretty severe and made transportation difficult, so development of major mining was hindered until advanced mining techniques were established, and there was more widespread use of planes.

In the 1990s, students from Kiana interviewed residents about their culture. One of the Elders said that the village had moved long ago to its present site because the old one was too isolated. There was no school, but a church and store were located at the new village. The Elder told the story of Maniilaq who prophesied that a big ship would come from the air, and the warm countries would become cold. Maniilaq also said that many people would come from around the bend during the gold rush. When the first planes did arrive, they were called swallows, and the people were afraid of them. The Elder also spoke of the old days when people were starving because they couldn't find enough food. They learned from childhood that a person had to catch as much fish as possible, and put most of it away for the winter.[41]

Natives practice a subsistence lifestyle, hunting and fishing, and gathering berries. Some are employed with year-round jobs at the school, city office and the Maniilaq Association. A few are developing small businesses. Some excavation is carried out at the Red Dog Mine and provides occasional employment. In the late 1990s, the community was looking at developing tourism, mainly guided river tours to the Great Kobuk Sand Dunes. The Kobuk River is only navigable from the end of May until early October. Barges bring supplies only during summer, and some of the stores have their own boats that bring in the necessary goods.

KLAWOK

Seven miles north of Craig on Prince of Wales Island, this village was known by many names: Klawerak, Clevak, Klawak, and Tievak. Klawock was originally a Tlingit summer fishing camp named for a native man named Kloo-wah, which eventually evolved as Klawock.

In 1868, a salmon saltery and trading post were established by George Hamilton. He sold it ten years later to a San Francisco company, which built the first cannery in Alaska and also packed the first can of salmon in the state. In addition, the cannery operated a sawmill that produced up to 15,000 feed of lumber per day to make the boxes for packing salmon. [42]

Most of the employees were natives, and when labor moved around because of the work seasons, the cannery was given funding under the Wheeler Howard Act in order to keep operations going all year. The one stipulation for the grant was that no liquor be allowed in the town. About 1897, a red salmon hatchery was built and operated for about twenty years. Other canneries were built in the region, but they used mainly Chinese labor because they were more easily controlled. The employers didn't want to deal with the demand for wage increases or strikes by the natives which would cause a decrease in their packs.

The Alaska Timber Corporation built a sawmill here in 1971, and was followed by three more timber companies. The facilities were expanded to include a log sorting yard and a deep-water dock. A salmon hatchery was also established. The 1980s saw the demise of the last of the canneries, but in the early 1990s, Klawock was working on reopening the cannery and renovating its dock. In the meantime, logging supplements Klawock's economy, with the Klawock Timber Company one of the largest employers in the area. Commercial fishing is one of the village's main sources of income, but timber has taken more importance in recent years. The deep-draft dock at Klawock island is mainly used for loading lumber. Subsistence also includes hunting deer.

The Elizabeth Peratrovich Celebration is held in Klawock every February. It is sponsored by the Alaska Native Brotherhood and Sisterhood, of which Elizabeth was once the Grand President. In 1945, she spoke before the territorial Senate and lobbied for the passage of the Alaska Anti-Discrimination Act. Through her efforts, the bill was passed in February 16, 1945.

KNIK

Knik is situated about seventeen miles northeast of Anchorage on Cook Inlet on the Iditarod Trail that was developed during the gold rush between 1898 and 1916. Knik is a Tanaina Indian word meaning "fire." The fur trade and mining operations in the area caused old Knik to be founded when Russians began trade there before the purchase of Alaska by the United States. The Alaska Commercial Company (ACC) also came and bought out some of the Russian posts. After American occupation, the ACC established a trading post, known as Knik-Knik, on the east branch of Knik Arm. It was later called Old Knik after the new village was reestablished on the west bank.

A prospector named George Palmer came to the area in the 1890s, worked with the ACC and eventually owned his own trading post. It is believed he was partly responsible for moving ACC's trading post to the west side of Knik Arm. Because of the deeper channel on this side, it enabled larger vessels to come to the newly relocated post. Although this was an ideal location, when Lake George overflowed the water rushed down the Knik River and threatened the post. Eventually, ACC left and Palmer bought the business.

When the Klondike gold rush was in its heyday, Knik was a distribution center for the miners who came through on their way to the gold fields in the Talkeetna Mountains. A post office was then established, with George Palmer as its first postmaster. He also had a boat named *Lucy*, which carried supplies, furs, and gold dust back and forth between Knik and San Francisco. In the middle 1900s, Knik began to wane with the decline of the gold fields, and another town by the name of Anchorage began to grow. Many of the residents from Knik moved to Anchorage in 1915 when a railroad was being built.

Known as the "Mushing Center of the World" because many dog mushers live here, Knik is situated on the Ididarod Trail and is the Number 4 checkpoint for the Iditarod Sled Dog Race. It also houses the Sled Dog Mushers' Hall of Fame.

KODIAK ISLAND

The town of Kodiak is located on the tip of Kodiak Island. This site was known as 'Kikhtowik' from which the name is derived, and is an Eskimo word for "island." The name Kodiak was adopted in 1901 by the U.S. Board on Geographic Names because of its popular usage.

Colonization of the island began in the 1700s. Led by Stefhen Glotov, the Russians arrived in 1763 and mistook the resident Sugpiaq Eskimos for Aleuts. While the ship lay out in anchor, some of natives paddled out and tried to communicate with the men. The interpreter couldn't understand them because he only spoke Aleut. The Eskimos left, but returned later with a slave Aleut boy so they could talk to the ship's officers. The Russians told the natives they should pay homage to the Empress but they refused. Glotov tried to explain to them he wanted to be friends and conduct trade with them, which they did reluctantly. Glotov and his men spent the winter here, but the natives were too hostile and there was so little food that on May 24, 1763, the Russians left.

It wasn't until 1784 that the first white settlement was established. Grigorii Shelikov and his ambitious wife Natalia, along with more than 100 Russian men, came to a place called Three Saints Bay. In 1791, Alexander Baranov was sent to Three Saints Bay to run the company. When the settlement almost sank into the sea after an earthquake and tidal wave, Baranov moved the community to the present site of Kodiak and called it Pavlovsk.[43] In less than twenty years, the Russians had all but depleted the sea otter population. During their tenure here, the Russians subjected the people to undue hardships. The native women were held ransom while their husbands brought in pelts to pay for the women's return. With no more otter to be had, the Russians left the village and headed for Sitka. The white man also brought diseases to which the natives were not immune. All these activities had a devastating effect on the population, and by the late 1800s there were very few people left.

In April 1861, a Russian named Pavel Golovin, traveling around the world reporting on the state of affairs of the Russian American Company, stopped at Kodiak. In a letter he wrote to his loved ones, he stated, "Well, here we are, . . . we are now abiding on Kodiak Island, . . . The pure Aleuts are those who live on the islands . . . Formerly these were quite warlike people, who often fought among themselves with great ferocity. . . Russian promyshlenniks who came to the Aleutian Islands at first lived on friendly terms, . . . began to lord it over them as if they were in their own land. . . They stole the catch of furs from the Aleuts, insulted them, took their wives and daughters, and finally provoked the islanders beyond endurance. . ."[44]

The opening of a cannery at the Karluk Spit in 1882 sparked the development of commercial fishing. Kodiak was rebuilt economically when about a dozen canneries were established by the early 1900s, but the town suffered a setback when Novarupta Volcano erupted in 1912. Earthquakes preceded the eruption, and when the volcano blew, Mt. Katmai collapsed into the volcano, and many villages hundreds of miles away were completely buried in ash.

Good Friday, 1964, is a day Alaskans will never forget. On March 27, a massive earthquake rocked the south central area of Alaska. Kodiak Island didn't suffer much damage from the quake itself, but the series of tsunamis all but destroyed its waterfront and business district. The fishing fleet, canneries, and processing plant were demolished. The largest wave crested at thirty-five feet above mean low tide. There was more than $30 million worth of damage, but the infrastructure of Kodiak was rebuilt, and by 1968 the town was back on its feet, and ended up being the largest fishing port in the United States. Because of the Magnusson Act of 1976, which extended U.S. fishing rights 200 miles offshore and reduced competition, Kodiak was able to develop a groundfish processing industry.

KOYUKUK

With a population of about 130, Koyukuk is situated near the junction of the Koyukuk and Yukon Rivers, about 300 miles west of Fairbanks. This was originally a Koyukukhotana village. In 1838, a Russian trading post was established in the nearby village of Nulato. A year later, the dreaded smallpox hit the region and was only one of the many epidemics to visit the people. Koyukuk means "village under Meneelghaadze bluff." Meneelghaadze is defined as "something in the bluff," which may refer to clay.

A telegraph station was built at Koyukuk when the telegraph line was constructed along the Yukon River, then a trading post was opened in 1880 which served Koyukuk and the surrounding communities. The village became an outfitting and supply point for miners when the gold rush started. A few years later, the post office was established and operated until 1900. With an influx of miners, the Yukon River became quite a busy place, and at one time had more than forty-five steamboats plying the river.

Eventually, the gold prospectors left the area, but when galena was found, mining operations picked up again. In 1939, the first school was built which brought people to live permanently at Koyukuk. Because the village was located on a flood plain, many of the houses were built up, high off the ground.

Salmon was most important to the villagers. In recent years, the Alaska Cooperative Extension 4-H started a school program for students to learn about development of salmon. They raised the fish in incubators and recorded pertinent data. At the end of the project, the salmon had to be destroyed to keep them from damaging the wild salmon's genetic stock.

Residents today live a subsistence lifestyle. Unemployment is very high, because there are very few full-time jobs available. Supplies are delivered by barge in the summer. Winter trails are used by residents to visit other communities.

LITUYA BAY

One hundred miles west of Juneau, Lituya Bay, a Tlingit word meaning "lake within the point," is the place of gigantic waves. Ice-covered peaks tower over the narrow, T-shaped bay at about 12,000 feet. One peak that was called Mt. Fairweather by Captain Cook when he sailed here in 1778 rises about 15,000 feet. The bay was called L'tooa by the Russians, and then Frenchman's Bay by whalers.

In the 1740s, water that was dammed up in the glaciers around Mt. Crillon broke through the ice and swept down into the bay and out to the sea. This rush of water met the incoming surge, and was pushed back and forth, through the bay. Noticeable in later years was a new tree line that contrasted with the old, caused by the huge wave crests.

A Frenchman named Jean Francois de Galoup (Comte de La Perouse) led an expedition in 1786 looking for a northwest passage. In June he entered Lituya Bay and found a Tlingit village. The entrance to the bay was known by the Tlingits to be very dangerous. When attempting to map the waters, twenty-one surveyors got too close to the bay's mouth while taking soundings, their boat capsized, and they were swept away. Perouse put up a cross in their memory on a small island in the middle of the bay, which he named Cenotaph. The natives mourned Le Perouse's loss too because they also had some of their own people taken by the dangerous currents and waves.[45]

The Tlingits, who left in 1853, told of a legend about a giant wave that came and destroyed all traces of their village. They spoke of a giant monster called Kah Lituya that lived in a cave underneath the mouth of the bay and caused all the catastrophes. When strangers came near the entrance, the bears warned the monster by shaking the ground, which caused titanic waves.

After the Tlingits left the bay, it wasn't until 1917 that anyone attempted to settle there. A man named Jim Huscroft built his cabin and started a fox farm on Cenotaph Island on Lituya Bay. On October 27, 1936, a loud sound woke him, and the rumbling continued for about a half hour. Huscroft survived the 100-foot waves that crashed in on the island, but it destroyed his shed and most of his house. The waves were so powerful they cleaned the hillside down to bedrock.

In modern times, the waves still took their toll. In 1958, one of the largest waves was recorded. Bill and Vivian Swanson had their trawler, *Badger*, anchored inside the bay's entrance. An earthquake hit, dropping millions of tons of rock from 3,000 feet above into the inlet. When the rubble hit the bay the surge of water went across the bay and more than 1,700 feet up a hill. A wave picked up the Swansons' boat and lifted it so high the couple could look down more than eighty feet over the treetops. Their survival was a miracle. Because the boat did not sink right away, Bill and Vivian had a few minutes to get into their skiff, and they were later picked up.[46]

MANOKOTAK

Manokotak was an Eskimo village that didn't become a permanent settlement until the 1940s, when a number of other villages consolidated. The community is about twenty-five miles southwest of Dillingham, and situated on the east bank of the Igushik River that flows into Nushagak Bay. The natives originally wanted to establish their village near the mouth of Lake Amanka, but the river was too shallow and barges were unable to navigate to the site. Manokotak means "on the lap of" because the village sits on the 'lap' of Manokotak Mountain.

The majority of residents were pure-blooded Eskimos, and one of the Eskimo dialects was used exclusively for communication. English interpreters were used when the residents had to communicate with government officials. Although English was taught in school, the children spoke their native tongue otherwise.

As of 1966, the natives did not own the land and were considered squatters. The site was to have been surveyed and individual titles given, which would then make the residents eligible for home-building loans through various Federal agencies. Because the village didn't have a store, residents had to travel to Dillingham for their supplies. [47]

Modern times have brought three miles of road to the area. There are no docking facilities, and the barge that delivers supplies a few times a year simply pulls up on the beach. Today, snow machines and ATVs have replaced the dog sleds. Manokotak's economy base is fishing, and many of the fishermen participate in the Togiak herring and herring roe-on-kelp fisheries. During the salmon-fishing season, most of the residents live at the villages of Igushik or Ekuk. Other than fishing, subsistence comes from trapping and hunting caribou.

METLAKATLA

Situated on the west coast of Annette Island, Metlakatla is fifteen miles south of Ketchikan. The village was established when missionary William Duncan brought a group of Canadian Tsimshian Indians here from Queen Charlotte Island, which was called Old Metlakatla. The name means "saltwater channel passage."

Duncan was a Scottish lay preacher who thought he was going to India, but was instead sent to British Columbia in 1857. When he arrived, he found bodies laying on the beach that had been cut to pieces, the result of a fight between tribesmen the day before. Much to his dismay, he also found out they were cannibals, but Duncan was lucky and persevered. He went to live in one of the prosperous Indian villages, spent much of his time learning the Tsimshian language, and converted more than 1,000 Indians within twenty years. Bishop Ridley, newly appointed to the post in 1880, was sent to help Duncan with his ever-growing congregation. Because Duncan refused to use a standard Episcopalian ritual, it began a theological controversy with Bishop Ridley who did not understand the Indian traditions. They were not allowed intoxicants, and Duncan did not want them to partake of the ritual of drinking wine in the Sacrament of the Last Supper.[48]

With permission from the Anglican Church, Duncan and 400 of his converts migrated to Annette Island in 1887 and established their own community at a deserted Tlingit village. Duncan was a dynamic person who didn't let any grass grow under his feet. Once settled in New Metlakatla, he began platting the new town, laying out streets and lots for the natives, and had homes and a church built. About 1888, a sawmill and cannery were erected; the cannery didn't actually start producing until 1890 because funds had to be found to acquire the needed machinery. When Duncan got too old to take care of the village, the federal government took over the operation of the mill and cannery. Duncan died in Metlakatla in 1918. In recent years, Father Duncan's church was taken over by a charismatic group.

A large airfield was built on Annette Island during World War II. After the war, the Coast Guard built a search and rescue base that was in operation until 1976. The airfield was used by amphibious planes for a while, shuttling tourists back and forth from Ketchikan until 1973, when the Ketchikan Airport was built.

The natives turned down the Native Claims Settlement, so Metlakatla is the only federal reservation in Alaska for indigenous people, which makes them exempt from certain government laws and regulations.

Metlakatla is accessible by air and water, and scheduled float plane services shuttle to Ketchikan. The community commemorates Founder's day on August 7 of each year, celebrating the arrival of William Duncan and his converts.

NAKNEK

Yup'ik and Athabascan Indians settled here more than 6,000 years ago. Naknek is thought to be a Russian translation of the Eskimo word naugeik. It may come from a Yup'ik word that means "muddy." First noted by Capt. Lt. Vasiliev in 1821, the name was known as Kinuyak in 1880, and later changed by the Russian Navy to Naknek. Before the Alaska Purchase, Russians built a fort here, and other fur trappers also inhabited the area.

This community began in 1890 with the opening of the first cannery in the district operated by the Arctic Packing Company, which later sold it to the Alaska Packers Association. The Naknek Packing Company purchased a saltery owned by L. A. Pederson in 1894 and built its cannery a few miles from the village. By 1900, there were twelve canneries operating and many of the mechanics who worked on them came from Europe. Naknek grew up around the canneries that acquired the land due to the Homestead Act, and became a major center for commercial fishing and processing. Naknek was also the most important source for red canned salmon.[49]

As additional people came here, they found the land around the canneries was either already taken or unsuitable for their homes. As a result, they took squatters rights and built shelters on the Russian Orthodox Church's land. The church later divided its property into lots and sold them to the people who wished to own the land and build homes. This became the center of town where the post office was established in 1907.

Until World War II started, many of the canneries imported their workers, leaving the natives excluded from cash income from the salmon industry. The community of South Naknek developed when canneries were established across the Naknek River. This community's growth was gradual and somewhat haphazard with very poor housing. The homes were for the most part structurally unsound, and there were no community bonds such as a church or community center.

Naknek today is a major center for the Bristol Bay commercial sockeye salmon industry. With an average population of 575, Naknek's population jumps to more than 5,000 fishermen and cannery workers during the summer when the salmon are running.

NAPASKIAK

This Eskimo village is located on the east bank of the Kuskokwim River, about seven miles southeast of Bethel. Meaning "wood people," the word is derived from the word Napaskiagmute. The name was first reported by the U.S. Geodedic Survey in 1867. In Wendall Oswalt's book, he writes that Napaskiak was only a place name and had no meaning in Yuk.[50]

A Russian Orthodox Church was established in the 1800s. Moravian missionaries had come too, but they were unsuccessful, because the natives preferred the Orthodox church because their neighbors in Kwethluk embraced the religion. By 1906, all the residents had been baptized by the Orthodox priests. Services were first held in a ceremonial structure called a kashgee until the church was built in 1931.

There is no record of any Russian trading center here, but

some of the Elders recall one operated by a Russian at one time. In the early 1900s, Oscar Samuelson established a trading post and sold some of his personal supplies to the natives, and a few years later he moved the post across the river. Apparently, the natives liked Samuelson because he was a fair trader. When the people were low on funds, he extended credit to them and went out of his way to help them. Samuelson ran the post for about forty years, and then hired a Eskimo to manage the store. After Samuelson died, his daughter took over and fired the manager because they couldn't agree on the post's management.

The natives subsisted on hunting pelts. Traders would extend them credit, which covered any supplies the natives purchased for their hunting needs. When the pelts were delivered, the amount was deducted from, or added to, their credit. During the fall, the men would take their boats as far as Aniak to go moose hunting.

By the 1960s, modern man's problems besieged the residents. Many turned to alcohol, which was ordered by telegram from a liquor store in Anchorage. Disease was rampant, especially tuberculosis, which the people called "owk" disease, their word for blood. The Elders said that before the "gussuk" (white people) came they didn't have the illness. The Elders were also afraid to leave their village, because they believed that if they died away from their homes, the gussuks would throw their bodies away.[51]

Today, subsistence includes fishing and hunting. Some residents are employed by the school and some local businesses. Just west of the village is a 3,000 foot gravel airstrip and seaplane landing. During the summer months a barge delivers needed provisions.

NENANA

An Athabascan village at the base of Toghotthele Hill, Nenana is a crossroads community at the Nenana and Tanana Rivers, and situated along the George Banks Highway and Alaska Railroad tracks. It was first known as Tortella, the white man's interpretation of Toghotthele, defined as "mountain that parallels the river." The name was changed to

Nenana, derived from Nenashna, which means "a good place to camp between the rivers."

The Russian influence is evident in many of the Alaska villages, and Nenana is no exception. Before the Americans came in the 1870s, the Russians had already been here trading and bartering for furs with the natives. In 1902, a man named Jim Duke built a road house and trading post. Nenana became a busy river freighting station, supplying many of the interior areas that did not have access to a railroad or highways, and Duke supplied goods and lodging for the river's many travelers. St. Mark's Mission was built in 1905 by the Episcopal Church. The discovery of gold in Fairbanks further boosted Nenana's economy. Bill Cogwill arrived in Nenana about 1917, set up a clothing store, and outfitted the fur trappers and Russians who worked on the railroad. He later built a warehouse.

The town grew up around the construction of the northern division of the Alaska Railroad. In 1916, government surveyors came to Nenana and laid out the town. There was not much space for building as the level land was prone to flooding, but people came and bought lots anyway. The *Fairbanks Daily News-Miner* wrote that people were "buying lots in the jungle and covered with a foot of water for three and four hundred dollars."[52] Nenana became quite prosperous with a population of about 5,000 people, many of them railroad workers. After the railroad bridge was completed, the train depot was built in 1923, and President Harding came to Nenana and drove the golden spike on the bridge over the Tanana River. This railroad linked Nenana to Fairbanks and Seward. Nenana's population diminished when the rail workers left. It was further depleted when many of the men went off to war. Then there was too much flooding, utilities got too expensive for many of the residents, and the influenza hit. The town had to depend, in part, on being a hub for the barge traffic for its commerce.

What began in 1917 by surveyors for the Alaska Railroad became one of Alaska's best known events: The Nenana Ice Classic. Held every spring (April or May), only Alaskans may participate in the event. Thousands come to guess the exact time the ice will break up on the Nenana River for cash prizes. The Nenana Ice Building was constructed for this event and is connected by wire to a tripod anchored in the river's ice, which trips when the ice begins to break up.

Today, in addition to fishing for subsistence, residents work for a barge line, school district, and do some highway maintenance. The ice classic employs about 100 people. The largest employer is a barge line that supplies many of the villages with cargo and fuel on the Tanana and Yukon Rivers during the summer months.

NEWHALEN

This place was historically home to the Tanaina Indians. The community is situated on the north shore of Iliamna Lake, 320 miles southwest of Anchorage. The Yup'ik Eskimos were constantly fighting with the Tanainas and often went on raiding parties. After one raid, one of the Tanaina women was captured by the Eskimos who took her to the village of Naknek, where she was shabbily treated. When she was returned to her village, the Tanainas decided to make war on the Yup'iks. It wasn't until about three years later that the "great" battle occurred, but after the fight, both sides vowed never to make war with each other again.

Newhalen was established in the 1800s as a fishing village and takes its name from the Yup'ik word Noghelingamuit, which means "people of Noghelin." In turn, Noghelin is defined as "land of prosperity or abundance," and describes the wealth of caribou and fish at Lake Iliamna.

Today, Newhalen still retains its status as a fishing camp with a population of approximately 160 people, the majority of whom are Yup'ik Eskimos. They live a subsistence lifestyle and receive their main income from seasonal fishing and some tourism. A number of the residents travel to Bristol Bay for employment at the fisheries. Supplies are shipped in by barge by way of the Kvichak River and lightered to shore.

Until recently, there were no roads that connected Newhalen to any other community, except for a fifteen-mile gravel road that went to the airport. The 1990s brought the possibility of a road that would connect the communities of Iliamna and Nondalton, with a bridge crossing the Newhalen River.

Newhalen is noted for its great sports fishing and is

inundated with thousands of tourists and fisherman during the summer months. The village celebrates Village Carnival around the second week in February, and features dog races, Native crafts, and dances.

NINILCHIK

The community is about forty miles south of Kenai, on the west coast of Cook Inlet. Ninilchik means "peaceful settlement by a river." But according to a late Elder, the name originated from the Dena'ina word Niqnilchint, which he thought might mean "lodge is built place." It may have referred to the lodges the natives used while subsistence fishing and hunting. The Athabaskan Indians have historically conducted fur farming and fishing on the peninsula. [53]

Ninilchik was settled between 1830 and 1840 by Russian fur traders who had married native women. Some of the men could not afford to take their families back home and they would not leave their wives. They remained in Alaska after their retirement, or signed new contracts with their employers.

By 1880, the U.S. Census recorded fifty-three people living in Ninilchik. They subsisted on hunting, fur trapping, fishing, and gold panning. In 1896, a school was built. By the early 1900s, there were about 100 people living in Ninilchik. The post office was established about twenty-five years later and small canneries were built that employed many of the residents. In 1949, Berman Packing Company (later renamed Seward Fisheries) began canning operations.

The natives seldom left the village until the Sterling Highway was built. People came here to homestead after World War II, and when the highway was completed even more moved into the area. A road commission station was located on top of a hill above the village, and later the post office moved there from its location in a general store. In the 1950s, what was called a "coal road" that ran from the highway down to the beach was built by the residents so they could get coal for heating. Today, the users are campers and clam diggers, as the beaches in this area abound with large razor clams.

Today, residents subsist on commercial fishing, timber harvesting, and a bit of tourism. Most of the homes are used only seasonally. Because Ninilchik is near the Sterling Highway, the community has easy access to Anchorage and other towns.

Ninilchik celebrates its "Biggest Little Fair in Alaska," about the third week in August. Tourism is big in the spring, with thousands of people who come to dig razor clams during the minus tides.

NOORVIK

About 400 miles west of Fairbanks, "the place that is moved to" originated when a group of Kowagmiut Eskimo fisherman and hunters came from Deering about 1915. The party was led by Charles Replogle who was a missionary teacher. He negotiated with President Woodrow Wilson to acquire a reservation here, which consisted of 225 square miles. Replogle brought his group to Noorvik when the fishing became depleted in the Deering area due to mining hydraulic operations. He was also concerned with all the drinking and carrying on in Deering and wanted to get his people away from those less-than-desirable elements. The group originally settled at a place called Aksik, upriver from Noorvik, and later moved here because of better building sites.

Noorvik drew more people because of its wealth of game. A church was built in 1915 and the post office was established in 1937. At one time, a creative missionary installed a clock at Noorvik, which gave it the distinction of being the only village to have one. It was installed in order to teach the natives punctuality. Not long after, the clock stopped forever when someone apparently got angry about something, and belted it with a stick.

Noorvik was home to a native named Twok who had suffered a crippling accident when he was a teenager. Forced to live a different lifestyle, he began to draw. Well-known artist Rockwell Kent was in Alaska for a year during 1918, painting wilderness images. He said Twok's line drawings were unique and classified him as a ranking artist. Twok created his drawings on reindeer hides, and one of his works was on display at the Hotel Anchorage.[54]

During the winter months, the natives hunted for a living and the women spent their time making mukluks and parkas.

In the spring, they scattered to go muskrat hunting, and summer time was spent at the fish camps. Travel in the winter was
mainly by dog sled, and summer brought out rowboats and
motorboats.

After the commercial fishing season is over, the villagers
subsist by working seasonally at the Red Dog Mine, fire-fight-
ing, and go to the town of Kotzebue for employment. They also
hunt muskrat about three months out of the year. All transportation is by boat or plane, as there are no roads that link
Noorvik to any other community. Temperatures can be extreme
in the winter, and have been recorded as low as minus fifty-four
degrees.

NULATO

This name comes from an Athabascan word defined as "place
where the dog salmon come," referring to the Yukon River.
Located 220 miles east of Nome, Nulato was a traditional trading site between the Athabascans and Inupiat Eskimos who
came from the Kobuk area.

A Russian explorer named Malakof and his native guide
reached the Yukon via the Unalakleet River in 1837. A year
later, he went up the Yukon again and arrived at the present
site of Nulato, where he built a blockhouse and trading post.
Running low on provisions, Malakof traveled to St. Michael to
restock his supplies, and while he was away the natives came
and burned everything.

In the 1840s, Russian Navy Lieutenant Lavrentiy Zagoskin
presented a proposal for exploring the Alaskan interior. The
Russian American Company approved and Zagoskin's
expedition left on December 4, 1842. On January 15, 1843, they
arrived at Nulato after traveling through horrendous weather,
where they met Deryabin who was building a trading post.
Zagoskin's men pitched in and helped with the construction.
The expedition left on June 4, 1843, for more exploration. Just
before leaving the leader wrote in his journal, "We prayed to
God and took leave of our Nulato comrades."[55] He had no idea
that years later all the people would be wiped out.

The next commander of the post was another Russian who
was so cruel to the natives, they finally rebelled and murdered

everyone. Lieutenant John J. Bernard, part of a British party who came to the area searching for the lost Franklin Expedition, was also at the stockade and slain. His murder became an international incident, creating diplomatic tension between Russia and Great Britain. After the massacre, what few natives were left went into the Koyukuk Mountains. Eventually, they returned and reestablished their village about a mile from the original site.

In 1857, Western Union Telegraph Company came to explore the possibility of building an overland telegraph route from the United States to Asia and Europe. The massive project would have encompassed 6,000 miles, the majority of it through wilderness. Robert Kennicott, who was a scientist and explorer, was elected to explore the Yukon Basin and arrived at Nulato in 1865. Preparing to continue on to Fort Yukon, Kennicott died in May of 1866 due to overwork and exposure. Succeeding Kennicott was Doctor William Dall, who arrived six months later to take over the exploration. He believed that Kennicott was actually murdered by the Russians. When Dall returned to St. Michael, he learned that the Atlantic Cable had already been laid, and Western Union's telegraph project was abandoned. The Dall sheep of Alaska were named for William Dall.

Many people in Nulato are employed with the city, school and clinic. The Bureau of Land Management hires some natives during the summer for fire fighting. There is also fish processing and construction. Their mainstay though is trapping in the winter. The main mode of transportation is the river, and supplies are brought in by barge during the summer months.

NUNAPITCHUK

Twenty miles northwest of Bethel on a tributary of the Kuskokwim River on Johnson Slough sits the Yup'ik Eskimo village of Nunapitchuk. The land is mostly tundra with many lakes in the region. The name is a Yup'ik word, Nunapicuaq, meaning "small land."

The first people to settle at Nunapitchuk lived on the mushy tundra that was not really suitable for houses, but people kept moving in and building. They used this place more as a winter camp and went to the fish camps in the spring and summer months, bringing with them muskrat and other fur-bearing animals they had trapped during the winter for trade.[56]

Some of the first outside people were the Moravian missionaries and Russian Orthodox Church in the 1800s, who came to convert all the natives. Apparently, they succeeded because all the natives here today profess to be members of a church. During the hard years when food was scarce, the missionaries found some of the people starving. Their winter existence depended on fishing and hunting during the warmer months. Most of their food was dried or fermented. They also picked berries during the summer and stored them in barrels.[57]

Nunapitchuk began as a town in the 1920s when people from other villages came here to live after they survived the flu epidemic. The natives also came down with tuberculosis. Before any health services were available, there was only a nurse's aide who treated the sick as best she could. But most of the time, the people relied on their old ways. One of the remedies was to rub seal oil over one's body for a stomach ache. The nurse believed the people started getting sick because they were in permanent settlements and too close to one another. In the early days, the people migrated a lot and were more spread out.

There is no water piped to the homes because of freezing temperatures. Some do have storage tanks with pressure pumps, but the tanks have to be filled each day and the water must be hauled in from the local washateria. Today, residents subsistence by fishing, and there is occasional employment with city and local government.

NUNIVAK ISLAND & VILLAGE OF MEKORYUK

Inhabited for more than 2,000 years by the Nuniwarmiut people, or Cup'ik Eskimos, Nunivak means "big land." It is located in the Bering Sea, thirty miles offshore from the Kuskokwim and Yukon Rivers.[58] Radiocarbon-dated materials going back to 670 B.C. were recovered by Bureau of Indian Affairs (BIA) investigations. The island is treeless and shrouded in fog most of the time. Plant life consists of grasses, lichens, shrubs and sedge.

The first outside contact was a Russian named Vasilief in 1821, and a man named Etolin with the Russian American

Company followed the same year. But with the arrival of the white man, disease decimated the population in 1900, and left only four native survivors.[59]

Reindeer were imported to the island in the 1920s by an Eskimo-Russian trader. The BIA bought the operation and had a slaughterhouse constructed. These reindeer were later crossed with caribou, and as a result they were much larger and harder to handle. Thirty-four musk ox from Greenland were transferred to the island in 1934 to save the species from extinction, and were under the care of a local trader named Paul Ivanof. The last musk ox in Alaska was killed in Barrow in 1865. Today, they number more than 500. Their calves have been relocated to be used as breeding stock and establish herds in other areas of Alaska.

The Evangelical Covenant Church was built in the 1930s by an Eskimo missionary named Jacob Kenick. This church was established in the village of Mekoryuk, the only community on the island. It was followed by a BIA school, which brought people from other areas to the island.

The people of Mekoryuk live mostly off the land and the sea. Some are employed at seasonal fish camps on the island. They subsist on walrus, birds, and arctic fox, and participate in the reindeer roundups each July. The women carve ivory and knit the underwool from the musk ox to make lacy garments for sale. One of the major employers is the Bering Sea Reindeer Products Company.

The natives depend on boat or plane for transport and mail delivery. Barges from Bethel come to the island once or twice each summer to deliver supplies.

NUSHAGAK

Nushagak Bay is a former Eskimo village that was established as a trading post in 1819. Under orders of the Russian American Company, explorers came this way to find a lost race of Russians. It was believed that these people were descendants of survivors on an expedition in 1648 near Chukotsk Peninsula in Asia. In 1818, explorers arrived at this site and called it Redoubt Alexander. Russian Orthodox missionaries arrived about ten years later. Baron Ferdinand von Wrangell ordered a chapel constructed at Nushagak in 1832, but it wasn't until 1845 that it was actually built.

The Russian company decided move its operations to the Kuskokwim Valley, and by 1846 Nushagak was relegated to a trail house. The natives called this region Tahlekuk, which means "elbow," and referred to the bend in the river. [60]

Nushagak had salteries, canneries and cold storage facilities, and was a busy place until the United States purchased Alaska. The natives brought their pelts to the fort and exchanged them for blankets, where the rate was one blanket for four beaver pelts. The village was first called Fort Alexander, then changed to Nushagak when the post office was established in 1899. The homes were built in rows, one behind another on a terraced hill, connected by staircases. These stairs could be quite dangerous at times because they were very slippery when the fog came in.

In 1899, the Pacific Steam Whaling Company established a cannery on the shore of Nushagak Bay. A few years later it was sold to the Pacific Packing & Navigation Company, then sold again. Pacific American Fisheries was the final purchaser of the cannery, but never opened it. The area began to decline when other commercial fishing companies established themselves on the other side of the bay, and a larger community was developing that would be named Dillingham. In 1918-1919, hundreds of natives died when the influenza epidemic hit. Today, not much is left of the village.

QUINHAGAK

Quinhagak is located on the east shore of Kuskokwim Bay, seventy miles southwest of Bethel. It is a long-established village that dates back to 1,000 A.D., and is one of the largest communities in the area.

The Yup'ik name for this village is Kuinerraq, which means "new river channel." It was a semi-permanent winter settlement; the people went to different locations with the changing seasons to hunt seal, fish for salmon, and pick berries. Quinhagak was also the first village in the lower Kuskokwim that had sustained contact with the white man. A Russian named Gavril Sarichev reported the village on a map of 1826.[61]

After the purchase of Alaska by the United States, the Alaska Commercial Company supplied the Kuskokwim River trading post with merchandise, which was lightered to a warehouse a short distance from the village. The goods were then transported to the village by small boats. When the Kuskokwim was charted in 1915, the ships no longer stopped here, but went directly to Bethel.

With the intent of exploring the delta, Moravian missionaries came to the region in 1884 and built a mission about nine years later. In 1902, some businessmen came to Quinhagak and looked into the possibility of building a salmon cannery. The post office opened in 1905. Because there were no sidewalks, boards were laid out to provide access to buildings. The same year, about 1,600 reindeer were imported to Bethel for grazing during the summer. Three years later, 600 were sent here to graze on the tundra. In 1929, the Kuskokwim Reindeer Company branded more than 6,000 reindeer, but years later, most of the herds had scattered to other areas.

Quinhagak saw an upswing in its economy at the start of the gold rush with the influx of miners, then declined again when the gold deposits ran out. The natives relied on fur trapping for their livelihood. When World War I started, the demand for furs dropped and so did the residents' earnings. Some income was generated when a trail was cut between Bethel, Quinhagak, and Goodnews Bay and local residents were hired to build shelters and bridges along the trail as it was being graded.

Employment here is seasonal fishing. Subsistence includes hunting for seal; the natives prefer the bearded seal. Barges deliver freight a couple of times a year, and bring in supplies for the school.

Constant changing river patterns are a problem to the village because of erosion. Waves from storms undermine the slope, and melting of the underlying permafrost contributes to the erosion. Problems with sports fishermen prompted the residents to expand their jurisdiction over the more than 5,000 outsiders who use the Kanektok River.

SAVOONGA

Savoonga is called the "Walrus Capital of the World," and is located on St. Lawrence Island in the Bering Sea. Alaskan and Siberian Yup'ik Eskimos were the main inhabitants, but between 1878 and 1880 the population was severely reduced because of starvation. The origin of the area's name is unknown.

Famine came to the natives when traders who arrived in 1878, traded seal and walrus skins for liquor. Instead of hunting and fishing, the inhabitants spent their time drinking. By the time winter arrived, there was no food left. Each spring a revenue cutter would visit St. Lawrence Island. One spring, when the cutter arrived at Savoonga, all the natives were dead.

Seventy head of reindeer were imported to the island by the federal government in 1891. To better manage the growing herds, and because of better grazing lands, Savoonga was established as a reindeer herding station in 1916. By the following year, there were more than 10,000 animals. Savoonga was a place of good hunting, in addition to the reindeer, and drew many people from the community of Gambell.

Whalers visited the island from time to time and traded with the inhabitants. One time they traded cotton cloth, and the women made parka covers from the cloth. They had no thread and used sinew for stitching. Because the missionaries made the natives wash their clothes once a week, they were told to wash the parkas. In those days, clothes were washed by tossing them into boiling water until they were clean. Unfortunately, the missionaries didn't know that sinew melted in hot water. The parkas were taken out piece by piece and had to be sewn back together using cotton thread.

Archaeologist Ales Hrdlika visited Savoonga about 1928 during his travels through Alaska collecting artifacts. Calling it "Savonga," Hrdlika spent much of his time ministering to the natives, which for the most part entailed pulling teeth. He also collected some artifacts, as he wrote, ". . . find and purchase cheaply many smaller objects of fossil ivory, which they excavate from the 4 miles distant old site."[62]

Savoonga is pretty isolated and has no boat dock. Residents did not have plumbing in their homes until early 1999. In addition to subsistence fishing, the natives trap fox for extra income. The community is heavily dependent on air travel during the winter because it is so isolated, has no seaport, and experiences iced-in conditions. All supplies have to be lightered in from Kotzebue and then offloaded onto the beach.

This village becomes a busy place when the annual Savoonga Walrus Festival is celebrated each May. Tourists flock in, but pay a hefty fee to tour the island and watch the walrus herds.

SELEWIK

This community has a population of more than 700 people and is located at the mouth of the Selewik River, seventy miles southeast of Kotzebue. When Lieutenant Zagosin of the Russian Navy visited in the early 1800s, he noted the name as "Chilivik." The 1880 census called the people Selawigamutes. The name Selewik refers to a fish, the species of which is unknown. It was thought that a member of the Franklin Expedition gave the village its name.

Selewik was once the center of fox and mink raising. Sod houses were built on both sides of the Selewik River, so there was a lot of rowing back and forth. A federal school and Friends mission were built in 1908. Students often had to spend the night at the school because the area was prone to severe blizzards. It was not uncommon to have minus sixty-degree temperatures. At times, there was so much snow it almost covered the houses, and the only way the neighbors were able to find them was from the black stovepipes that stuck up in the air. The natives also had to dig ditches around their property to keep the spring snow runoff from flooding their homes.[63]

The extreme was in summer when temperatures went over 85 degrees. It got so hot that most of the families had cook stoves outside the home. Mosquitoes were horrible pests, and one of the residents stated that occasionally their dogs died from loss of blood because the mosquitoes were so thick. Poor housing did not help their situation, because most of the homes had only one room for an entire family.

In the spring, the villagers headed for the fish camps using log rafts on which they pitched tents, living on them as they went from camp to camp. The natives also hunted muskrat and their pelts were used to pay off the debts they had incurred during the winter.

Today, residents subsist on fishing and berry picking. The school, city and a grocery store provide some employment. Some of the villagers do beadwork and other handicrafts they sell to the gift shops in the larger cities. Selewick can be reached by barge or plane. In recent years, boardwalks have been constructed throughout the village.

SHUNGNAK

Shungnak was originally founded in 1899 as a supply station for mining activities in the Cosmos Hills. When the Kobuk River began to erode the village because of annual flooding, it was moved ten miles downstream and called Kochuk before being changed to Shungnak. Jade was mined and cut at the Shungnak River and Dahl Creek. Shungnak is derived from the Eskimo word Isinnag, which means "jade." The village is located 300 miles west of Fairbanks and situated on a bluff overlooking the Kobuk River.

Deanna Robyn Davis of Shungnak and another young girl who were with the Summer Youth Program in 1998 wrote the following: "The first school was built in 1918 at the old site, now called Kobuk, and the school was moved to the present site in 1920. The first missionaries arrived in 1922. In the early days, some of the natives lived down the hill (bluff). Gas lights were used because there was no electricity "down the hill." The natives had no fishing poles, so they made what was called ice-fishing sticks. Some of the Elders make parkas, mukluks, and wolf or beaver mittens. And today, there just a few people that still live down the hill. Long ago the Eskimo people used to have big dances around here in Shungnak. Nowadays, the younger generation doesn't know how to dance like the Eskimo people long ago."[64]

Subsistence is mainly fishing, trapping and hunting. The Bureau of Land Management hires firefighters seasonally. Most full-time employment is with the school district. The residents are known for their basketry and beadwork. Local conveyance is usually by dog sled, small boats, or ATVs. Shungnak is accessible by boat or plane, and a marine service delivers supplies by barge during the summer months.

SITKA

The Tlingits, who may have been members of the Kiksadi clan, came here from Kiks Bay. When tribal disputes arose, some members of the clan, along with their frog totem, came to the region to settle, built a fortification, and called it Knootlian. It was later named New Archangel by the Russians, and then renamed Sitka, which means "near the sea."[65]

In July 1741, Captain Alexei Chirikof brought his ship into the harbor. One of the gigs was sent to explore the area, but the men didn't return. Another gig was sent, and it also did not come back. After three weeks, Chirikof finally left, never knowing what happened to his crew. Indian folklore has it that one of their chiefs lured the unsuspecting crew members by wearing a bearskin and killed the white men.[66]

When the Russians got to Sitka in 1799, they met Richard Cleveland, an American who came only to get otter skins. But the Russians were here to colonize the area, so they stayed and named the site New Archangel. Alexander Baranov, who managed the Russian American Company, arrived at Sitka with a number of Aleuts and company employees. The Russians had overhunted the south central part of Alaska and came here for the sea otter. The local natives began to grow hostile after the Russians began killing off their prime hunting. They torched the town of New Archangel and killed every white man they could find. Baranov was gone when the attack occurred and when he returned he forced the Tlingits to flee. The Russian reign came to an end when the U.S. purchased Alaska in 1867.

A report written by a Russian named Kyrill Khlebnikov substantiated the Tlingit attitude toward the Russians. He wrote, "The fort is strongly guarded. Everyone relies on guards. Inspectors and watchmen must be attentive at all times."[67] Kyrill noted that the Kalosh were clever enough in that they were not overt in their attitude, but it would be wise for the white man not to kill the natives because of the devastating vengeance that would be wrought upon them.

During the 1800s, Sitka was a busy port of call for ships from

U.S. Navy, Forest Service Geological Survey Photo
Aerial view of Sitka (1930s). Russians, British and American traders plied these waters, selling and shipping furs, salmon and lumber.

all over the world. Furs were exported to Europe and Asia, and lumber and salmon exported to Hawaii, Mexico, and California, but Sitka's popularity diminished somewhat with the decline of fur-bearing animals. The town then went into the timber industry and also built one of the first salmon canneries in Alaska in 1878. After two years of operation, the cannery closed down. When gold was discovered Sitka came alive again. Prospectors rushed here when gold-bearing quartz was discovered on Silver bay, just southeast of town.

In 1912, the whaling industry added to Sitka's economy. The U.S. Whaling Company established a station at the south end of Baranov Island, and harvested more than 300 whales the first year using bow-mounted harpoons. In 1923, whaling operations ceased and the plant became a herring reduction facility.

Today, in addition to fishing and retail businesses, Sitka depends on tourism for its economy.

SKAGWAY

During 1897, Skagway became one of the most famous cities in the world because of the gold fields in the Yukon. Skagway is a Tlingit word that could mean many things: "place where the north wind blows," "rough water," "cruel wind," "end of salt water." A Tlingit leader believes it means "lady relieving herself on a rock;" yet another thinks it stands for "sound a sled runner makes when it breaks loose from the snow and ice." Skagway has also been spelled many different ways: Cquque, Schkague, Sch-kawai and Skagwa. At any rate, it has been Skagway since 1899.[68]

A German named Captain William Moore went to Skagway in 1887 and filed a claim on 160 acres in anticipation of the gold rush, ten years before it happened. When the rush did occur, Skagway became the temporary home to more than 20,000 people, which made it the largest town in Alaska at that time. Custom records of 1898 show that at least 5,000 people arrived in a one-month period.

The gold seekers used two trails that went to the headwaters of the Yukon: the Chilkoot Trail, thirty-three miles long, originating from the little town of Dyea; and the forty-mile White Pass Trail out of Skagway. Many of the prospectors had little knowledge of how to survive in this region. Most of the equipment they were hauling was abandoned because they couldn't carry it over the passes. In 1898, an avalanche buried more than 100 men and women who had left Sheep Camp and were on their way up the summit of Chilkoot Pass. The men who were still at camp went up to rescue the prospectors, but many of the bodies were never found.[69]

Skagway was known as a rip-snortin', shoot-em-up town loaded with con men. One of the most famous was Soapy Smith, known for his many devious ways of relieving prospectors of their wealth. The town got fed up with its bad reputation and formed a vigilante committee called "Committee of One-Hundred and One." Soapy met his end in a shoot-out at the hands of Frank Reid, the town surveyor, who was a member of the committee. During its heyday, Skagway sported more than seventy saloons and was run by organized criminals.[70]

In 1898, Michael Heney, who was an Irishman and a

railroad contractor, along with some English businessmen, built a 110-mile railroad through White Pass to Whitehorse in May 1898, and Skagway was its southern terminus. Heney was also a member of the Copper River & Northwestern Railway project in the early 1900s at Chitina.

Skagway might have become a ghost town had it not been for the White Pass and Yukon Railroad, which provided fuel, freight, and transportation to Whitehorse. It also served the Anvil Gold Mines in the Yukon until they closed in 1982. The Klondike Highway gave Skagway its link to the Alaska Highway and state ferry connection to the southeast. Skagway brings many tourists by maintaining all of its historic sites from the gold-rush era.

SLEETMUTE

Sleetmute is about 240 miles west of Anchorage on the east bank of the Kuskokwim River, and was founded by the Ingalik Indians. Because of the slate deposits in the area, the village was named Sleetmute, meaning "whetstone people." The name was also spelled Steelmut, Steitmute and Sikmiut. When the Russians arrived, they built a trading post about a mile from the village at the junction of the Holitna and Kuskokwim Rivers in the early 1830s. The post was later relocated downriver about 100 miles. A man named Frederick Bishop started another trading post at Sleetmute in 1906. A school was established in 1921, followed by a post office a few years later, and within ten years the Russian Orthodox church was built. Because there was no commercial fishing activity at Sleetmute, in order for the natives to get their subsistence they had to travel to outlying fish camps in the summer months.

The Kuskokwim Corporation was formed as a result of a merger of ten middle Kuskokwim River villages, and the natives of Sleetmute were shareholders. They incorporated under the Alaska Native Claims Settlement Act. Sleetmute residents were also served by the Kuskokwim Native Association, which operated the Aniak Experimental Farm Project and a community mental health program.

In addition to subsistence fishing, the natives hunt moose, bear and porcupine. A primary employer is the school. In the summer months, barges bring in supplies via the Kuskokwim River. During winter, natives use snow machines on the river.

TANAKEE SPRINGS

Tanakee is derived from a Tlingit word, tinaghu, which means "coppery shield bay." This was in reference to three highly prized copper shields the natives lost in a storm. The "Springs" was added to the name later. Tanakee Springs is located on the east side of Chichagof Island, forty-five miles southwest of Juneau.

Officially founded in 1899, prospectors and fishermen came here to wait out the winters and use the natural hot-sulfur springs. In 1895, a large building and tub were constructed to provide a warm bathing place, and later rocks were blasted to enlarge the springs. Pictographs in the area show there were early battles between different tribes at this site. The winners soaked in the hot mineral springs while their enemies lay decapitated nearby on the beach.

A man named Ed Snyder built a general store in 1899, and shortly thereafter a cannery opened. A logging camp operated in the area, and a few years later, the post office opened.

The summer of 1993 was extremely dry and caused a terrible fire. Tanakee Springs suffered a disaster when a big portion of the town burned down. A barge captain saw the fire and blew his air horn, which woke up the residents so they could save the remainder of their town. Unfortunately, many jobs went up in smoke, too.

The community is mainly a retirement place. Some of the people live on pensions, others are engaged in tourism and a few of the residents make their living as commercial fishermen. The only vehicles allowed in town are the ATVs and bicycles owned by residents. There is no running water except what flows naturally down the hill, and their outhouses are situated on the beach over the tide.[71]

The village is dependent on seaplanes and the Alaska Marine Highway for transportation. There are no landing facilities or local roads, and the state ferry provides transportation for passengers only. About six times a year barges deliver fuel and supplies.

TANANA

Tanana is an Athabascan village that started out as a trading post built by the Alaska Commercial Company and headed
by one of its agents, Arthur Harper. In 1881, Fort Gibbon was
built by the U.S. Army. Before that time, a man named Francois
Mercier established a trading post in the area about 1868. The
St. James Episcopal Mission was built years later about three
miles above the village, by Reverend J. L. Prevost.

Located at the junction of the Tanana and Yukon Rivers, this
village was originally called Nuchalawoya, and Athabascan
word that means "the place where the two rivers meet." Later,
the name was changed to Tanana and is derived from Tananah,
defined as "river trail."[72] The village was strung out for about a
mile along the right bank of the Yukon River.

Tanana became a placer mining district and more trading
posts popped up in the region with the coming of the gold rush.
But after 1906 the gold seekers left the area. Fort Gibbon was
closed in 1923. During World War II, an air base was constructed near the village and used as a refueling stop for the
lend-lease aircraft program.

During the 1930s, the natives made their living fishing,
hunting, trapping and ratting. Mail was delivered by planes in
the winter. When the Yukon River froze, usually by mid-
November, mail planes used the river as a landing strip until
April. When the ice broke, mail was delivered via steamers,
which also brought fresh fruit and other supplies.[73]

Today, some residents are employed at local businesses and
in construction work, in addition to commercial fishing during
the season. The village is accessible only by air or river. There
is a small harbor where barges deliver supplies and freight.

TOGIAK

According to an 1826 atlas, this Eskimo village was once
called Tugiatok. Situated on flat tundra at the head of Togiak
Bay about sixty-five miles west of Dillingham, the community
was originally located on the other side of the bay, and called
Togiagamute (Togiaga people). Because it was so difficult to
gather wood during heavy snowfalls, the natives relocated to
the present site across the bay, which also had a slough that

protected their boats. They called it Nasaurluq, which means "young girl."

When a Moravian missionary named John Kilbuck arrived in 1888, the people were very friendly and treated him like a king. He also noted that their culture had not been touched by any Russian influence. Surrounding villages suffered from the white man's illnesses. When the 1918-1919 flu epidemic broke out, many of the natives from the communities of the Yukon-Kuskokwim area came here to escape the disease.

A saltery was established by the Alaska Packers Association in 1895, but it operated for only one year. During the summer months, the village men moved their families to the town of Dillingham for fishing, where they set up a tent city. They engaged in this activity until commercial fisheries were established at Togiak in the 1950s.[74]

Winter storms with sixty-seventy-mph winds are not uncommon as this area has an unprotected coastline. In 1964, a very strong pressure gradient occurred during one of the highest tides, and a devastating flood hit Togiak. The fish racks, fuel oil, and stores of gas were demolished. The Togiak Fisheries were also destroyed by the storm. The cannery was rebuilt with the help of the native population. In 1965, the Bureau of Indian Affairs (BIA) loaned reindeer to three natives so they could start a herd on Hagemeister Island. It was hoped this venture would turn into a commercial business.

TYONEK

Forty-three miles southwest of Anchorage lies the Tanaina Athabascan village of Tyonek, which is located on the northwest shore of Cook Inlet. In 1880, the name was reported as Toyonok, which means "little chief."

The Russian American Company had a trading post here until the late 1800s, but dissension between the Russians and natives occurred, and sometime later the Alaska Commercial Company took over the post. Captain Cook had visited the area in 1778 and found the residents possessed iron knives and glass beads. He believed they had been trading with the Russians.

In the 1880s, Tyonek became a supply and disembarkation point when gold was discovered at Resurrection Creek. Placer mining was also conducted in the Willow Creek district, run by the Klondike & Boston Gold Mining & Manufacturing Company. In 1896, a saltery was established north of the village at the mouth of Chuitna River with the advent of successful commercial fishing.

The area natives suffered multiple tragedies. During the years 1836-1840, half of the population was lost to smallpox. In 1918, the influenza epidemic hit hard and left very few survivors. About twelve years later, the place was flooded which precipitated the village's move on the top of a bluff in 1934. When Anchorage was founded, the population again declined.

Tyonek's last traditional chief was Simeon Chickalusion, but everyone called him "Ole Man." He was loved by all his people because he tried to do his best for the their welfare. He moved the village to its present site when high tides kept flooding their homes. Chickalusion was instrumental in getting an airstrip built. He also succeeded in getting a church built by starting out with just a bible, cross, a few dollars and some candles. The people have said Tyonek may mean "little chief," but Simeon Chickalusion was a "Great Chief."[75]

The natives subsist on salmon, beluga whale and other seafood. In recent years, they became involved as guides for fishing and hunting. The village owns a 3,000-foot gravel airstrip, and permission is required to land. There are no roads to Tyonek, and supplies are delivered by barge.

UGASHIK

Once one of the largest villages in the region, Ugashik is situated on the Alaska Peninsula. Ivan Petroff recorded the name of this village as "Oogashik" in 1880. It was also called Ougatik and located where the Ugashik River empties into the Bering Sea, as noted on an old map dating to about 1822. Henry W. Elliott wrote in 1887, "At Oogashik, where we find a small settlement of Aleuts from Oonalashka . . ."[76]

The 1922 census report noted there was a Russian Orthodox church that had been at Ugashik since about 1837. A pioneer in the salmon business was C. A. Johnson, who started a saltery in 1889 on the Ugashik River, which serpentines itself past the community.[77] The Johnson Saltery merged with the cannery owned by the Bering Sea Packing Company. Later, Johnson established and operated another saltery on another section of the river, which in turn was sold to the Alaska Packers Association. More than 1,000 barrels of salmon were shipped out of the village in 1890. Ugashik was one of the communities established when the Red Salmon Company built its cannery during this time period. [78]

The Bering Sea Packing Company built the first cannery on the left bank of the Ugashik River, near the site where Johnson had his first saltery. Construction delays occurred when machinery on the schooner *Premier* went ashore on Stepovak Bay instead of the Ugashik. It did not reach the village until 1891, but then it was decided this site was not suitable and the cannery closed. It was later moved to another point on the river and operated for only two years.

The Alaska Packers Association established a cannery here in 1895 known as the Ugashik Fishing Station. It was built using machinery from the Russian American Packing's cannery once operated at Afognak. The cannery operated until 1907 and was later used as a saltery.

Like many of the native villages, Ugashik was almost decimated by the 1918 flu epidemic. Most of the survivors moved up to the Pilot Point fish camp. Archaeologist Ales Hrdlicka referred to Ugashik as "a large dead village." Behind the village were wooden crosses that spanned more than half a mile. Hard times came when Alaska Packers closed its cannery.

As of 1966, there were a total of nine houses in Ugashik, with a population of approximately forty-six. The residents did not live in the village year-round, but went to spend time at Pilot Point. Wrecks of fishing and cannery boats dotted the banks of the river, and no businesses existed except for the post office. There was only a dirt road that went from the village to a small airstrip, reportedly built by a bush pilot.

Present-day permanent residents in Ugashik number about six. Because there is no school, the people moved away so their children could attend school elsewhere. It was also difficult for the village to get fuel. The population is about seventy when the people return to Ugashik during the fishing season in the summer.

Courtesy Roy Matsuno, Anchorage, Alaska
Aerial view of Ugashik and frozen Ugashik River (1999).

Courtesy Roy Matsuno, Anchorage, Alaska
Fish-drying racks at Ugashik (1966).

UMNAK ISLAND

This island is located just west of Unalaska and is part of the Fox Islands. In the 1750s, Russian explorers came to claim the territory, and while here they mistreated the natives. But a Russian named Stepan Glotov nurtured a good relationship with the Aleut villages, and today some of them still carry his

Courtesy Roy Matsuno, Anchorage, Alaska
Jerry Engiak and David Matsuno with Elder John Kignulguk, at his Ugashik house in 1966.

name. In 1764, Umnak natives asked Glotov to get rid of the people who lived in the village of Uliaga because they were thieves, which he did, by killing them all off. Modern Aleuts believe the name Umnak means "fish line." The early natives called the area Agunalaksh, which meant "the shores where the sea breaks its neck."

By the 1800s, the Russians had introduced livestock to the island. Because there were no natural predators and plenty of forage, the stock thrived. A man named Henry Tucker was the first rancher on the island. He said Umnak was "only wind, fog and rain," and that "This country is a perfect hell." Eventually, he abandoned the site, as did the many others who followed him. The cattle were left to fend for themselves. The animals evolved into wild range steers.[79]

In the 1930s, Carlyle Eubank came here from Utah and began running a sheep ranch with about 15,000 head. Seven years later, Eubank was getting about 120,000 pounds of wool.

Apparently, the only enemies the sheep had on the island were ravens, which were known to fly at the sheep and pluck out their eyes. The birds would feast on the remains after the sheep panicked and fell down into gullies.

During World War II, Fort Glen was established as a tactical air base. American forces were stationed here in case of Japanese attack, and were deployed to protect Dutch Harbor. After the war, the sheep industry was still making a profit with the wool. But in 1969, a New York investor bought out the sheep ranch, turned one of the Army's buildings into a slaughter-house, and killed all the sheep. The investor left in 1976.

The 1990s brought two businessmen who got together, and with money from investors, started the Bering Pacific Ranch. The State of Alaska gave the company a loan for a slaughter-house. Today, the meat is in demand as a premium beef that is Alaska-grown and naturally raised, with no antibiotics or growth hormones given to the animals.

UNALAKLEET

Unalakleet is situated on Norton Sound at the mouth of Unalakleet River, 148 miles southeast of Nome. The younger generation of natives believe the name means "place where the east wind blows." According to the Elders, it was originally called Ungalaklik, which meant "south side." Because it was too difficult for white men to speak Inupiaq, the name was pronounced Unalakleet.

A long time ago there was a battle fought between the people of Ungalaklik and another tribe of Indians. After the fight, one of the women (named Masu) heard a sound, and she discovered a little Indian boy not of their village. She took him home and adopted him, where she taught the boy to speak Inupiaq and the Eskimo way. The boy was named Nulthkutuk, and when he grew up he became headman of Ungalaklik.[80]

Natives moved from the original village across the river when an epidemic almost wiped out the community. The Russian American Company built a trading post in the 1830s. In 1898, reindeer herds were imported from Lapland. The Lapps taught the people how to herd the animals and many of them became experts. The natives subsisted on reindeer herding, fishing and trapping. They lived in sod houses, and the support beams for their homes were gathered from the driftwood logs that floated down the river.

The area has been inhabited for more than 7,000 years according to archaeologists who have dated artifacts beginning in 200 B.C. The natives who settled here came from many places. The languages spoken here were Inupiaq, Yup'ik and Malimiut; newer generations have blended the three dialects.

On February 2, 1925, because of the diphtheria epidemic, 300,0000 units of serum were transported by dog sled to Nome. Five days later, a second batch arrived in Seward, which was then shipped by train to Nenana and then relayed by dog team to Unalakleet.

Today Unalakleet's main economy is commercial fishing. The natives also maintain a herd of musk ox, where their underwool is spun and hand-knit into garments. Subsistence includes trapping of lynx, wolves, and fox, where the fur is used for clothing and trimming. [81]

UNALASKA

This village was founded by Solovief, who established a fur trading post in the 1760s. It was first called Iliuliuk, meaning "harmony" or "good understanding." The name might be an Aleut word for "great land."[82]

Unalaska is located on Unalaska Island in the Aleutian Chain, approximately 800 miles from Anchorage, and was once one of the largest Aleut communities. The Russians came to harvest the sea otter fur. Some of the Aleut hunters were enslaved and taken to the Pribilof Islands.[83]

During the Klondike gold rush in 1898, Unalaska became a station for ships sailing between Seattle and the Klondike. Food and fuel were also stored in warehouses for emergencies.

In 1919, the killer Spanish influenza epidemic hit Unalaska residents. Coast Guard personnel, headed by Captain F. G. Dodge of the cutter *Unalga*, were sent to the island with medical assistance. When they arrived, they couldn't believe the devastation and chaos. They had to call for volunteers to help bury the dead and feed the people who were ill. The day after the Coast Guard arrived, the whole village was stricken.

Department of Interior Photo (from "Alaska, the Last Frontier,"
Federal Writer's Project, Macmillan Co., 1939)
Fish house and racks at Unalakleet (1930s). Today, fishing is still a major component of the town's economy.

Captain Dodge wrote in his report, "About three hundred sick in this regions, all natives, one hundred orphans, many unburied bodies being eaten by dogs, have sent burial detail ashore to bury dead and shoot dogs. . ."[84] The Coast Guard was at Unalaska for more than a month. If it hadn't been for Dodge and his men, everyone in the village might have died.

During World War II, Unalaska was attacked by the Japanese. The native population was relegated to southeast Alaska during the war when thousands of armed troops occupied the island. Today, relics such as old rusted quonset huts lay scattered across the island as a reminder. The Russian Orthodox Church was almost destroyed by evacuating U.S. Army troops.

Today, the population of Unalaska is predominantly white. The natives who still live here subsist mainly on commercial fishing. Some employment is provided at off-shore processors. Dutch Harbor provides safe shelter for the fishing fleet. There has been an influx of people to Unalaska because of the pollock fishery that has developed, and tourism is coming into its own because it has become a port of call for cruise ships.

YAKUTAT

This community sits at the mouth of Yakutat Bay and is about 215 miles northwest of Juneau. It was probably first inhabited by Eyak-speaking people who came from the Copper River area, and were later conquered by the Tlingits. Yakutat means "the place where the canoes rest," or it might be derived from an Athabaskan word that means "great river."[85]

When the Russians arrived in 1788 they came to hunt sea otters, and the Russian American Company established a fort in 1805. The Tlingits destroyed the fort when the Russians denied them access to their traditional fishing areas.[86]

The Russians later set up an penal colony on the southeast shore of the bay, called Glory of Russia, which was fortified with a blockhouse. The Tlingits were unhappy about they way they were being treated and killed forty of the colonists, and the Russians never returned.

The Alaska Commercial Company opened a store in 1884, and two years later miners came to look for gold on the beaches in the area. By 1889, the Swedish Free Mission Church had established a school and sawmill. Later, the Stimson Lumber Company constructed a cannery, sawmill and store. Many of the natives moved to the new site so they could be near the cannery. In the 1920s, the Yakutat & Southern Railroad, built with lumber capital, began hauling timber to the sawmill, then hauled fish to a salmon cannery, which boosted Yakutat's economy. During World War II, a large aviation garrison and paved runway were constructed. Troops were withdrawn after the war, but the runway is still in use.[87]

This is the place where the earth shook in 1899. The first shaking started on September 3, with the grand finale on September 10, and it didn't completely subside for twenty days. When the earthquake was over, the land of Yakutat had risen forty-seven feet. Fortunately no lives were lost. Because there were no seismographs in 1899, the magnitude of the quake was estimated to be about 8.6, based on assessing the damage from various areas from the epicenter.

People could see the trees swaying and hear their houses creak and shake. One of the missionaries was going to postpone his services, but the natives insisted they hold church, believing that their God, Ankow, was angry at the earth and was shaking it. When the land shook on September 10, it lasted about one-and-a-half minutes, which resulted in tidal waves, and people said that the bay rose about fifteen feet. The quake was felt as far south as Lake Chelan, Washington.

Just across the bay is the Malaspina Glacier, which is larger than the state of Rhode Island. But probably the better known ice field is the Hubbard Glacier. In 1986, this glacier blocked the entrance to Russell Fiord, trapping many sea mammals. A dammed lake was created by this phenomenon, but it gave way about five months later. Hubbard moved again in 1989, but this time the glacier did not close the fiord. Experts believe that eventually the glacier will cause complete closure of Russell Fiord, which will severely affect the salmon on the Situk River.

Yakutat natives depend on fishing for their subsistence in addition to hunting. A cold storage plant is one of the largest employers in the area.

Chapter four notes

[1] James W. Phillips, *Alaska-Yukon Place Names*, University of Washington Press, 1973, p. 3.

[2] Alaska Department of Community & Regional Affairs (DCRA), web site: www.comregaf.state.ak.us/CF-ComDB.htm. (Note: Basic data for the majority of Alaska communities can be read at this website, therefore, no further endnotes will be cited.)

[3] Armed Forces, website: www.armedforces.com/sitesmus/AKADAK/INSTL.htm

[4] Sister Margaret Cantwell, S.S.A., in collaboration with Sister Mary George Edmond, S.S.A., *North to Share: The Sisters of Saint Ann in Alaska and the Yukon Territory*, 1992, pp. 71-75.

[5] Miscellaneous typescripts, Town of Akutan. See also *Pathfinder of Alaska*, Vol 5, #11, 1924.

[6] The Longest Village on the Lower Yukon, by Mike Stockburger, website: www.lysd.schoolzone.net/lysd/auk.htm

[7] Jan S. Doward, *They Came To Wrong Way Home*, Pacific Press, 1961, p. 111.

[8] Presbyterian Church, website: www.yukonpresbytery.com/YukonPresbytery/Arctic/

[9] Sam Wright, *Koviashuvik: A time and place of joy*, Sierra Club Books, 1988, pp. 188-189.

[10] Admiralty Island: Fortress of the Bears, *Alaska Geographic Quarterly.*, Vol. 18, No. 3, 1991, p. 11-12.

[11] Federal Writers' Project, *Alaska: Last American Frontier*, Macmillan Company, 1939, pp. 147-148. (hereafter cited as WPA Alaska)

[12] *Angoon: Its History, Population and Economy*, Bureau of Indian Affairs (BIA), Village Study, June 1975.

[13] Donna MacAlpine, "A Brief History of the Anvik Mission," Anvik Historical Society., June, 1987.

[14] Ales Hrdlika, *Alaska Diary: 1926-1931*, Jaques Cattell Press, PA, 1943, p. 47.

[15] Donna MacAlpine, email to author, Sept., 1999.

[16] James W. Phillips, Op. cit., p. 12.

[17] WPA Alaska, Op. cit., pp. 342-343.

[18] Then and Now in Atqasuk, website: www.nsbsd.k12.ak.us/projects/arctic_year/atqasuk/

[19] WPA Alaska, Op. cit., p. 343.

[20] Mineral Management Service, Shipwrecks Off Alaska's Coast, Alaska OCS region, website: www.mms.gov/alaska/ref/ships/tables/

[21] Gary C. Stein, *Uprooted: Native Casualties of the Aleutian Campaign of World War II*, Alaska State Library Archives; see also The Aleutians Campaign: June 1942-August 1943, 1945, Washington; Publications Branch.

[22] Stewart O'Nan, "Scratch the Island from the Maps," *Outside Magazine*, November, 1998, online edition: www.outsidemag.com/magazine/1198/9811scratch.html

[23] Patricia Wade, Chicaloon Village Traditional Council, email to author, Dec., 1998.

[24] WPA Alaska, Op. cit., pp. 243-244.

[25] *Egegik, Alaska - Village Study*, BIA 1966.

[26] James W. Phillips, Op. cit., p. 44.

[27] Ann Chandonnet, *On the Trail of Eklutna*, User-Friendly Press, 1979, p. 14.

[28] Marjorie Cochrane, *Between Two Rivers: The Growth of Chugiak-Eagle River*, 1983, p. 4.

[29] Ibid., p. 52.

[30] WPA Alaska, Op. cit., p. 159.

[31] Hoonah History, Hoonah High School, Alaska History Class, 1973.

[32] "Lake Clark-Iliamna Country, *Alaska Geographic Quarterly*, Vol. 8, No. 3, 1981, pp. 136, 142.

[33] James W. Phillips, Op. cit., p. 70.

[34] Minerals Management Service, Op. cit.

[35] Ann Vick, *The Cama-i Book*, Anchor Books, 1983, p. 114.

[36] Herbert W. Krieger, *Indian Villages of Southeast Alaska*, Facsimile, Shorey Pub., 1966., pp. 484, 488.

[37] WPA Alaska, Op. cit., pp. 71, 223.

[38] History of Kenai, Alaska, Kenai Visitors & Convention Bureau.

[39] Sarah Eppenbach, *Alaska's Southeast*, Pacific Search Press, 1983, pp.164-165.

[40] Miscellaneous Ketchikan brochures.

[41] The Kiana Project, website: www.alaskool.org/projects/kiana/kiana.htm

[42] Silver Years of the Alaska Canned Salmon Industry, *Alaska Geographic Quarterly.*, Vol. 3, No. 4, 1976, p. 14.

[43] Peggy Wayburn, *Adventuring in Alaska*, Sierra Club Books, 1994, pp. 246-247.

[44] Basil Dmytryshyn & E.A.P. Crownhart-Vaughn, trans., *Civil and Savage Encounters: The Worldly Travel Letters of an Imperial Russian Navy Officer, 1860-1861*, Western Imprints, 1983, p. 132.

[45] WPA Alaska, Op. cit., pp. 216-217.

[46] Dale Brown, *Wild Alaska*, Time Inc., 5th Ptg., 1976, p. 38.

[47] *Manokotak, Alaska - Village Study*, BIA, 1966.

[48] Kathryn Winslow, *Alaska Bound*, Dodd, Mead & Co., 1960, pp. 168-169; see also WPA, Op. cit., pp. 126-127.

[49] *Naknek and South Naknek - Village Study*, BIA, August, 1966.

[50] Wendell Oswalt, *Napaskiak: An Alaskan Eskimo Community*, University of Arizona Press, 1963, pp. 9-10.

[51] Ibid., p. 113.

[52] William H. Wilson, *Railroad in the Clouds: The Alaska Railroad in the Age of Steam, 1914-1945*, Pruett Pub., 1977, pp. 110-111.

[53] Elsa Pedersen & Walt Pedersen, eds., *A Larger History of the Kenai Peninsula*, Walt & Elsa Pedersen, 1983, pp. 101, 103.

[54] WPA Alaska, Op. cit., p. 397.

[55] Theodore J. Karamanski, *Fur Trade and Exploration: Opening the Far Northwest, 1821-1852*, University of Oklahoma Press, 1983, pp. 227-228.

[56] Ann Vick, Op. cit., pp. 272-273.

[57] Paul E. Thompson, Alaska Villages, unpublished manuscript, No. 4, 1937, p. 58, Courtesy Alaska State Library.

[58] James W. Phillips, Op. cit., p. 98.

[59] WPA Alaska, Op. cit., p. 359.

[60] Nushagak River, *Alaska Geographic Quarterly*, Vol. 17, No. 1, pp. 33, 37.

[61] Quinhagak, Traditional Village Council Report, 1990.

[62] Ales Hrdlika, Op. cit., pp. 93-94.

[63] Paul E. Thompson, Op. cit., p. 76.

[64] Deanna Robyn Davis, letter to author, July, 1998.

[65] David Wharton, *They Don't Speak Russian in Sitka: A New Look at the History of Southern Alask*a, Markgraf Pub., 1991, pp. 3-5.

[66] WPA Alaska, Op. cit., pp. 160-161.

[67] Basil Dmytryshyn and E.A.P. Crownhart-Vaughan, trans., *Colonial Russian America: Kyrill T. Khlebnikov's Reports*, 1817-1832, Oregon Historical Society., 1976, p. 104.

[68] David Wharton, Op. cit., p. 147.

[69] Sarah Eppenbach, Op. cit., pp. 254-255.

[70] Richard Erdoes, *Saloons of the Old West*, Alfred A. Knopf, 1979, p. 108.

[71] Sarah Eppenbach, Op. cit., p. 281.

[72] James W. Phillips, Op. cit., p. 128.

[73] Paul E. Thompson, Op. cit., p. 83.

[74] *Togiak, Alaska - Village Study*, BIA, August, 1966.

[75] E.L. Bartlett High School, Native Village of Tyonek, 1983: A Review of Our Athabascan Heritage.

[76] Robert Ekstrom, "Ugashik-Our History," *Riverbank Chatter*, Vol. 1, Issue 1, Spring, 1997.

[77] Jefferson F. Moser, Alaska Salmon Investigations in 1900 and 1901, p. 215.

[78] *Ugashik, Alaska - Village Study*, BIA, August, 1966.

[79] WPA Alaska, Op. cit., pp. 341-343.

[80] Patricia Partnow, Indian Education Program, Anchorage School Dist., 1986.

[81] Doris Ivanoff, Unalakleet Librarian, email to author, April, 1999.

[82] James W. Phillips, Op. cit., p. 135.

[83] WPA Alaska, Op. cit., p. 339-340.

[84] Dennis L. Noble, Fog, Men, and Cutters: A Short History of the Bering Sea Patrol, website: www.uscg.mil/hq/g-cp/history/BeringSea.html

[85] James W. Phillips, Op. cit., p. 145.

[86] Yakutat's History, website: www.italio.com/where_yakutathistory_content.htm

[87] Yakutat History, website: www.johnnyseastriverlodge.com/yakutat

PERSONAL COMMUNICATIONS

Roy Matsuno, President, Ugashik Village Council, Alaska
John Harder, Kahlotus, Washington
Boyd Peterson, Pasco, Washington (Kahlotus)
Elizabeth Riley, Chewelah, Washington
Walt E. Goodman, Chewelah, Washington
Phyliss Griffith, Entiat, Washington
David Bigger, VISTA Volunteer, Quinhagak, Alaska
Deana Davis, Shungnak, Alaska
Elaine Poole, Menan, Idaho
Irene Martin, Skamokawa, Washington
James Hermanston, Port Townsend, Washington (Chimacum)
Opal McConnell, Mukilteo, Washington
Ruth Rushton, Orting, Washington
The Bishop Family, Chimacum, Washington
Lillian Pethtel, Kamiah, Idaho
Janie Tippett, Joseph, Oregon (Imnaha)
Van McDaniel, Salkum, Washington
Bud Purdy, Picabo, Idaho
Jack Fosmark, Salem, Oregon (Necanicum)

INDEX

THE AUTHOR

Born in Allentown, Pennsylvania, Sandra (Sandy) Nestor spent most of her life in Southern California, and now makes her home in Medford, Oregon. She worked for ten years in the publications department at the Rockwell International Science Center in Thousand Oaks, California. During part of that time, Sandy spent six years living on a thirty-foot sailboat and hopes to do it again someday.

She has always had a fascination with history, and began her exploration into name origins in the mid 1980s. Sandy discovered a little place called Rabbit Hash, Kentucky, and wrote an historical article which was published in *Kentucky Living* in August of 2000. She also self-published a cookbook, *The Floating Gourmet*, which was a big hit with boaters. Her inquisitiveness and a series of events led her to explore the origin of Indian place names. Sandy's toughest and most rewarding experience was in the research. Being told time and time again there was no information, her attitude was that "If the place exists, it has a history somewhere." Determination and patience brought otherwise obscure material to light. Along her research travels, she met wonderful people from their respective communities who were enthusiastic and shared the history of their towns.

In addition to pursuing her writing career, she works in the office of the First Presbyterian Church in Medford.

When she can find some leisure, Sandy spends her time reading books written by her favorite authors, Douglas Preston and Lincoln Childs. She is currently working on another book that covers towns with Indian names in the West and Plains states. Sandy's email is halekai@wave.net and welcomes comments and criticism.

For a free Caxton catalog write to:

CAXTON PRESS
312 Main Street
Caldwell, ID 83605-3299

or

Visit our Internet Website:

www.caxtonpress.com

Caxton Press is a division of The CAXTON PRINTERS, Ltd.

WC